"If you are looking for a job ... before you go to the newspapers and the help-wanted ads, listen to Bob Adams, publisher of *The Metropolitan New York JobBank*."

-Tom Brokaw, *NBC*

"Help on the job hunt ... Anyone who is job-hunting in the New York area can find a lot of useful ideas in a new paperback called *The Metropolitan New York JobBank* ..."

-Angela Taylor, *New York Times*

"One of the better publishers of employment almanacs is Adams Media Corporation ... publisher of *The Metropolitan New York JobBank* and similarly named directories of employers in Texas, Boston, Chicago, Northern and Southern California, and Washington DC. A good buy ..."

-Wall Street Journal's
National Business Employment Weekly

"For those graduates whose parents are pacing the floor, conspicuously placing circled want ads around the house and typing up resumes, [*The Carolina JobBank*] answers job-search questions."

-Greensboro News and Record

"A timely book for Chicago job hunters follows books from the same publisher that were well received in New York and Boston ... [*The Chicago JobBank* is] a fine tool for job hunters ..."

-Clarence Peterson, *Chicago Tribune*

"Because our listing is seen by people across the nation, it generates lots of resumes for us. We encourage unsolicited resumes. We'll always be listed [in *The Chicago JobBank*] as long as I'm in this career."

-Tom Fitzpatrick, Director of Human Resources
Merchandise Mart Properties, Inc.

"Job-hunting is never fun, but this book can ease the ordeal ... [*The Los Angeles JobBank*] will help allay fears, build confidence, and avoid wheel-spinning."

-Robert W. Ross, *Los Angeles Times*

"*The Seattle JobBank* is an essential resource for job hunters."

-Gil Lopez, Staffing Team Manager
Battelle Pacific Northwest Laboratories

"*The Phoenix JobBank* is a first-class publication. The information provided is useful and current."

> **-Lyndon Denton**
> **Director of Human Resources and Materials Management**
> **Apache Nitrogen Products, Inc.**

"Job hunters can't afford to waste time. *The Minneapolis-St. Paul JobBank* contains information that used to require hours of research in the library."

> **-Carmella Zagone**
> **Minneapolis-based Human Resources Administrator**

"*The Florida JobBank* is an invaluable job-search reference tool. It provides the most up-to-date information and contact names available for companies in Florida. I should know -- it worked for me!"

> **-Rhonda Cody, Human Resources Consultant**
> **Aetna Life and Casualty**

"I read through the 'Basics of Job Winning' and 'Resumes' sections [in *The Dallas-Fort Worth JobBank*] and found them to be very informative, with some positive tips for the job searcher. I believe the strategies outlined will bring success to any determined candidate."

> **-Camilla Norder, Professional Recruiter**
> **Presbyterian Hospital of Dallas**

"Through *The Dallas-Fort Worth JobBank,* we've been able to attract high-quality candidates for several positions."

> **-Rob Bertino, Southern States Sales Manager**
> **CompuServe**

"Packed with helpful contacts, *The Houston JobBank* empowers its reader to launch an effective, strategic job search in the Houston metropolitan area."

> **-Andrew Ceperley, Director**
> **College of Communication Career Services**
> **The University of Texas at Austin**

"*The San Francisco Bay Area JobBank* ... is a highly useful guide, with plenty of how-to's ranging from resume tips to interview dress codes and research shortcuts."

> **-A.S. Ross, *San Francisco Examiner***

"[*The Atlanta JobBank* is] one of the best sources for finding a job in Atlanta!"

> **-Luann Miller, Human Resources Manager**
> **Prudential Preferred Financial Services**

What makes the JobBank series the nation's premier line of employment guides?

With vital employment information on thousands of employers across the nation, the JobBank series is the most comprehensive and authoritative set of career directories available today.

Each book in the series provides information on **dozens of different industries** in a given city or area, with the primary employer listings providing contact information, telephone and fax numbers, e-mail addresses, Websites, a summary of the firm's business, internships, and in many cases descriptions of the firm's typical professional job categories.

All of the reference information in the JobBank series is as up-to-date and accurate as possible. Every year, the entire database is thoroughly researched and verified by mail and by telephone. Adams Media Corporation publishes **more local employment guides more often** than any other publisher of career directories.

The JobBank series offers **28 regional titles**, from Minneapolis to Houston, and from Boston to San Francisco as well as **two industry-specific titles**. All of the information is organized geographically, because most people look for jobs in specific areas of the country.

A condensed, but thorough, review of the entire job search process is presented in the chapter **The Basics of Job Winning**, a feature which has received many compliments from career counselors. In addition, each JobBank directory includes a section on **resumes and cover letters** the *New York Times* has acclaimed as "excellent."

The JobBank series gives job hunters the most comprehensive, timely, and accurate career information, organized and indexed to facilitate your job search. An entire career reference library, JobBank books are designed to help you find optimal employment in any market.

Top career publications from Adams Media Corporation

13th Edition

THE Seattle

JobBank

Editor:	Erik L. Herman
Assistant Editor:	Sarah Rocha
Researchers:	Maurice Curran
	Megan Danahy
	Emily Mozzone

Adams Media
AVON, MASSACHUSETTS

Published by Adams Media, an F+W Publications Company
57 Littlefield Street, Avon, MA 02322 U.S.A.
www.adamsmedia.com

ISBN: 1-58062-958-X
ISSN: 1098-979X
Manufactured in the United States of America.

Product or brand names used in this book are proprietary property of the applicable firm, subject to trademark protection, and registered with government offices. Any use of these names does not convey endorsement by or other affiliation with the name holder.

Because addresses and telephone numbers of smaller companies change rapidly, we recommend you call each company and verify the information before mailing to the employers listed in this book. Mass mailings are not recommended.

While the publisher has made every reasonable effort to obtain and verify accurate information, occasional errors are possible due to the magnitude of the data. Should you discover an error, or if a company is missing, please write the editors at the above address so that we may update future editions.

"This publication is designed to provide accurate and authoritative information with regard to the subject matter covered. It is sold with the understanding that the publisher is not engaged in rendering legal, accounting, or other professional advice. If legal advice or other expert assistance is required, the services of a competent professional person should be sought."

--From a *Declaration of Principles* jointly adopted by a Committee of the American Bar Association and a Committee of Publishers and Associations

This book is available on standing order and at quantity discounts for bulk purchases.
For information, call 800/872-5627 (in Massachusetts, 508/427-7100)
or email at jobbank@adamsmedia.com

TABLE OF CONTENTS

- *Automotive Repair Shops*
- *Automotive Stampings*
- *Industrial Vehicles and Moving Equipment*
- *Motor Vehicles and Equipment*
- *Travel Trailers and Campers*

Banking/Savings and Loans/82

Biotechnology, Pharmaceuticals, and Scientific R&D/88
- *Clinical Labs*
- *Lab Equipment Manufacturers*
- *Pharmaceutical Manufacturers and Distributors*

Business Services and Non-Scientific Research/94
- *Adjustment and Collection Services*
- *Cleaning, Maintenance, and Pest Control Services*
- *Credit Reporting Services*
- *Detective, Guard, and Armored Car Services/Security Systems Services*
- *Miscellaneous Equipment Rental and Leasing*
- *Secretarial and Court Reporting Services*

Charities and Social Services/98
- *Job Training and Vocational Rehabilitation Services*

Chemicals/Rubber and Plastics/102
- *Adhesives, Detergents, Inks, Paints, Soaps, Varnishes*
- *Agricultural Chemicals and Fertilizers*
- *Carbon and Graphite Products*
- *Chemical Engineering Firms*
- *Industrial Gases*

Communications: Telecommunications and Broadcasting/107
- *Cable/Pay Television Services*
- *Communications Equipment*
- *Radio and Television Broadcasting Stations*
- *Telephone, Telegraph, and Other Message Communications*

Computer Hardware, Software, and Services/114
- *Computer Components and Hardware Manufacturers*
- *Consultants and Computer Training Companies*
- *Internet and Online Service Providers*
- *Networking and Systems Services*
- *Repair Services/Rental and Leasing*
- *Resellers, Wholesalers, and Distributors*
- *Software Developers/Programming Services*

Educational Services/128
- *Business/Secretarial/Data Processing Schools*
- *Colleges/Universities/Professional Schools*
- *Community Colleges/Technical Schools/Vocational Schools*
- *Elementary and Secondary Schools*
- *Preschool and Child Daycare Services*

Electronic/Industrial Electrical Equipment/135
- *Electronic Machines and Systems*
- *Semiconductor Manufacturers*

Environmental and Waste Management Services/144
- *Environmental Engineering Firms*
- *Sanitary Services*

Fabricated/Primary Metals and Products/148
- *Aluminum and Copper Foundries*
- *Die-Castings*
- *Iron and Steel Foundries/Steel Works, Blast Furnaces, and Rolling Mills*

Financial Services/152
- *Consumer Financing and Credit Agencies*
- *Investment Specialists*

SECTION FOUR: INDEX

INTRODUCTION

HOW TO USE THIS BOOK

Right now, you hold in your hands one of the most effective job-hunting tools available anywhere. In *The Seattle JobBank*, you will find valuable information to help you launch or continue a rewarding career. But before you open to the book's employer listings and start calling about current job openings, take a few minutes to learn how best to use the resources presented in *The Seattle JobBank*.

The Seattle JobBank will help you to stand out from other jobseekers. While many people looking for a new job rely solely on newspaper help-wanted ads, this book offers you a much more effective job-search method -- direct contact. The direct contact method has been proven twice as effective as scanning the help-wanted ads. Instead of waiting for employers to come looking for you, you'll be far more effective going to them. While many of your competitors will use trial and error methods in trying to set up interviews, you'll learn not only how to get interviews, but what to expect once you've got them.

In the next few pages, we'll take you through each section of the book so you'll be prepared to get a jump-start on your competition.

Basics of Job Winning

Preparation. Strategy. Time management. These are three of the most important elements of a successful job search. *Basics of Job Winning* helps you address these and all the other elements needed to find the right job.

One of your first priorities should be to define your personal career objectives. What qualities make a job desirable to you? Creativity? High pay? Prestige? Use *Basics of Job Winning* to weigh these questions. Then use the rest of the chapter to design a strategy to find a job that matches your criteria.

In *Basics of Job Winning*, you'll learn which job-hunting techniques work, and which don't. We've reviewed the pros and cons of mass mailings, help-wanted ads, and direct contact. We'll show you how to develop and approach contacts in your field; how to research a prospective employer; and how to use that information to get an interview and the job.

Also included in *Basics of Job Winning*: interview dress code and etiquette, the "do's and don'ts" of interviewing, sample interview questions, and more. We also deal with some of the unique problems faced by those jobseekers who are currently employed, those who have lost a job, and college students conducting their first job search.

Resumes and Cover Letters

The approach you take to writing your resume and cover letter can often mean the difference between getting an interview and never being noticed. In this section, we discuss different formats, as well as what to put on (and what to leave off) your resume. We review the benefits and drawbacks of professional resume writers, and the importance of a follow-up letter. Also included in this section are sample resumes and cover letters which you can use as models.

The Employer Listings

Employers are listed alphabetically by industry. When a company does business under a person's name, like "John Smith & Co.," the company is usually listed by the surname's spelling (in this case "S"). Exceptions occur when a company's name is widely recognized, like "JCPenney" or "Howard Johnson Motor Lodge." In those cases, the company's first name is the key ("J" and "H" respectively).

The *Seattle JobBank* covers a very wide range of industries. Each company profile is assigned to one of the industry chapters listed below.

Accounting and Management Consulting
Advertising, Marketing, and Public Relations
Aerospace
Apparel, Fashion, and Textiles
Architecture, Construction, and Engineering
Arts, Entertainment, Sports, and Recreation
Automotive
Banking/Savings and Loans
Biotechnology, Pharmaceuticals, and
    Scientific R&D
Business Services and Non-Scientific
    Research
Charities and Social Services
Chemicals/Rubber and Plastics
Communications: Telecommunications and
    Broadcasting
Computer Hardware, Software, and Services
Educational Services
Electronic/Industrial Electrical Equipment
Environmental and Waste Management
    Services

Fabricated/Primary Metals and Products
Financial Services
Food and Beverages/Agriculture
Government
Health Care: Services, Equipment, and
    Products
Hotels and Restaurants
Insurance
Legal Services
Manufacturing: Miscellaneous Consumer
Manufacturing: Miscellaneous Industrial
Mining/Gas/Petroleum/Energy Related
Paper and Wood Products
Printing and Publishing
Real Estate
Retail
Stone, Clay, Glass, and Concrete Products
Transportation/Travel
Utilities: Electric/Gas/Water
Miscellaneous Wholesaling

Many of the company listings offer detailed company profiles. In addition to company names, addresses, and phone numbers, these listings also include contact names or hiring departments, and descriptions of each company's products and/or services. Many of these listings also feature a variety of additional information including:

Positions advertised - A list of job titles that the company was advertising for at the time our research was conducted. Note: Keep in mind that *The Seattle JobBank* is a directory of major employers in the area, not a directory of openings currently available. Positions listed in this book that were advertised at the time research was conducted may no longer be open. Many of the companies listed will be hiring, others will not. However, since most professional job openings are filled without the placement of help-wanted ads, contacting the employers in this book directly is still a more effective method than browsing the Sunday papers.

Special programs - Does the company offer training programs, internships, or apprenticeships? These programs can be important to first time jobseekers and college students looking for practical work experience. Many employer profiles will include information on these programs.

Parent company - If an employer is a subsidiary of a larger company, the name of that parent company will often be listed here. Use this information to supplement your company research before contacting the employer.

Number of employees - The number of workers a company employs.

Company listings may also include information on other U.S. locations and any stock exchanges the firm may be listed on.

A note on all employer listings that appear in *The Seattle JobBank*: This book is intended as a starting point. It is not intended to replace any effort that you, the jobseeker, should devote to your job hunt. Keep in mind that while a great deal of effort has been put into collecting and verifying the company profiles provided in this book, addresses and contact names change regularly. Inevitably, some contact names listed herein have changed even before you read this. We recommend you contact a company before mailing your resume to ensure nothing has changed.

Index

The Seattle JobBank index is listed alphabetically by industry.

THE JOB SEARCH

THE BASICS OF JOB WINNING: A CONDENSED REVIEW

This chapter is divided into four sections. The first section explains the fundamentals that every jobseeker should know, especially first-time jobseekers. The next three sections deal with special situations faced by specific types of jobseekers: those who are currently employed, those who have lost a job, and college students.

THE BASICS:
Things Everyone Needs to Know

Career Planning

The first step to finding your ideal job is to clearly define your objectives. This is better known as career planning (or life planning if you wish to emphasize the importance of combining the two). Career planning has become a field of study in and of itself.

If you are thinking of choosing or switching careers, we particularly emphasize two things. First, choose a career where you will enjoy most of the day-to-day tasks. This sounds obvious, but most of us have at some point found the idea of a glamour industry or prestigious job title attractive without thinking of the key consideration: Would we enjoy performing the *everyday* tasks the position entails?

The second key consideration is that you are not merely choosing a career, but also a lifestyle. Career counselors indicate that one of the most common problems people encounter in jobseeking is that they fail to consider how well-suited they are for a particular position or career. For example, some people, attracted to management consulting by good salaries, early responsibility, and high-level corporate exposure, do not adapt well to the long hours, heavy travel demands, and constant pressure to produce. Be sure to ask yourself how you might adapt to the day-to-day duties and working environment that a specific position entails. Then ask yourself how you might adapt to the demands of that career or industry as a whole.

Choosing Your Strategy

Assuming that you've established your career objectives, the next step of the job search is to develop a strategy. If you don't take the time to develop a plan, you may find yourself going in circles after several weeks of randomly searching for opportunities that always seem just beyond your reach.

The most common jobseeking techniques are:

- following up on help-wanted advertisements (in the newspaper or online)
- using employment services
- relying on personal contacts
- contacting employers directly (the Direct Contact method)

Each of these approaches can lead to better jobs. However, the Direct Contact method boasts twice the success rate of the others. So unless you have specific reasons to employ other strategies, Direct Contact should form the foundation of your job search.

If you choose to use other methods as well, try to expend at least half your energy on Direct Contact. Millions of other jobseekers have already proven that Direct Contact has been twice as effective in obtaining employment, so why not follow in their footsteps?

Setting Your Schedule

Okay, so now that you've targeted a strategy it's time to work out the details of your job search. The most important detail is setting up a schedule. Of course, since job searches aren't something most people do regularly, it may be hard to estimate how long each step will take. Nonetheless, it is important to have a plan so that you can monitor your progress.

When outlining your job search schedule, have a realistic time frame in mind. If you will be job-searching full-time, your search could take at least two months or more. If you can only devote part-time effort, it will probably take at least four months.

You probably know a few people who seem to spend their whole lives searching for a better job in their spare time. Don't be one of them. If you are presently working and don't feel like devoting a lot of energy to jobseeking right now, then wait. Focus on enjoying your present position, performing your best on the job, and storing up energy for when you are really ready to begin your job search.

> **The first step in beginning your job search is to clearly define your objectives.**

Those of you who are currently unemployed should remember that *job-hunting is tough work, both physically and emotionally.* It is also intellectually demanding work that requires you to be at your best. So don't tire yourself out by working on your job campaign around the clock. At the same time, be sure to discipline yourself. The most logical way to manage your time while looking for a job is to keep your regular working hours.

If you are searching full-time and have decided to choose several different strategies, we recommend that you divide up each week, designating some time for each method. By trying several approaches at once, you can evaluate how promising each seems and alter your schedule accordingly. Keep in mind that the *majority of openings are filled without being advertised.* Remember also that positions advertised on the Internet are just as likely to already be filled as those found in the newspaper!

If you are searching part-time and decide to try several different contact methods, we recommend that you try them sequentially. You simply won't have enough time to put a meaningful amount of effort into more than one method at once. Estimate the length of your job search, and then allocate so many weeks or months for each contact method, beginning with Direct Contact. The purpose of setting this schedule is not to rush you to your goal but to help you periodically evaluate your progress.

The Direct Contact Method

Once you have scheduled your time, you are ready to begin your search in earnest. Beginning with the Direct Contact method, the first step is to develop a checklist for categorizing the types of firms for which you'd like to work. You might categorize firms by product line, size, customer type (such as industrial or consumer), growth prospects, or geographical location. Keep in mind, the shorter the list the easier it will be to locate a company that is right for you.

Next you will want to use this *JobBank* book to assemble your list of potential employers. Choose firms where *you* are most likely to be able to find a job. Try matching your skills with those that a specific job demands. Consider where your skills might be in demand, the degree of competition for employment, and the employment outlook at each company.

Separate your prospect list into three groups. The first 25 percent will be your primary target group, the next 25 percent will be your secondary group, and the remaining names will be your reserve group.

After you form your prospect list, begin working on your resume. Refer to the Resumes and Cover Letters section following this chapter for more information.

Once your resume is complete, begin researching your first batch of prospective employers. You will want to determine whether you would be happy working at the firms you are researching and to get a better idea of what their employment needs might be. You also need to obtain enough information to sound highly informed about the company during phone conversations and in mail correspondence. But don't go all out on your research yet! You probably won't be able to arrange interviews with some of these firms, so save your big research effort until you start to arrange interviews. Nevertheless, you should plan to spend several hours researching each firm. Do your research in batches to save time and energy. Start with this book, and find out what you can about each of the firms in your primary target group. For answers to specific questions, contact any pertinent professional associations that may be able to help you learn more about an employer. Read industry publications looking for articles on the firm. (Addresses of associations and names of important publications are listed after each section of employer listings in this book.) Then look up the company on the Internet or try additional resources at your local library. Keep organized, and maintain a folder on each firm.

> **The more you know about a company, the more likely you are to catch an interviewer's eye. (You'll also face fewer surprises once you get the job!)**

Information to look for includes: company size; president, CEO, or owner's name; when the company was established; what each division does; and benefits that are important to you. An abundance of company information can now be found electronically, through the World Wide Web or commercial online services. Researching companies online is a convenient means of obtaining information quickly and easily. If you have access to the Internet, you can search from your home at any time of day.

You may search a particular company's Website for current information that may be otherwise unavailable in print. In fact, many companies that maintain a site update their information daily. In addition, you may also search articles written about the company online. Today, most of the nation's largest newspapers, magazines, trade publications, and regional business periodicals have online versions of their publications. To find additional resources, use a search engine like Yahoo! or Alta Vista and type in the keyword "companies" or "employers."

If you discover something that really disturbs you about the firm (they are about to close their only local office), or if you discover that your chances of getting a job there are practically nil (they have just instituted a hiring freeze), then cross them off your prospect list. If possible, supplement your research efforts by contacting individuals who know the firm well. Ideally you should make an informal contact with someone at that particular firm, but often a direct competitor or a major customer will be able to supply you with just as much information. At the very least, try to obtain whatever printed information the company has available -- not just annual reports, but product brochures, company profiles, or catalogs. This information is often available on the Internet.

Getting the Interview

Now it is time to make Direct Contact with the goal of arranging interviews. If you have read any books on job-searching, you may have noticed that most of these books tell you to avoid the human resources office like the plague. It is said that the human resources office never hires people; they screen candidates. Unfortunately, this is often the case. If you can identify the appropriate manager with the authority to hire you, you should try to contact that person directly.

The obvious means of initiating Direct Contact are:

- Mail (postal or electronic)
- Phone calls

Mail contact is a good choice if you have not been in the job market for a while. You can take your time to prepare a letter, say exactly what you want, and of course include your resume. Remember that employers receive many resumes every day. Don't be surprised if you do not get a response to your inquiry, *and don't spend weeks waiting for responses that may never come.* If you do send a letter, follow it up (or precede it) with a phone call. This will increase your impact, and because of the initial research you did, will underscore both your familiarity with and your interest in the firm. Bear in mind that your goal is to make your name a familiar one with prospective employers, so that when a position becomes available, your resume will be one of the first the hiring manager seeks out.

DEVELOPING YOUR CONTACTS: NETWORKING

Some career counselors feel that the best route to a better job is through somebody you already know or through somebody to whom you can be introduced. These counselors recommend that you build your contact base beyond your current acquaintances by asking each one to introduce you, or refer you, to additional people in your field of interest.

The theory goes like this: You might start with 15 personal contacts, each of whom introduces you to three additional people, for a total of 45 additional contacts. Then each of these people introduces you to three additional people, which adds 135 additional contacts. Theoretically, you will soon know every person in the industry.

Of course, developing your personal contacts does not work quite as smoothly as the theory suggests because some people will not be able to introduce you to anyone. The further you stray from your initial contact base, the weaker your references may be. So, if you do try developing your own contacts, try to begin with as many people that you know personally as you can. Dig into your personal phone book and your holiday greeting card list and locate old classmates from school. Be particularly sure to approach people who perform your personal business such as your lawyer, accountant, banker, doctor, stockbroker, and insurance agent. These people develop a very broad contact base due to the nature of their professions.

If you send a fax, always follow with a hard copy of your resume and cover letter in the mail. Often, through no fault of your own, a fax will come through illegibly and employers do not often have time to let candidates know.

Another alternative is to make a "cover call." Your cover call should be just like your cover letter: concise. Your first statement should interest the employer in you. Then try to subtly mention your familiarity with the firm. Don't be overbearing; keep your introduction to three sentences or less. Be pleasant, self-confident, and relaxed. This will greatly increase the chances of the person at the other end of the line developing the conversation. But don't press. If you are asked to follow up with "something in the mail," this signals the conversation's natural end. Don't try to prolong the conversation once it has ended, and don't ask what they want to receive in the mail. Always send your resume and a highly personalized follow-up letter, reminding the addressee of the phone conversation. *Always* include a cover letter if you are asked to send a resume, and treat your resume and cover letter as a total package. Gear your letter toward the specific position you are applying for and prove why you would be a "good match" for the position.

> **Always include a cover letter if you are asked to send a resume.**

Unless you are in telephone sales, making smooth and relaxed cover calls will probably not come easily. Practice them on your own, and then with your friends or relatives.

DON'T BOTHER WITH MASS MAILINGS OR BARRAGES OF PHONE CALLS

Direct Contact does not mean burying every firm within a hundred miles with mail and phone calls. Mass mailings rarely work in the job hunt. This also applies to those letters that are personalized -- but dehumanized -- on an automatic typewriter or computer. Don't waste your time or money on such a project; you will fool no one but yourself.

The worst part of sending out mass mailings, or making unplanned phone calls to companies you have not researched, is that you are likely to be remembered as someone with little genuine interest in the firm, who lacks sincerity -- somebody that nobody wants to hire.

If you obtain an interview as a result of a telephone conversation, be sure to send a thank-you note reiterating the points you made during the conversation. You will appear more professional and increase your impact. However, unless specifically requested, don't mail your resume once an interview has been arranged. Take it with you to the interview instead.

You should never show up to seek a professional position without an appointment. Even if you are somehow lucky enough to obtain an interview, you will appear so unprofessional that you will not be seriously considered.

HELP WANTED ADVERTISEMENTS

Only a small fraction of professional job openings are advertised. Yet the majority of jobseekers -- and quite a few people not in the job market -- spend a lot of time studying the help wanted ads. As a result, the competition for advertised openings is often very severe.

A moderate-sized employer told us about their experience advertising in the help wanted section of a major Sunday newspaper:

It was a disaster. We had over 500 responses from this relatively small ad in just one week. We have only two phone lines in this office and one was totally knocked out. We'll never advertise for professional help again.

If you insist on following up on help wanted ads, then research a firm before you reply to an ad. Preliminary research might help to separate you from all of the other professionals responding to that ad, many of whom will have only a passing interest in the opportunity. It will also give you insight about a particular firm, to help you determine if it is potentially a good match. That said, your chances of obtaining a job through the want ads are still much smaller than they are with the Direct Contact method.

Preparing for the Interview

As each interview is arranged, begin your in-depth research. You should arrive at an interview knowing the company upside-down and inside-out. You need to know the company's products, types of customers, subsidiaries, parent company, principal locations, rank in the industry, sales and profit trends, type of ownership, size, current plans, and much more. By this time you have probably narrowed your job search to one industry. Even if you haven't, you should still be familiar with common industry terms, the trends in the firm's industry, the firm's principal competitors and their relative performance, and the direction in which the industry leaders are headed.

Dig into every resource you can! Surf the Internet. Read the company literature, the trade press, the business press, and if the company is public, call your stockbroker (if you have one) and ask for additional information. If possible, speak to someone at the firm before the interview, or if not, speak to someone at a competing firm. The more time you spend, the better. Even if you feel extremely pressed for time, you should set aside several hours for pre-interview research.

> **You should arrive at an interview knowing the company upside-down and inside-out.**

If you have been out of the job market for some time, don't be surprised if you find yourself tense during your first few interviews. It will probably happen every time you re-enter the market, not just when you seek your first job after getting out of school.

Tension is natural during an interview, but knowing you have done a thorough research job should put you more at ease. Make a list of questions that you think might be asked in each interview. Think out your answers carefully and practice them with a friend. Tape record your responses to the problem questions. (*See also in this chapter: Informational Interviews.*) If you feel particularly unsure of your interviewing skills, arrange your first interviews at firms you are not as interested in. (But remember it is common courtesy to seem enthusiastic about the possibility of working for any firm at which you interview.) Practice again on your own after these first few interviews. Go over the difficult questions that you were asked.

Take some time to really think about how you will convey your work history. Present "bad experiences" as "learning experiences." Instead of saying "I hated my position as a salesperson because I had to bother people on the phone," say "I realized that cold-calling was not my strong suit. Though I love working with people, I decided my talents would be best used in a more face-to-face atmosphere." Always find some sort of lesson from previous jobs, as they all have one.

Interview Attire

How important is the proper dress for a job interview? Buying a complete wardrobe, donning new shoes, and having your hair styled every morning are not enough to guarantee you a career position as an investment banker. But on the other hand, if you can't find a clean, conservative suit or won't take the time to wash your hair, then you are just wasting your time by interviewing at all.

Personal grooming is as important as finding appropriate clothes for a job interview. Careful grooming indicates both a sense of thoroughness and self-confidence. This is not the time to make a statement -- take out the extra earrings and avoid any garish hair colors not found in nature. Women should not wear excessive makeup, and both men and women should refrain from wearing any perfume or cologne (it only takes a small spritz to leave an allergic interviewer with a fit of sneezing and a bad impression of your meeting). Men should be freshly shaven, even if the interview is late in the day, and men with long hair should have it pulled back and neat.

Men applying for any professional position should wear a suit, preferably in a conservative color such as navy or charcoal gray. It is easy to get away with wearing the same dark suit to consecutive interviews at the same company; just be sure to wear a different shirt and tie for each interview.

Women should also wear a business suit. Professionalism still dictates a suit with a skirt, rather than slacks, as proper interview garb for women. This is usually true even at companies where pants are acceptable attire for female employees. As much as you may disagree with this guideline, the more prudent time to fight this standard is after you land the job.

The final selection of candidates for a job opening won't be determined by dress, of course. However, inappropriate dress can quickly eliminate a first-round candidate. So while you shouldn't spend a fortune on a new wardrobe, you should be sure that your clothes are adequate. The key is to dress at least as formally or slightly more formally and more conservatively than the position would suggest.

What to Bring

Be complete. Everyone needs a watch, a pen, and a notepad. Finally, a briefcase or a leather-bound folder (containing extra, *unfolded*, copies of your resume) will help complete the look of professionalism.

Sometimes the interviewer will be running behind schedule. Don't be upset, be sympathetic. There is often pressure to interview a lot of candidates and to quickly fill a demanding position. So be sure to come to your interview with good reading material to keep yourself occupied and relaxed.

The Interview

The very beginning of the interview is the most important part because it determines the tone for the rest of it. Those first few moments are especially crucial. Do you smile when you meet? Do you establish enough eye contact, but not too much? Do you walk into the office with a self-assured and confident stride? Do you shake hands firmly? Do you make small talk easily without being garrulous? It is

---

BE PREPARED:
Some Common Interview Questions

Tell me about yourself.

Why did you leave your last job?

What excites you in your current job?

Where would you like to be in five years?

How much overtime are you willing to work?

What would your previous/present employer tell me about you?

Tell me about a difficult situation that you
faced at your previous/present job.

What are your greatest strengths?

What are your weaknesses?

Describe a work situation where you took initiative
and went beyond your normal responsibilities.

Why should we hire you?

---

human nature to judge people by that first impression, so make sure it is a good one. But most of all, try to be yourself.

Often the interviewer will begin, after the small talk, by telling you about the company, the division, the department, or perhaps, the position. Because of your detailed research, the information about the company should be repetitive for you, and the interviewer would probably like nothing better than to avoid this regurgitation of the company biography. So if you can do so tactfully, indicate to the interviewer that you are very familiar with the firm. If he or she seems intent on providing you with background information, despite your hints, then acquiesce.

But be sure to remain attentive. If you can manage to generate a brief discussion of the company or the industry at this point, without being forceful, great. It will help to further build rapport, underscore your interest, and increase your impact.

> **The interviewer's job is to find a reason to turn you down; your job is to not provide that reason.**
>
> -John L. LaFevre, author,
> *How You Really Get Hired*
>
> Reprinted from the 1989/90 *CPC Annual,* with permission of the National Association of Colleges and Employers (formerly College Placement Council, Inc.), copyright holder.

Soon (if it didn't begin that way) the interviewer will begin the questions, many of which you will have already practiced. This period of the interview usually falls into one of two categories (or somewhere in between): either a structured interview, where the interviewer has a prescribed set of questions to ask; or an unstructured interview, where the interviewer will ask only leading questions to get you to talk about yourself, your experiences, and your goals. Try to sense as quickly as possible in which direction the interviewer wishes to proceed. This will make the interviewer feel more relaxed and in control of the situation.

Remember to keep attuned to the interviewer and make the length of your answers appropriate to the situation. If you are really unsure as to how detailed a response the interviewer is seeking, then ask.

As the interview progresses, the interviewer will probably mention some of the most important responsibilities of the position. If applicable, draw parallels between your experience and the demands of the position as detailed by the interviewer. Describe your past experience in the same manner that you do on your resume: emphasizing results and achievements and not merely describing activities. But don't exaggerate. Be on the level about your abilities.

The first interview is often the toughest, where many candidates are screened out. If you are interviewing for a very competitive position, you will have to make an impression that will last. Focus on a few of your greatest strengths that are relevant to the position. Develop these points carefully, state them again in different words, and then try to summarize them briefly at the end of the interview.

Often the interviewer will pause toward the end and ask if you have any questions. Particularly in a structured interview, this might be the one chance to really show your knowledge of and interest in the firm. Have a list prepared of specific questions that are of real interest to you. Let your questions subtly show your research and your knowledge of the firm's activities. It is wise to have an extensive list of questions, as several of them may be answered during the interview.

Do not turn your opportunity to ask questions into an interrogation. Avoid reading directly from your list of questions, and ask questions that you are fairly certain the interviewer can answer (remember how you feel when you cannot answer a question during an interview).

Even if you are unable to determine the salary range beforehand, do not ask about it during the first interview. You can always ask later. Above all, don't ask about fringe benefits until you have been offered a position. (Then be sure to get all the details.)

Try not to be negative about anything during the interview, particularly any past employer or any previous job. Be cheerful. Everyone likes to work with someone who seems to be happy. Even if you detest your current/former job or manager, do not make disparaging comments. The interviewer may construe this as a sign of a potential attitude problem and not consider you a strong candidate.

Don't let a tough question throw you off base. If you don't know the answer to a question, simply say so -- do not apologize. Just smile. Nobody can answer every question -- particularly some of the questions that are asked in job interviews.

Before your first interview, you may be able to determine how many rounds of interviews there usually are for positions at your level. (Of course it may differ quite a bit even within the different levels of one firm.) Usually you can count on attending at least two or three interviews, although some firms are known to give a minimum of six interviews for all professional positions. While you should be more relaxed as you return for subsequent interviews, the pressure will be on. The more prepared you are, the better.

Depending on what information you are able to obtain, you might want to vary your strategy quite a bit from interview to interview. For instance, if the first interview is a screening interview, then be sure a few of your strengths really stand out. On the other hand, if later interviews are primarily with people who are in a position to veto your hiring, but not to push it forward, then you should primarily focus on building rapport as opposed to reiterating and developing your key strengths.

If it looks as though your skills and background do not match the position the interviewer was hoping to fill, ask him or her if there is another division or subsidiary that perhaps could profit from your talents.

After the Interview

Write a follow-up letter immediately after the interview, while it is still fresh in the interviewer's mind (see the sample follow-up letter format found in the Resumes and Cover Letters chapter). Not only is this a thank-you, but it also gives you the chance to provide the interviewer with any details you may have forgotten (as long as they can be tactfully added in). If you haven't heard back from the interviewer within a week of sending your thank-you letter, call to stress your continued interest in the firm and the position. If you lost any points during the interview for any reason, this letter can help you regain footing. Be polite and make sure to stress your continued interest and competency to fill the position. Just don't forget to proofread it thoroughly. If you are unsure of the spelling of the interviewer's name, call the receptionist and ask.

THE BALANCING ACT:
Looking for a New Job While Currently Employed

For those of you who are still employed, job-searching will be particularly tiring because it must be done in addition to your normal work responsibilities. So don't overwork yourself to the point where you show up to interviews looking exhausted or start to slip behind at your current job. On the other hand, don't be tempted to quit your present job! The long hours are worth it. Searching for a job while you have one puts you in a position of strength.

Making Contact

If you must be at your office during the business day, then you have additional problems to deal with. How can you work interviews into the business day? And if you work in an open office, how can you even call to set up interviews? Obviously, you should keep up the effort and the appearances on your present job. So maximize your use of the lunch hour, early mornings, and late afternoons for calling. If you keep trying, you'll be surprised how often you will be able to reach the executive you are trying to contact during your out-of-office hours. You can catch people as early as 8 a.m. and as late as 6 p.m. on frequent occasions.

Scheduling Interviews

Your inability to interview at any time other than lunch just might work to your advantage. If you can, try to set up as many interviews as possible for your lunch hour. This will go a long way to creating a relaxed atmosphere. But be sure the interviews don't stray too far from the agenda on hand.

Lunchtime interviews are much easier to obtain if you have substantial career experience. People with less experience will often find no alternative to taking time off for interviews. If you have to take time off, you have to take time off. But try to do this as little as possible. Try to take the whole day off in order to avoid being blatantly obvious about your job search, and try to schedule two to three interviews for the same day. (It is very difficult to maintain an optimum level of energy at more than three interviews in one day.) Explain to the interviewer why you might have to juggle your interview schedule; he/she should honor the respect you're showing your current employer by minimizing your days off and will probably appreciate the fact that another prospective employer is interested in you.

> **Try calling as early as 8 a.m. and as late as 6 p.m. You'll be surprised how often you will be able to reach the executive you want during these times of the day.**

References

What do you tell an interviewer who asks for references from your current employer? Just say that while you are happy to have your former employers contacted, you are trying to keep your job search confidential and would rather that your current employer not be contacted until you have been given a firm offer.

IF YOU'RE FIRED OR LAID OFF:
Picking Yourself Up and Dusting Yourself Off

If you've been fired or laid off, you are not the first and will not be the last to go through this traumatic experience. In today's changing economy, thousands of professionals lose their jobs every year. Even if you were terminated with just cause, do not lose heart. Remember, being fired is not a reflection on you as a person. It is usually a reflection of your company's staffing needs and its perception of your recent job performance and attitude. And if you were not performing up to par or enjoying your work, then you will probably be better off at another company anyway.

> **Be prepared for the question "Why were you fired?" during job interviews.**

A thorough job search could take months, so be sure to negotiate a reasonable severance package, if possible, and determine to what benefits, such as health insurance, you are still legally entitled. Also, register for unemployment compensation immediately. Don't be surprised to find other professionals collecting unemployment compensation -- it is for everyone who has lost their job.

Don't start your job search with a flurry of unplanned activity. Start by choosing a strategy and working out a plan. Now is not the time for major changes in your life. If possible, remain in the same career and in the same geographical location, at least until you have been working again for a while. On the other hand, if the only industry for which you are trained is leaving, or is severely depressed in your area, then you should give prompt consideration to moving or switching careers.

Avoid mentioning you were fired when arranging interviews, but be prepared for the question "Why were you fired?" during an interview. If you were laid off as a result of downsizing, briefly explain, being sure to reinforce that your job loss was not due to performance. If you were in fact fired, be honest, but try to detail the reason as favorably as possible and portray what you have learned from your mistakes. If you are confident one of your past managers will give you a good reference, tell the interviewer to contact that person. Do not to speak negatively of your past employer and try not to sound particularly worried about your status of being temporarily unemployed.

Finally, don't spend too much time reflecting on why you were let go or how you might have avoided it. Think positively, look to the future, and be sure to follow a careful plan during your job search.

THE COLLEGE STUDENT:
Conducting Your First Job Search

While you will be able to apply many of the basics covered earlier in this chapter to your job search, there are some situations unique to the college student's job search.

> ### THE GPA QUESTION
>
> You are interviewing for the job of your dreams. Everything is going well: You've established a good rapport, the interviewer seems impressed with your qualifications, and you're almost positive the job is yours. Then you're asked about your GPA, which is pitifully low. Do you tell the truth and watch your dream job fly out the window?
>
> *Never* lie about your GPA (they may request your transcript, and no company will hire a liar). You can, however, explain if there is a reason you don't feel your grades reflect your abilities, and mention any other impressive statistics. For example, if you have a high GPA in your major, or in the last few semesters (as opposed to your cumulative college career), you can use that fact to your advantage.

Perhaps the biggest problem college students face is lack of experience. Many schools have internship programs designed to give students exposure to the field of their choice, as well as the opportunity to make valuable contacts. Check out your school's career services department to see what internships are available. If your school does not have a formal internship program, or if there are no available internships that appeal to you, try contacting local businesses and offering your services. Often, businesses will be more than willing to have an extra pair of hands (especially if those hands are unpaid!) for a day or two each week. Or try contacting school alumni to see if you can "shadow" them for a few days, and see what their daily duties are like.

Informational Interviews

Although many jobseekers do not do this, it can be extremely helpful to arrange an informational interview with a college alumnus or someone else who works in your desired industry. You interview them about their job, their company, and their industry with questions you have prepared in advance. This can be done over the phone but is usually done in person. This will provide you with a contact in the industry who may give you more valuable information -- or perhaps even a job opportunity -- in the future. Always follow up with a thank you letter that includes your contact information.

The goal is to try to begin building experience and establishing contacts as early as possible in your college career.

What do you do if, for whatever reason, you weren't able to get experience directly related to your desired career? First, look at your previous jobs and see if there's anything you can highlight. Did you supervise or train other employees? Did you reorganize the accounting system, or boost productivity in some way? Accomplishments like these demonstrate leadership, responsibility, and innovation -- qualities that most companies look for in employees. And don't forget volunteer activities and school clubs, which can also showcase these traits.

On-Campus Recruiting

Companies will often send recruiters to interview on-site at various colleges. This gives students a chance to interview with companies that may not have interviewed them otherwise. This is particularly true if a company schedules "open" interviews, in which the only screening process is who is first in line at the sign-ups. Of course, since many more applicants gain interviews in this format, this also means that many more people are rejected. The on-campus interview is generally a screening interview, to see if it is worth the company's time to invite you in for a second interview. So do everything possible to make yourself stand out from the crowd.

The first step, of course, is to check out any and all information your school's career center has on the company. If the information seems out of date, check out the company on the Internet or call the company's headquarters and ask for any printed information.

Many companies will host an informational meeting for interviewees, often the evening before interviews are scheduled to take place. DO NOT MISS THIS MEETING. The recruiter will almost certainly ask if you attended. Make an effort to stay after the meeting and talk with the company's representatives. Not only does this give you an opportunity to find out more information about both the company and the position, it also makes you stand out in the recruiter's mind. If there's a particular company that you had your heart set on, but you weren't able to get an interview with them, attend the information session anyway. You may be able to persuade the recruiter to squeeze you into the schedule. (Or you may discover that the company really isn't the right fit for you after all.)

Try to check out the interview site beforehand. Some colleges may conduct "mock" interviews that take place in one of the standard interview rooms. Or you may be able to convince a career counselor (or even a custodian) to let you sneak a peek during off-hours. Either way, having an idea of the room's setup will help you to mentally prepare.

Arrive at least 15 minutes early to the interview. The recruiter may be ahead of schedule, and might meet you early. But don't be surprised if previous interviews have run over, resulting in your 30-minute slot being reduced to 20 minutes (or less). Don't complain or appear anxious; just use the time you do have as efficiently as possible to showcase the reasons *you* are the ideal candidate. Staying calm and composed in these situations will work to your advantage.

LAST WORDS

A parting word of advice. Again and again during your job search you will face rejection. You will be rejected when you apply for interviews. You will be rejected after interviews. For every job offer you finally receive, you probably will have been rejected many times. Don't let rejections slow you down. Keep reminding yourself that the sooner you go out, start your job search, and get those rejections flowing in, the closer you will be to obtaining the job you want.

RESUMES AND COVER LETTERS

When filling a position, an employer will often have 100-plus applicants, but time to interview only a handful of the most promising ones. As a result, he or she will reject most applicants after only briefly skimming their resumes.

Unless you have phoned and talked to the employer -- which you should do whenever you can -- you will be chosen or rejected for an interview entirely on the basis of your resume and cover letter. *Your cover letter must catch the employer's attention, and your resume must hold it.* (But remember -- a resume is no substitute for a job search campaign. *You* must seek a job. Your resume is only one tool, albeit a critical one.)

RESUME FORMAT:
Mechanics of a First Impression

The Basics

Employers dislike long resumes, so unless you have an unusually strong background with many years of experience and a diversity of outstanding achievements, keep your resume length to one page. If you must squeeze in more information than would otherwise fit, try using a smaller typeface or changing the margins. Watch also for "widows" at the end of paragraphs. You can often free up some space if you can shorten the information enough to get rid of those single words taking up an entire line. Another tactic that works with some word processing programs is to decrease the font size of your paragraph returns and changing the spacing between lines.

Print your resume on standard 8 1/2" x 11" paper. Since recruiters often get resumes in batches of hundreds, a smaller-sized resume may be lost in the pile. Oversized resumes are likely to get crumpled at the edges, and won't fit easily in their files.

First impressions matter, so make sure the recruiter's first impression of your resume is a good one. Never hand-write your resume (or cover letter)! Print your resume on quality paper that has weight and texture, in a conservative color such as white, ivory, or pale gray. Good resume paper is easy to find at many stores that sell stationery or office products. It is even available at some drug stores. Use *matching* paper and envelopes for both your resume and cover letter. One hiring manager at a major magazine throws out all resumes that arrive on paper that differs in color from the envelope!

Do not buy paper with images of clouds and rainbows in the background or anything that looks like casual stationery that you would send to your favorite aunt. Do not spray perfume or cologne on your resume. Do not include your picture with your resume unless you have a specific and appropriate reason to do so.

Another tip: Do a test print of your resume (and cover letter), to make sure the watermark is on the same side as the text so that you can read it. Also make sure it is right-side up. As trivial as this may sound, some recruiters check for this! One recruiter at a law firm in New Hampshire sheepishly admitted this is the first thing he checks. *"I open each envelope and check the watermarks on the resume and cover letter. Those candidates that have it wrong go into a different pile."*

Getting it on Paper

Modern photocomposition typesetting gives you the clearest, sharpest image, a wide variety of type styles, and effects such as italics, bold-facing, and book-like justified margins. It is also too expensive for many jobseekers. The quality of today's laser printers means that a computer-generated resume can look just as impressive as one that has been professionally typeset.

A computer with a word processing or desktop publishing program is the most common way to generate your resume. This allows you the flexibility to make changes almost instantly and to store different drafts on disk. Word processing and desktop publishing programs also offer many different fonts to choose from, each taking up different amounts of space. (It is generally best to stay between 9-point and 12-point font size.) Many other options are also available, such as bold-facing or italicizing for emphasis and the ability to change and manipulate spacing. It is generally recommended to leave the right-hand margin unjustified as this keeps the spacing between the text even and therefore easier to read. It is not wrong to justify both margins of text, but if possible try it both ways before you decide.

For a resume on paper, the end result will be largely determined by the quality of the printer you use. Laser printers will generally provide the best quality. Do not use a dot matrix printer.

Many companies now use scanning equipment to screen the resumes they receive, and certain paper, fonts, and other features are more compatible with this technology. White paper is preferable, as well as a standard font such as Courier or Helvetica. You should use at least a 10-point font, and avoid bolding, italics, underlining, borders, boxes, or graphics.

Household typewriters and office typewriters with nylon or other cloth ribbons are *not* good enough for typing your resume. If you don't have access to a quality word processing program, hire a professional with the resources to prepare your resume for you. Keep in mind that businesses such as Kinko's (open 24 hours) provide access to computers with quality printers.

Don't make your copies on an office photocopier. Only the human resources office may see the resume you mail. Everyone else may see only a copy of it, and copies of copies quickly become unreadable. Furthermore, sending photocopies of your resume or cover letter is completely unprofessional. Either print out each copy individually, or take your resume to a professional copy shop, which will generally offer professionally-maintained, extra-high-quality photocopiers and charge fairly reasonable prices. You want your resume to represent you with the look of polished quality.

Proof with Care

Whether you typed it or paid to have it produced professionally, mistakes on resumes are not only embarrassing, but will usually remove you from consideration (particularly if something obvious such as your name is misspelled). No matter how much you paid someone else to type, write, or typeset your resume, *you* lose if there is a mistake. So proofread it as carefully as possible. Get a friend to help you. Read your draft aloud as your friend checks the proof copy. Then have your friend read aloud while you check. Next, read it letter by letter to check spelling and punctuation.

If you are having it typed or typeset by a resume service or a printer, and you don't have time to proof it, pay for it and take it home. Proof it there and bring it back later to get it corrected and printed.

If you wrote your resume with a word processing program, use the built-in spell checker to double-check for spelling errors. Keep in mind that a spell checker will not find errors such as "to" for "two" or "wok" for "work." Many spell check programs do not recognize missing or misused punctuation, nor are they set to check the spelling of capitalized words. It's important that you still proofread your resume to check for grammatical mistakes and other problems, even <u>after</u> it has been spellchecked. If you find mistakes, do not make edits in pen or pencil or use white-out to fix them on the final copy!

Electronic Resumes

As companies rely increasingly on emerging technologies to find qualified candidates for job openings, you may opt to create an electronic resume in order to remain competitive in today's job market. Why is this important? Companies today sometimes request that resumes be submitted by e-mail, and many hiring managers regularly check online resume databases for candidates to fill unadvertised job openings. Other companies enlist the services of electronic employment database services, which charge jobseekers a nominal fee to have their resumes posted to the database to be viewed by potential employers. Still other companies use their own automated applicant tracking systems, in which case your resume is fed through a scanner that sends the image to a computer that "reads" your resume, looking for keywords, and files it accordingly in its database.

Whether you're posting your resume online, e-mailing it directly to an employer, sending it to an electronic employment database, or sending it to a company you suspect uses an automated applicant tracking system, you must create some form of electronic resume to take advantage of the technology. Don't panic! An electronic resume is simply a modified version of your conventional resume. An electronic resume is one that is sparsely formatted, but filled with keywords and important facts.

In order to post your resume to the Internet -- either to an online resume database or through direct e-mail to an employer -- you will need to change the way your resume is formatted. Instead of a Word, WordPerfect, or other word processing document, save your resume as a plain text, DOS, or ASCII file. These three terms are basically interchangeable, and describe text at its simplest, most basic level, without the formatting such as boldface or italics that most jobseekers use to make their resumes look more interesting. If you use e-mail, you'll notice that all of your messages are written and received in this format. First, you should remove all formatting from your resume including boldface, italics, underlining, bullets, differing font sizes, and graphics. Then, convert and save your resume as a plain text file. Most word processing programs have a "save as" feature that allows you to save files in different formats. Here, you should choose "text only" or "plain text."

Another option is to create a resume in HTML (hypertext markup language), the text formatting language used to publish information on the World Wide Web. However, the real usefulness of HTML resumes is still being explored. Most of the major online databases do not accept HTML resumes, and the vast majority of companies only accept plain text resumes through their e-mail.

Finally, if you simply wish to send your resume to an electronic employment database or a company that uses an automated applicant tracking system, there is no need to convert your resume to a plain text file. The only change you need to make is to organize the information in your resume by keywords. Employers are likely to do keyword searches for information, such as degree held or knowledge of particular types of software. Therefore, using the right keywords or key phrases in your resume is critical to its ultimate success. Keywords are usually nouns or short phrases that the computer searches for which refer to experience, training, skills, and abilities. For example, let's say an employer searches an employment database for a sales representative with the following criteria:

BS/BA
exceeded quota
cold calls
high energy
willing to travel

Even if you have the right qualifications, neglecting to use these keywords would result in the computer passing over your resume. Although there is no way to know for sure which keywords employers are most likely to search for, you can make educated guesses by checking the help-wanted ads or online job postings for your type of job. You should also arrange keywords in a keyword summary, a paragraph listing your qualifications that immediately follows your name and address (see sample letter in this chapter). In addition, choose a nondecorative font with clear, distinct characters, such as Helvetica or Times. It is more difficult for a scanner to accurately pick up the more unusual fonts. Boldface and all capital letters are best used only for major section headings, such as "Experience" and "Education." It is also best to avoid using italics or underlining, since this can cause the letters to bleed into one another.

For more specific information on creating and sending electronic resumes, see *The Adams Internet Job Search Almanac.*

Types of Resumes

The most common resume formats are the functional resume, the chronological resume, and the combination resume. (Examples can be found at the end of this chapter.) A functional resume focuses on skills and de-emphasizes job titles, employers, etc. A functional resume is best if you have been out of the work force for a long time or are changing careers. It is also good if you want to highlight specific skills and strengths, especially if all of your work experience has been at one company. This format can also be a good choice if you are just out of school or have no experience in your desired field.

Choose a chronological format if you are currently working or were working recently, and if your most recent experiences relate to your desired field. Use reverse chronological order and include dates. To a recruiter your last job and your latest schooling are the most important, so put the last first and list the rest going back in time.

A combination resume is perhaps the most common. This resume simply combines elements of the functional and chronological resume formats. This is used by many jobseekers with a solid track record who find elements of both types useful.

Organization

Your name, phone number, e-mail address (if you have one), and a complete mailing address should be at the top of your resume. Try to make your name stand out by using a slightly larger font size or all capital letters. Be sure to spell out everything. Never abbreviate St. for Street or Rd. for Road. If you are a college student, you should also put your home address and phone number at the top.

Change your message on your answering machine if necessary -- RUSH blaring in the background or your sorority sisters screaming may not come across well to all recruiters. If you think you may be moving within six months then include a second address and phone number of a trusted friend or relative who can reach you no matter where you are.

Remember that employers will keep your resume on file and
may contact you months later if a position opens that fits your qualifications.
All too often, candidates are unreachable because they have moved and had not
previously provided enough contact options on their resume.

Next, list your experience, then your education. If you are a recent graduate, list your education first, unless your experience is more important than your education. (For example, if you have just graduated from a teaching school, have some business experience, and are applying for a job in business, you would list your business experience first.)

Keep everything easy to find. Put the dates of your employment and education on the left of the page. Put the names of the companies you worked for and the schools you attended a few spaces to the right of the dates. Put the city and state, or the city and country, where you studied or worked to the right of the page.

The important thing is simply to break up the text in some logical way that makes your resume visually attractive and easy to scan, so experiment to see which layout works best for your resume. However you set it up, *stay consistent.* Inconsistencies in fonts, spacing, or tenses will make your resume look sloppy. Also, be sure to use tabs to keep your information vertically lined up, rather than the less precise space bar.

RESUME CONTENT:
Say it with Style
Sell Yourself

You are selling your skills and accomplishments in your resume, so it is important to inventory yourself and know yourself. If you have achieved something, say so. Put it in the best possible light, but avoid subjective statements, such as "I am a hard worker" or "I get along well with my coworkers." Just stick to the facts.

While you shouldn't hold back or be modest, don't exaggerate your achievements to the point of misrepresentation. Be honest. Many companies will immediately drop an applicant from consideration (or fire a current employee) upon discovering inaccurate or untrue information on a resume or other application material.

Write down the important (and pertinent) things you have done, but do it in as few words as possible. Your resume will be scanned, not read, and short, concise phrases are much more effective than long-winded sentences. Avoid the use of "I" when emphasizing your accomplishments. Instead, use brief phrases beginning with action verbs.

While some technical terms will be unavoidable, you should try to avoid excessive "technicalese." Keep in mind that the first person to see your resume may be a human resources person who won't necessarily know all the jargon -- and how can they be impressed by something they don't understand?

Keep it Brief

Also, try to hold your paragraphs to six lines or less. If you have more than six lines of information about one job or school, put it in two or more paragraphs. A short resume will be examined more carefully. Remember: Your resume usually has between eight and 45 seconds to catch an employer's eye. So make every second count.

Job Objective

A functional resume may require a job objective to give it focus. One or two sentences describing the job you are seeking can clarify in what capacity your skills will be best put to use. Be sure that your stated objective is in line with the position you're applying for.

Examples:

> An entry-level editorial assistant position in the publishing industry.
> A senior management position with a telecommunications firm.

Don't include a job objective on a chronological resume unless your previous work experiences are <u>completely</u> unrelated to the position for which you're applying. The presence of an overly specific job objective might eliminate you from consideration for other positions that a recruiter feels are a better match for your qualifications. But even if you don't put an objective on paper, having a career goal in mind as you write can help give your resume a solid sense of direction.

USE ACTION VERBS

How you write your resume is just as important as *what* you write. In describing previous work experiences, the strongest resumes use short phrases beginning with action verbs. Below are a few you may want to use. (This list is not all-inclusive.)

achieved	developed	integrated	purchased
administered	devised	interpreted	reduced
advised	directed	interviewed	regulated
arranged	distributed	launched	represented
assisted	established	managed	resolved
attained	evaluated	marketed	restored
budgeted	examined	mediated	restructured
built	executed	monitored	revised
calculated	expanded	negotiated	scheduled
collaborated	expedited	obtained	selected
collected	facilitated	operated	served
compiled	formulated	ordered	sold
completed	founded	organized	solved
computed	generated	participated	streamlined
conducted	headed	performed	studied
consolidated	identified	planned	supervised
constructed	implemented	prepared	supplied
consulted	improved	presented	supported
controlled	increased	processed	tested
coordinated	initiated	produced	trained
created	installed	proposed	updated
determined	instructed	published	wrote

Some jobseekers may choose to include both "Relevant Experience" and "Additional Experience" sections. This can be useful, as it allows the jobseeker to place more emphasis on certain experiences and to de-emphasize others.

Emphasize continued experience in a particular job area or continued interest in a particular industry. De-emphasize irrelevant positions. It is okay to include one opening line providing a general description of each company you've worked at. Delete positions that you held for less than four months (unless you are a very recent college grad or still in school). Stress your <u>results</u> and your achievements, elaborating on how you contributed in your previous jobs. Did you increase sales, reduce costs, improve a product, implement a new program? Were you promoted? Use specific numbers (i.e., quantities, percentages, dollar amounts) whenever possible.

Education

Keep it brief if you have more than two years of career experience. Elaborate more if you have less experience. If you are a recent college graduate, you may choose to include any high school activities that are directly relevant to your career. If you've been out of school for a while you don't need to list your education prior to college.

Mention degrees received and any honors or special awards. Note individual courses or projects you participated in that might be relevant for employers. For example, if you are an English major applying for a position as a business writer, be sure to mention any business or economics courses. Previous experience such as Editor-in-Chief of the school newspaper would be relevant as well.

If you are uploading your resume to an online job hunting site such as CareerCity.com, action verbs are still important, but the key words or key nouns that a computer would search for become more important. For example, if you're seeking an accounting position, key nouns that a computer would search for such as "Lotus 1-2-3" or "CPA" or "payroll" become very important.

Highlight Impressive Skills

Be sure to mention any computer skills you may have. You may wish to include a section entitled "Additional Skills" or "Computer Skills," in which you list any software programs you know. An additional skills section is also an ideal place to mention fluency in a foreign language.

Personal Data

This section is optional, but if you choose to include it, keep it brief. A one-word mention of hobbies such as fishing, chess, baseball, cooking, etc., can give the person who will interview you a good way to open up the conversation.

Team sports experience is looked at favorably. It doesn't hurt to include activities that are somewhat unusual (fencing, Akido, '70s music) or that somehow relate to the position or the company to which you're applying. For instance, it would be worth noting if you are a member of a professional organization in your industry of interest. Never include information about your age, alias, date of birth, health, physical characteristics, marital status, religious affiliation, or political/moral beliefs.

References

The most that is needed is the sentence "References available upon request" at the bottom of your resume. If you choose to leave it out, that's fine. This line is not really necessary. It is understood that references will most likely be asked for and provided by you later on in the interviewing process. Do not actually send references with your resume and cover letter unless specifically requested.

HIRING A RESUME WRITER:
Is it the Right Choice for You?

If you write reasonably well, it is to your advantage to write your own resume. Writing your resume forces you to review your experiences and figure out how to explain your accomplishments in clear, brief phrases. This will help you when you explain your work to interviewers. It is also easier to tailor your resume to each position you're applying for when you have put it together yourself.

If you write your resume, everything will be in your own words; it will sound like you. It will say what you want it to say. If you are a good writer, know yourself well, and have a good idea of which parts of your background employers are looking for, you should be able to write your own resume better than someone else. If you decide to write your resume yourself, have as many people as possible review and proofread it. Welcome objective opinions and other perspectives.

When to Get Help

If you have difficulty writing in "resume style" (which is quite unlike normal written language), if you are unsure which parts of your background to emphasize, or if you think your resume would make your case better if it did not follow one of the standard forms outlined either here or in a book on resumes, then you should consider having it professionally written.

Even some professional resume writers we know have had their resumes written with the help of fellow professionals. They sought the help of someone who could be objective about their background, as well as provide an experienced sounding board to help focus their thoughts.

If You Hire a Pro

The best way to choose a writer is by reputation: the recommendation of a friend, a personnel director, your school placement officer, or someone else knowledgeable in the field.

Important questions:
- "How long have you been writing resumes?"
- "If I'm not satisfied with what you write, will you go over it with me and change it?"
- "Do you charge by the hour or a flat rate?"

There is no sure relation between price and quality, except that you are unlikely to get a good writer for less than $50 for an uncomplicated resume and you shouldn't have to pay more than $300 unless your experience is very extensive or complicated. There will be additional charges for printing. Assume nothing no matter how much you pay. It is your career at stake if there are mistakes on your resume!

Few resume services will give you a firm price over the phone, simply because some resumes are too complicated and take too long to do for a predetermined price. Some services will quote you a price that applies to almost all of their customers. Once you decide to use a specific writer, you should insist on a firm price quote *before* engaging their services. Also, find out how expensive minor changes will be.

COVER LETTERS:
Quick, Clear, and Concise

Always mail a cover letter with your resume. In a cover letter you can show an interest in the company that you can't show in a resume. You can also point out one or two of your skills or accomplishments the company can put to good use.

Make it Personal

The more personal you can get, the better, so long as you keep it professional. If someone known to the person you are writing has recommended that you contact the company, get permission to include his/her name in the letter. If you can get the name of a person to send the letter to, address it directly to that person (after first calling the company to verify the spelling of the person's name, correct title, and mailing address). Be sure to put the person's name and title on both the letter and the envelope. This will ensure that your letter will get through to the proper person, even if a new person now occupies this position. It will not always be possible to get the name of a person. Always strive to get at least a title.

Be sure to mention something about why you have an interest in the company - - *so many candidates apply for jobs with no apparent knowledge of what the company does!* This conveys the message that they just want any job.

Type cover letters in full. Don't try the cheap and easy ways, like using a computer mail merge program or photocopying the body of your letter and typing in the inside address and salutation. You will give the impression that you are mailing to a host of companies and have no particular interest in any one.

Print your cover letter on the same color and same high-quality paper as your resume.

Cover letter basic format

Paragraph 1: State what the position is that you are seeking. It is not always necessary to state how you found out about the position -- often you will apply without knowing that a position is open.

Paragraph 2: Include what you know about the company and why you are interested in working there. Mention any prior contact with the company or someone known to the hiring person if relevant. Briefly state your qualifications and what you can offer. (Do not talk about what you cannot do).

Paragraph 3: Close with your phone number and where/when you can be reached. Make a request for an interview. State when you will follow up by phone (or mail or e-mail if the ad requests no phone calls). Do not wait long -- generally five working days. If you say you're going to follow up, then actually do it! This phone call can get your resume noticed when it might otherwise sit in a stack of 225 other resumes.

Cover letter do's and don'ts

- *Do* keep your cover letter brief and to the point.
- *Do* be sure it is error-free.
- *Do* accentuate what you can offer the company, not what you hope to gain.
- *Do* be sure your phone number and address is on your cover letter just in case it gets separated from your resume (this happens!).
- *Do* check the watermark by holding the paper up to a light -- be sure it is facing forward so it is readable -- on the same side as the text, and right-side up.
- *Do* sign your cover letter (or type your name if you are sending it electronically). Blue or black ink are both fine. Do not use red ink.
- *Don't* just repeat information verbatim from your resume.
- *Don't* overuse the personal pronoun "I."
- *Don't* send a generic cover letter -- show your personal knowledge of and interest in that particular company.

THANK YOU LETTERS:
Another Way to Stand Out

As mentioned earlier, *always* send a thank you letter after an interview (see the sample later in this section). So few candidates do this and it is yet another way for you to stand out. Be sure to mention something specific from the interview and restate your interest in the company and the position.

It is generally acceptable to handwrite your thank you letter on a generic thank you card (but *never* a postcard). Make sure handwritten notes are neat and legible. However, if you are in doubt, typing your letter is always the safe bet. If you met with several people it is fine to send them each an individual thank you letter. Call the company if you need to check on the correct spelling of their names.

Remember to:
- Keep it short.
- Proofread it carefully.
- Send it *promptly.*

FUNCTIONAL RESUME

C.J. RAVENCLAW
129 Pennsylvania Avenue
Washington DC 20500
202/555-6652
e-mail: ravenclaw@dcpress.net

Objective
A position as a graphic designer commensurate with my acquired skills and expertise.

Summary
Extensive experience in plate making, separations, color matching, background definition, printing, mechanicals, color corrections, and personnel supervision. A highly motivated manager and effective communicator. Proven ability to:

- **Create Commercial Graphics**
- **Produce Embossed Drawings**
- **Color Separate**
- **Control Quality**
- **Resolve Printing Problems**
- **Analyze Customer Satisfaction**

Qualifications
Printing:
Knowledgeable in black and white as well as color printing. Excellent judgment in determining acceptability of color reproduction through comparison with original. Proficient at producing four- or five-color corrections on all media, as well as restyling previously reproduced four-color artwork.

Customer Relations:
Routinely work closely with customers to ensure specifications are met. Capable of striking a balance between technical printing capabilities and need for customer satisfaction through entire production process.

Specialties:
Practiced at creating silk screen overlays for a multitude of processes including velo bind, GBC bind, and perfect bind. Creative design and timely preparation of posters, flyers, and personalized stationery.

Personnel Supervision:
Skillful at fostering atmosphere that encourages highly talented artists to balance high-level creativity with maximum production. Consistently beat production deadlines. Instruct new employees, apprentices, and students in both artistry and technical operations.

Experience
Graphic Arts Professor, Ohio State University, Columbus OH (1992-1996).
Manager, Design Graphics, Washington DC (1997-present).

Education
Massachusetts Conservatory of Art, Ph.D. 1990
University of Massachusetts, B.A. 1988

CHRONOLOGICAL RESUME

HARRY SEABORN
557 Shoreline Drive
Seattle, WA 98404
(206) 555-6584
e-mail: hseaborn@centco.com

EXPERIENCE

THE CENTER COMPANY   Seattle, WA
Systems Programmer   1996-present
• Develop and maintain customer accounting and order tracking database using a Visual Basic front end and SQL server.
• Plan and implement migration of company wide transition from mainframe-based dumb terminals to a true client server environment using Windows NT Workstation and Server.
• Oversee general local and wide area network administration including the development of a variety of intranet modules to improve internal company communication and planning across divisions.

INFO TECH, INC.   Seattle, WA
Technical Manager   1994-1996
• Designed and managed the implementation of a network providing the legal community with a direct line to Supreme Court cases across the Internet using SQL Server and a variety of Internet tools.
• Developed a system to make the entire library catalog available on line using PERL scripts and SQL.
• Used Visual Basic and Microsoft Access to create a registration system for university registrar.

EDUCATION

SALEM STATE UNIVERSITY   Salem, OR
    M.S. in Computer Science.   1993
    B.S. in Computer Science.   1991

COMPUTER SKILLS

• Programming Languages: Visual Basic, Java, C++, SQL, PERL
• Software: SQL Server, Internet Information Server, Oracle
• Operating Systems: Windows NT, UNIX, Linux

FUNCTIONAL RESUME

Donna Hermione Moss
703 Wizard's Way
Chicago, IL 60601
(312) 555-8841
e-mail: donna@cowfire.com

OBJECTIVE:
To contribute over five years of experience in promotion, communications, and administration to an entry-level position in advertising.

SUMMARY OF QUALIFICATIONS:
- Performed advertising duties for small business.
- Experience in business writing and communications skills.
- General knowledge of office management.
- Demonstrated ability to work well with others, in both supervisory and support staff roles.
- Type 75 words per minute.

SELECTED ACHIEVEMENTS AND RESULTS:
Promotion:
Composing, editing, and proofreading correspondence and public relations materials for own catering service. Large-scale mailings.

Communication:
Instruction; curriculum and lesson planning; student evaluation; parent-teacher conferences; development of educational materials. Training and supervising clerks.

Computer Skills:
Proficient in MS Word, Lotus 1-2-3, Excel, and Filemaker Pro.

Administration:
Record-keeping and file maintenance. Data processing and computer operations, accounts receivable, accounts payable, inventory control, and customer relations. Scheduling, office management, and telephone reception.

PROFESSIONAL HISTORY:
Teacher; Self-Employed (owner of catering service); Floor Manager; Administrative Assistant; Accounting Clerk.

EDUCATION:
Beloit College, Beloit, WI, BA in Education, 1991

CHRONOLOGICAL RESUME

PERCY ZIEGLER
16 Josiah Court
Marlborough CT 06447
203/555-9641 (h)
203/555-8176, x14 (w)

EDUCATION

Keene State College, Keene NH
Bachelor of Arts in Elementary Education, 1998
- Graduated *magna cum laude*
- English minor
- Kappa Delta Pi member, inducted 1996

EXPERIENCE
September 1998-
Present

Elmer T. Thienes Elementary School, Marlborough CT
Part-time Kindergarten Teacher
- Instruct kindergartners in reading, spelling, language arts, and music.
- Participate in the selection of textbooks and learning aids.
- Organize and supervise class field trips and coordinate in-class presentations.

Summers
1995-1997

Keene YMCA, Youth Division, Keene NH
Child-care Counselor
- Oversaw summer program for low-income youth.
- Budgeted and coordinated special events and field trips, working with Program Director to initiate variations in the program.
- Served as Youth Advocate in cooperation with social worker to address the social needs and problems of participants.

Spring 1997

Wheelock Elementary School, Keene NH
Student Teacher
- Taught third-grade class in all elementary subjects.
- Designed and implemented a two-week unit on Native Americans.
- Assisted in revision of third-grade curriculum.

Fall 1996

Child Development Center, Keene NH
Daycare Worker
- Supervised preschool children on the playground and during art activities.
- Created a "Wishbone Corner," where children could quietly look at books or take a voluntary "time-out."

ADDITIONAL INTERESTS

Martial arts, Pokemon, politics, reading, skiing, writing.

ELECTRONIC RESUME

GRIFFIN DORE
69 Dursley Drive
Cambridge, MA 02138
(617) 555-5555

KEYWORD SUMMARY

Senior financial manager with over ten years experience in Accounting and Systems Management, Budgeting, Forecasting, Cost Containment, Financial Reporting, and International Accounting. MBA in Management. Proficient in Lotus, Excel, Solomon, and Windows.

EXPERIENCE

COLWELL CORPORATION, Wellesley, MA
Director of Accounting and Budgets, 1990 to present
    Direct staff of twenty in General Ledger, Accounts Payable, Accounts Receivable, and International Accounting.
    Facilitate month-end closing process with parent company and auditors.
    Implemented team-oriented cross-training program within accounting group, resulting in timely month-end closings and increased productivity of key accounting staff.
    Developed and implemented a strategy for Sales and Use Tax Compliance in all fifty states.
    Prepare monthly financial statements and analyses.

FRANKLIN AND DELANEY COMPANY, Melrose, MA
Senior Accountant, 1987-1990
    Managed Accounts Payable, General Ledger, transaction processing, and financial reporting. Supervised staff of five.

Staff Accountant, 1985-1987
    Managed Accounts Payable, including vouchering, cash disbursements, and bank reconciliation.
    Wrote and issued policies.
    Maintained supporting schedules used during year-end audits.
    Trained new employees.

EDUCATION

MBA in Management, Northeastern University, Boston, MA, 1989
BS in Accounting, Boston College, Boston, MA, 1985

ASSOCIATIONS

National Association of Accountants

GENERAL MODEL
FOR A COVER LETTER

Your mailing address
Date

Contact's name
Contact's title
Company
Company's mailing address

Dear Mr./Ms. _____:

Immediately explain why your background makes you the best candidate for the position that you are applying for. Describe what prompted you to write (want ad, article you read about the company, networking contact, etc.). Keep the first paragraph short and hard-hitting.

Detail what you could contribute to this company. Show how your qualifications will benefit this firm. Describe your interest in the corporation. Subtly emphasizing your knowledge about this firm and your familiarity with the industry will set you apart from other candidates. Remember to keep this letter short; few recruiters will read a cover letter longer than half a page.

If possible, your closing paragraph should request specific action on the part of the reader. Include your phone number and the hours when you can be reached. Mention that if you do not hear from the reader by a specific date, you will follow up with a phone call. Lastly, thank the reader for their time, consideration, etc.

Sincerely,

(signature)

Your full name (typed)

Enclosure (use this if there are other materials, such as your resume, that are included in the same envelope)

SAMPLE COVER LETTER

16 Josiah Court
Marlborough CT 06447
January 16, 2000

Ms. Leona Malfoy
Assistant Principal
Laningham Elementary School
43 Mayflower Drive
Keene NH 03431

Dear Ms. Malfoy:

Toby Potter recently informed me of a possible opening for a third grade teacher at Laningham Elementary School. With my experience instructing third-graders, both in schools and in summer programs, I feel I would be an ideal candidate for the position. Please accept this letter and the enclosed resume as my application.

Laningham's educational philosophy that every child can learn and succeed interests me, since it mirrors my own. My current position at Elmer T. Thienes Elementary has reinforced this philosophy, heightening my awareness of the different styles and paces of learning and increasing my sensitivity toward special needs children. Furthermore, as a direct result of my student teaching experience at Wheelock Elementary School, I am comfortable, confident, and knowledgeable working with third-graders.

I look forward to discussing the position and my qualifications for it in more detail. I can be reached at 203/555-9641 evenings or 203/555-8176, x14 weekdays. If I do not hear from you before Tuesday of next week, I will call to see if we can schedule a time to meet. Thank you for your time and consideration.

Sincerely,

Percy Ziegler

Percy Ziegler

Enclosure

GENERAL MODEL FOR A
THANK YOU/FOLLOW-UP LETTER

Your mailing address
Date

Contact's name
Contact's title
Company
Company's mailing address

Dear Mr./Ms._____:

Remind the interviewer of the reason (i.e., a specific opening, an informational interview, etc.) you were interviewed, as well as the date. Thank him/her for the interview, and try to personalize your thanks by mentioning some specific aspect of the interview.

Confirm your interest in the organization (and in the opening, if you were interviewing for a particular position). Use specifics to re-emphasize that you have researched the firm in detail and have considered how you would fit into the company and the position. This is a good time to say anything you wish you had said in the initial meeting. Be sure to keep this letter brief; a half page is plenty.

If appropriate, close with a suggestion for further action, such as a desire to have an additional interview, if possible. Mention your phone number and the hours you can be reached. Alternatively, you may prefer to mention that you will follow up with a phone call in several days. Once again, thank the person for meeting with you, and state that you would be happy to provide any additional information about your qualifications.

Sincerely,

(signature)

Your full name (typed)

PRIMARY EMPLOYERS

ACCOUNTING AND MANAGEMENT CONSULTING

You can expect to find the following types of companies in this chapter:

Consulting and Research Firms
Industrial Accounting Firms
Management Services
Public Accounting Firms
Tax Preparation Companies

DELOITTE & TOUCHE
700 Fifth Avenue, Suite 4500, Seattle WA 98104-5044. 206/292-1800. **Contact:** Human Resources Manager. **World Wide Web address:** http://www.us.deloitte.com. **Description:** An international firm of certified public accountants providing professional accounting, auditing, tax, and management consulting services to widely diversified clients. The company has a specialized program consisting of national industry groups and functional groups that cross industry lines. Groups are involved in various disciplines including accounting, auditing, taxation management advisory services, small and growing businesses, mergers and acquisitions, and computer applications. **Corporate headquarters location:** Wilton CT.

ERNST & YOUNG LLP
999 Third Avenue, Suite 3500, Seattle WA 98104. 206/621-1800. **Contact:** Human Resources. **World Wide Web address:** http:/www.ey.com. **Description:** A certified public accounting firm that also provides management consulting services. Services include data processing, financial modeling, financial feasibility studies, production planning and inventory management, management sciences, health care planning, human resources, cost accounting, and budgeting systems. **Positions advertised include:** Technology & Security Risk Services Manager; Tax Consulting Manager. **Corporate headquarters location:** New York NY. **Number of employees nationwide:** 25,000. **Number of employees worldwide:** 73,000.

KPMG
3100 Two Union Square, 601 Union Street, Seattle WA 98101. 206/292-1500. **Contact:** Human Resources. **World Wide Web address:** http://www.kpmg.com. **Description:** Delivers a wide range of value-added assurance, tax, and consulting services. **Corporate headquarters location:** Montvale NJ. **Parent company:** KPMG International is a leader among professional services firms engaged in capturing, managing, assessing, and delivering information to create knowledge that will help its clients maximize shareholder value. **Listed on:** NASDAQ. **Stock exchange symbol:** KCIN.

LEMASTER & DANIELS
601 West Riverside Avenue, Suite 700, Spokane WA 99201. 509/624-4315. **Contact:** Human Resources. **World Wide Web address:** http://www.lemasterdaniels.com. **Description:** An accounting firm providing accounting, auditing, and tax services to

clients. Founded in 1908. **Positions advertised include:** Accountant; Director of Reimbursement. **Corporate headquarters location:** This location.

MERRILL LYNCH HOWARD JOHNSON

1700 Seventh Avenue, Suite 2200, Seattle WA 98101. 206/625-1040. **Contact:** Human Resources. **World Wide Web address:** http://www.ml.com. **Description:** An international benefits consulting company. The company works mainly with 401(k) plans and group benefits for corporations.

MILLIMAN USA

1301 Fifth Avenue, Suite 3800, Seattle WA 98101. 206/624-7940. **Contact:** Personnel Department. **E-mail address:** seattle.office@milliman.com. **World Wide Web address:** http://www.milliman.com. **Description:** A nationwide actuarial and consulting firm. **Positions advertised include:** Actuary; Pension Analyst. **Corporate headquarters location:** This location. **Operations at this facility include:** Administration; Service.

MOSS ADAMS LLP

1001 Fourth Avenue, Suite 2830, Seattle WA 98154. 206/223-1820. **Contact:** Human Resources. **World Wide Web address:** http://www.mossadams.com. **Description:** One of the nation's largest accounting and consulting firms. Founded in 1913. **Positions advertised include:** Assurance Services Manager; Tax Analyst; Research and Development Manager; Senior IT Consultant. **Corporate headquarters location:** This location. **Other U.S. locations:** CA; OR.

MOSS ADAMS LLP

1301 A Street, Suite 600, Tacoma WA 98402. 253/572-4100. **Contact:** Human Resources. **World Wide Web address:** http://www.mossadams.com. **Description:** One of the nation's largest accounting and consulting firms. Founded in 1913. **Corporate headquarters location:** Seattle WA. **Other U.S. locations:** CA; OR.

PRICEWATERHOUSECOOPERS

1001 Fourth Avenue, Suite 4200, Seattle WA 98154-1101. 206/622-1505. **Fax:** 206/398-3100. **Contact:** Human Resources Department. **World Wide Web address:** http://www.pricewaterhousecoopers.com. **Description:** One of the largest certified public accounting firms in the world. PricewaterhouseCoopers provides public accounting, business advisory, management consulting, and taxation services. **Corporate headquarters location:** New York NY. **Other U.S. locations:** Nationwide.

PRICEWATERHOUSECOOPERS

999 Third Avenue, Suite 1800, Seattle WA 98104-4045. 206/622-8700. **Contact:** Personnel. **World Wide Web address:** http://www.pricewaterhousecoopers.com. **Description:** One of the largest certified public accounting firms in the world. PricewaterhouseCoopers provides public accounting, business advisory, management consulting, and taxation services. **Corporate headquarters location:** New York NY. **Other U.S. locations:** Nationwide.

ADVERTISING, MARKETING, AND PUBLIC RELATIONS

You can expect to find the following types of companies in this chapter:

Advertising Agencies
Direct Mail Marketers
Market Research Firms
Public Relations Firms

ACKERLEY PARTNERS
1301 Fifth Avenue, Suite 4000, Seattle WA 98101. 206/624-2888. **Contact:** Personnel Department. **World Wide Web address:** http://www.ackerleypartners.com. **Description:** Operates a group of media and entertainment companies. The Ackerley Group's national operations include an outdoor advertising agency, 14 television stations, three radio stations, and a sports/entertainment division that operates the NBA's Seattle SuperSonics and the WNBA's Seattle Storm. **Corporate headquarters location:** This location. **Listed on:** New York Stock Exchange. **Stock exchange symbol:** AK.

ADVO, INC.
6020 South 226th Street, Kent WA 98032-4814. 253/872-0553. **Contact:** Human Resources. **World Wide Web address:** http://www.advo.com. **Description:** One of the nation's largest full-service direct mail marketing companies. **Company slogan:** The targeter of choice. **Corporate headquarters location:** Windsor CT. **Listed on:** New York Stock Exchange. **Stock exchange symbol:** AD.

BURKE GIBSON INC.
702 Third Street SW, Auburn WA 98001. 253/735-4444. **Contact:** Human Resources. **World Wide Web address:** http://www.burkegibsoninc.com. **Description:** Designs and manufactures point-of-purchase advertising displays for retail and warehouse sales. **Corporate headquarters location:** This location.

DDB SEATTLE
1008 Western Avenue, Suite 601, Seattle WA 98104. 206/442-9900. **Contact:** Human Resources. **World Wide Web address:** http://www.ddbseattle.com. **Description:** An advertising agency. **Positions advertised include:** Online Coordinator. **Parent company:** DDB Needham Worldwide, Inc.

EXHIBITGROUP/GILTSPUR
2902 North 26th Street, Tacoma WA 98407. 253/879-0131. **Contact:** Human Resources. **World Wide Web address:** http://www.e-g.com. **Description:** Produces signs, exhibits, and other advertising media.

FCB SEATTLE
1011 Western Avenue, Suite 1000, Seattle WA 98104. 206/223-6464. **Contact:** Human Resources. **E-mail address:** jobs@seattle.fcb.com. **World Wide Web address:** http://www.seattle.fcb.com.

Description: A full-service advertising agency. FCB Seattle also offers public relations services including corporate relations, marketing support, employee relations, financial relations, government affairs, and community relations. The staff includes specialists in marketing, media, account service, creative work, research, public relations, finance, agriculture, and broadcast affairs. **Corporate headquarters location:** New York NY.

JWT SPECIALIZED COMMUNICATIONS
720 Olive Way, Suite 500, Seattle WA 98101. 206/623-2620. **Contact:** Human Resources. **World Wide Web address:** http://www.jwtworks.com. **Description:** A national advertising agency specializing in personnel recruitment advertising, human resources management systems, and employee communications. **Corporate headquarters location:** Los Angeles CA.

PUBLICIS
424 Second Avenue West, Seattle WA 98119. 206/285-2222. **Contact:** Personnel Department. **World Wide Web address:** http://www.publicisseattle.com. **Description:** An advertising and public relations agency specializing in the areas of technology, health care, retail, and consumer goods. **Corporate headquarters location:** New York NY.

WHITE RUNKLE ASSOCIATES
518 West Riverside, Spokane WA 99201. 509/747-6767. **Fax:** 509/747-9211. **Contact:** Human Resources. **World Wide Web address:** http://www.whiterunkle.com. **Description:** A full-service advertising, marketing, and public relations firm serving clients throughout the Northwest. Founded in 1980. **Special programs:** Internships. **Corporate headquarters location:** This location. **Number of employees at this location:** 20.

WILLIAMS & HELDE
711 Sixth Avenue North, Suite 200, Seattle WA 98109. 206/285-1940. **Fax:** 206/283-8897. **Contact:** Human Resources Department. **World Wide Web address:** http://www.williams-helde.com. **Description:** An advertising agency. Founded in 1970. **Number of employees at this location:** 10.

AEROSPACE

You can expect to find the following types of companies in this chapter:

Aerospace Products and Services
Aircraft Equipment and Parts

AIM AVIATION INC.

P.O. Box 9011, Renton WA 98057. 425/235-2750. **Physical address:** 705 SW Seventh Street, Renton WA 98055. **Contact:** Human Resources Department. **E-mail address:** recruiting@ aimseattle.com. **World Wide Web address:** http://www.aimaviation. com. **Description:** Manufactures a wide variety of products for aircraft interiors. **Corporate headquarters location:** England.

AIM AVIATION INC.

1530 22nd Street NW, Auburn WA 98001-3300. 253/804-3355. **Contact:** Human Resources. **World Wide Web address:** http://www. aimaviation.com. **Description:** Manufactures a wide variety of products for aircraft interiors. **Corporate headquarters location:** England.

THE BOEING COMPANY

P.O. Box 3707, Mail Stop 6H-PH, Seattle WA 98124-2207. 206/655-1131. **Contact:** Employment Office. **World Wide Web address:** http://www.boeing.com. **Description:** One of the world's largest aerospace firms. Boeing applies advanced aerospace technology to a wide range of space, defense, electronic, and computing programs. The Boeing Company is divided into four business segments: Commercial Airplanes, Missile Aircraft and Missile Systems, Space and Communications, and Phantom Works, the company's advanced research and development segment. The Commercial Airplane Group is the company's largest operating unit. **Positions advertised include:** Strategy Analyst; Maintenance Analyst; Human Resources Specialist; Internal Auditor. **Corporate headquarters location:** Chicago IL. **Listed on:** New York Stock Exchange. **Stock exchange symbol:** BA. **Annual sales/revenues:** More than $100 million.

ESTERLINE TECHNOLOGIES

10800 NE Eighth Street, Suite 600, Bellevue WA 98004. 425/453-9400. **Fax:** 425/453-2916. **Contact:** Personnel Department. **E-mail address:** hr@esterline.com. **World Wide Web address:** http:// www.esterline.com. **Description:** A manufacturing company serving several market areas including commercial aerospace, the defense industry, and the electronics industries. The company is divided into three business groups: Advanced Materials, Aerospace, and Automation. **Corporate headquarters location:** This location. **Subsidiaries include:** Armtec Defense Products Company, Coachella CA; Auxitrol S.A., France; Excellon Automation Company, Torrance

CA; Kirkhill Rubber Company, Brea CA; Korry Electronics Company, Seattle WA; W.A. Whitney Company, Rockford IL. **Listed on:** New York Stock Exchange. **Stock exchange symbol:** ESL. **CEO:** Wendell P. Hurlbut.

EXOTIC METALS FORMING COMPANY
5411 South 226th Street, Kent WA 98032. 253/395-3710. **Contact:** Human Resources. **World Wide Web address:** http://www.emfcowa. com. **Description:** Manufactures aircraft engine parts. **Positions advertised include:** Material Manager; Programmer/Analyst; NDT Technician. **Corporate headquarters location:** This location.

GENERAL DYNAMICS
P.O. Box 97009, Redmond WA 98073-9709. 425/885-5000. **Fax:** 425/882-5746. **Contact:** Employment. **World Wide Web address:** http://www.generaldynamics.com. **Description:** The Aerospace & Electronics Division develops space propulsion, solid propellant, and electronics systems for the aerospace, defense, and electronics industries. Overall, General Dynamics is a defense and aerospace company that, in addition to this division, also operates through its Ordinance and Tactical Systems Division. **Corporate headquarters location:** Falls Church VA.

GOODRICH AVIATION
3100 112th Street, Everett WA 98204. 425/347-3030. **Contact:** Human Resources. **World Wide Web address:** http://www.goodrich. com. **Description:** Provides aircraft systems, components, and services, and manufactures a wide range of specialty chemicals. Goodrich Aviation operates an international network of sales offices and aircraft service centers and has manufacturing facilities in seven countries. **Listed on:** New York Stock Exchange. **Positions advertised include:** Senior Tooling Engineer. **Stock exchange symbol:** GR.

HEXCEL CORPORATION
P.O. Box 97004, Kent WA 98064. 253/872-7500. **Contact:** Human Resources. **World Wide Web address:** http://www.hexcel.com. **Description:** Manufactures structural materials including aerospace products, nonaerospace honeycomb, resin-impregnated industrial fabrics, and nonimpregnated fabrics; and specialty chemicals including bulk pharmaceuticals, custom and special-purpose chemicals, specialty resins, and industrial maintenance chemicals. **Corporate headquarters location:** Stamford CT.

HONEYWELL

15001 NE 36th Street, Redmond WA 98073. 425/885-3711. **Fax:** 425/885-8781. **Contact:** Human Resources. **World Wide Web address:** http://www.honeywell.com. **Description:** Honeywell is engaged in the research, development, manufacture, and sale of advanced technology products and services in the fields of chemicals, electronics, automation, and controls. The company's major businesses are home and building automation and control, performance polymers and chemicals, industrial automation and control, space and aviation systems, and defense and marine systems. **Other U.S. locations:** Nationwide. **Operations at this facility include:** This location designs and manufactures avionics systems for commercial and military aircraft.

IDD AEROSPACE CORPORATION

P.O. Box 97056, Redmond WA 98073. 425/885-4353. **Contact:** Human Resources. **World Wide Web address:** http://www.iddaerospace.com. **Description:** Manufactures illuminated displays and other lighting products and electrical components for the aerospace industry.

NORTHWEST AIRLINES

Seattle-Tacoma International Airport, Seattle WA 98158. **Recorded jobline:** 612/726-3600. **Contact:** Human Resources. **World Wide Web address:** http://www.nwa.com. **Description:** One of the world's largest airlines and one of America's oldest carriers. Northwest Airlines serves more than 250 cities in Asia, Europe, North America, and Australia. The U.S. system spans 49 states and the District of Columbia. Hub cities are located in Detroit, Minneapolis/St. Paul, Memphis, and Tokyo. Maintenance bases are in Atlanta and Minneapolis/St. Paul. Crew bases are in Anchorage, Chicago, Detroit, Memphis, San Francisco, Minneapolis/St. Paul, New York, Seattle/Tacoma, Boston, Los Angeles, Honolulu, and several international cities. The company maintains a fleet of over 400 aircraft that fly approximately 2,600 flights each day. Founded in 1926. **NOTE:** The company recommends calling the jobline or viewing postings on the Website first. Resumes should be sent to Northwest Airlines, 5101 Northwest Drive, Mail Stop A1410, St. Paul MN 55111-3034. **Corporate headquarters location:** Eagan MN. **Listed on:** NASDAQ. **Stock exchange symbol:** NWAC. **Number of employees worldwide:** 53,000.

NORTHWEST COMPOSITES, INC.

12810 Smokey Point Boulevard, Marysville WA 98271. 360/653-2211. **Fax:** 360/653-2112. **Contact:** Human Resources. **E-mail address:** hr@nwcomposites.com. **World Wide Web address:** http://www.nwcomposites.com. **Description:** Manufactures composite products for airplane interiors including luggage bins and door latches.

NEUVANT AEROSPACE

P.O. Box 70645, Seattle WA 98107. 425/353-8080. **Contact:** Elizabeth Hollar, Human Resources. **E-mail address:** elizabeth.hollar@neuvant.com. **World Wide Web address:** http://www.neuvant.com. **Description:** Manufactures aerostructure details. Allfab Aerospace builds parts for airplanes and missiles for commercial clients.

PIONEER INDUSTRIES

7440 West Marginal Way South, Seattle WA 98106. 206/768-1990. **Fax:** 206/768-8910. **Contact:** Human Resources Department. **World Wide Web address:** http://www.pioneerhumanserv.com. **Description:** A contract manufacturer of aircraft components and sheet metal products for a variety of industrial uses. Founded in 1966. **NOTE:** Second and third shifts are offered. **Positions advertised include:** Chemical Dependency Counselor; Residential Supervisor; Case Manager; Sheet Metal Instructor. **Special programs:** Training. **Corporate headquarters location:** This location. **Parent company:** Pioneer Human Services operates rehabilitation and job training programs for work-release prisoners and people recovering from addictions. **Listed on:** Privately held. **Annual sales/revenues:** $11 - $20 million. **Number of employees at this location:** 300.

RAYTHEON SYSTEMS COMPANY

1050 NE Hostmark, Poulsbo WA 98370. 360/697-6600. **Contact:** Personnel. **World Wide Web address:** http://www.raytheon.com. **Description:** Manufactures defense and commercial electronics systems and business aviation and special mission aircraft. **Corporate headquarters location:** Lexington MA.

SMITHS AEROSPACE

2720 West Washington Avenue, Yakima WA 98903. 509/248-5000. **Contact:** Cheryl Dale, Human Resources Director. **World Wide Web address:** http://www.dowty.com. **Description:** Manufactures hydraulic and pneumatic valves used in military and commercial fixed-wing aircraft and helicopters, tanks, and the national aerospace program. **Positions advertised include:** Systems Engineer; Video/Graphics Engineer; Avionics Systems Engineer; Test Equipment Builder; Business Development Manager. **Operations at this facility include:** Administration; Manufacturing; Sales.

UNIVERSITY SWAGING CORPORATION
840 NW 45th Street, Seattle WA 98107. 206/784-8000. **Contact:** Human Resources Department. **World Wide Web address:** http://www.universityswaging.com. **Description:** Manufactures aerospace and marine parts by performing a highly specialized cold metal forming process for fitting various types of metal fittings to multistrand cable. University Swaging Corporation is one of the few companies worldwide to utilize the swaging process to make a variety of aerospace parts from aluminum tubing for applications where minimal weight and maximum strength are a necessity, such as for braces and for moving parts. **Annual sales/revenues:** $11 - $20 million. **Number of employees at this location:** 60.

APPAREL, FASHION, AND TEXTILES

You can expect to find the following types of companies in this chapter:

Broadwoven Fabric Mills
Knitting Mills
Curtains and Draperies
Footwear
Nonwoven Fabrics
Textile Goods and Finishing
Yarn and Thread Mills

DIADORA AMERICA, INC.
6419 South 228th Street, Kent WA 98032-1874. 253/520-8868. **Contact:** Human Resources. **World Wide Web address:** http://www.diadoraamerica.com. **Description:** One of the world's largest manufacturers of soccer shoes and apparel, athletic clothing, and shoes for a variety of sports. Internationally, the company also produces a line of outdoor footwear, ski apparel, and cycling gear. **Parent company:** Diadora SpA.

HELLY HANSEN INC.
3326 160th Avenue SE, Suite 200, Bellevue WA 98008. 425/883-8823. **Contact:** Human Resources. **World Wide Web address:** http://www.hellyhansen.com. **Description:** Manufactures outdoor apparel. Product types include waterproof, winter, and work apparel. Founded in 1877. **International locations:** Moss, Norway.

KL MANUFACTURING COMPANY
2726 North Monroe Street, Spokane WA 99205-3355. 509/326-2350. **Fax:** 509/326-2350. **Contact:** Christine M. Green, Personnel Manager. **Description:** A garment mill engaged in the manufacture of clothing and backpacks. **NOTE:** Entry-level positions are offered. **Office hours:** Monday - Friday, 7:30 a.m. - 5:00 p.m. **Corporate headquarters location:** This location. **Other area locations:** Chewelah WA. **Facilities Manager:** Michael E. Doohan. **Number of employees at this location:** 135. **Number of employees nationwide:** 225.

MALLORY AND CHURCH CORPORATION
676 South Industrial Way, Seattle WA 98108. 206/587-2100. **Toll-free phone:** 800/255-TIES. **Fax:** 206/467-0290. **Contact:** Human Resources. **World Wide Web address:** http://www.malloryandchurch.com. **Description:** One of the world's largest manufacturers of neckties. Founded in 1908. **Corporate headquarters location:** This location. **Other U.S. locations:** Corona CA; Roswell GA; New York NY; Pittsburgh PA.

PACIFIC TRAIL INC.
1700 Westlake Avenue North, Suite 200, Seattle WA 98109. 206/270-5300. **Fax:** 206/805-2077. **Contact:** Human Resources. **Description:** Designs, manufactures, and markets outerwear for active, casual, and performance use. Founded in 1945. **Parent company:** London Fog.

PENDLETON WOOLEN MILLS
P.O. Box 145, Washougal WA 98671. 360/835-2131. **Fax:** 360/835-5451. **Contact:** Human Resources. **World Wide Web address:** http://www.pendleton-usa.com. **Description:** Processes and manufactures wool to create fabric and clothing.

UNIONBAY SPORTSWEAR
P.O. Box 58710, Seattle WA 98138. 206/282-8889. **Fax:** 206/298-2146. **Contact:** Human Resources. **World Wide Web address:** http://www.unionbay.com. **Description:** Manufactures a line of sportswear geared toward young men and women. **Positions advertised include:** Assistant Designer; Head Designer. **Office hours:** Monday - Friday, 7:30 a.m. - 5:30 p.m. **Corporate headquarters location:** Kent WA.

ARCHITECTURE, CONSTRUCTION, AND ENGINEERING

You can expect to find the following types of companies in this chapter:

Architectural and Engineering Services
Civil and Mechanical Engineering Firms
Construction Products, Manufacturers, and Wholesalers
General Contractors/ Specialized Trade Contractors

ANVIL CORPORATION
1675 West Bakerview Road, Bellingham WA 98226. 360/671-1450. **Contact:** Johanna Snyder, Human Resources. **E-mail address:** jsnyder@anvilcorp.com. **World Wide Web address:** http://www.anvilcorp.com. **Description:** An engineering and technical services company that provides a variety of services to the mining, environmental, utilities, transportation, and chemical industries. **Positions advertised include:** NDE Technician. **Corporate headquarters location:** This location.

ROBERT E. BAYLEY CONSTRUCTION
P.O. Box 9004, Mercer Island WA 98040-9004. 206/621-8884. **Contact:** Personnel Department. **World Wide Web address:** http://www.bayley.net. **Description:** A general building contractor specializing in commercial construction. **Corporate headquarters location:** This location.

R.W. BECK, INC.
1001 Fourth Avenue, Suite 2500, Seattle WA 98154. 206/695-4700. **Contact:** Mr. Van Finger, Director of Personnel. **World Wide Web address:** http://www.rwbeck.com. **Description:** A diversified professional, technical, and management consulting firm. The company provides construction, environmental, technical, energy, solid waste, and water/wastewater services nationwide. **Positions advertised include:** Senior Project Manager. **Corporate headquarters location:** This location. **Number of employees at this location:** 175. **Number of employees nationwide:** 500.

BERGER/ABAM ENGINEERS INC.
33301 Ninth Avenue South, Suite 300, Federal Way WA 98003-2600. 253/952-6100. **Fax:** 206/431-2250. **Contact:** Personnel. **E-mail address:** employment@abam.com. **World Wide Web address:** http://www.abam.com. **Description:** A civil engineering and consulting firm specializing in the design of piers and waterfront structures, tanks and reservoirs, bridges, transit guideways, buildings, floating structures, and offshore drilling platforms. Berger/Abam Engineers Inc. also performs concrete material research, advanced computer design analysis, and construction management services. **Positions advertised include:** Document Production Specialist; Civil Engineer. **Corporate headquarters location:** This location.

CH2M HILL

P.O. Box 91500, Bellevue WA 98009-2050. 425/453-5000. **Physical address:** 777 108th Avenue NE, Suite 800, Bellevue WA 98004. **Contact:** Human Resources. **World Wide Web address:** http://www.ch2m.com. **Description:** CH2M Hill is group of employee-owned companies operating under the names CH2M Hill, Inc., Industrial Design Corporation, Operations Management International, CH2M Hill International, and CH2M Hill Engineering. The company provides planning, engineering design, and operation and construction management services to help clients apply technology, safeguard the environment, and develop infrastructure. The professional staff includes specialists in environmental engineering and waste management, water management, transportation, industrial facilities, and a broad spectrum of infrastructure systems. Founded in 1946. **Corporate headquarters location:** Denver CO. **Other U.S. locations:** Nationwide. **Number of employees at this location:** 350. **Number of employees nationwide:** 4,000.

CALLISON ARCHITECTURE

1420 Fifth Avenue, Suite 2400, Seattle WA 98101. 206/623-4646. **Contact:** Human Resources. **E-mail address:** employment@callison.com. **World Wide Web address:** http://www.callison.com. **Description:** Provides architectural and design services to the healthcare, hospitality, residential, and retail markets. **Positions advertised include:** Administrative Assistant; Designer; Specification Writer. **Corporate headquarters location:** This location.

CAPITAL DEVELOPMENT COMPANY

P.O. Box 3487, Lacey WA 98509-0487. 360/491-6850. **Contact:** Human Resources. **Description:** Engaged in a variety of construction activities including contracting, leasing, and property development and management.

COCHRAN ELECTRIC COMPANY INC.

P.O. Box 33524, Seattle WA 98133-0524. 206/367-1900. **Physical address:** 12500 Aurora Avenue North, Seattle WA 98133. **Contact:** Personnel Department. **E-mail address:** jobs@cochraninc.com. **World Wide Web address:** http://www.cochran-inc.com. **Description:** Engaged in commercial and industrial electrical work and powerline engineering. **Corporate headquarters location:** This location.

DLR GROUP
900 Fourth Avenue, Suite 700, Seattle WA 98164. 206/461-6000. **Contact:** Jill Star, Recruiter. **E-mail address:** jstar@dlrgroup.com. **World Wide Web address:** http://www.dlrgroup.com. **Description:** An architectural design firm that specializes in educational, judicial, medical, and recreational projects.

WAYNE DALTON CORPORATION
2001 Industrial Drive, Centralia WA 98531. 360/736-7654. **Contact:** John Peterson, Human Resources. **World Wide Web address:** http://www.wayne-dalton.com. **Description:** Manufactures garage doors and related items. **Corporate headquarters location:** Mt. Hope OH. **Parent company:** Hardsco Corporation.

EDAW INC.
1505 Western Avenue, Suite 601, Seattle WA 98101. 206/622-1176. **Contact:** Human Resources. **E-mail address:** humanresources@edaw.com. **World Wide Web address:** http://www.edaw.com. **Description:** Engaged in landscape architecture, environmental planning, and urban design services worldwide. **Corporate headquarters location:** San Francisco CA. **Other U.S. locations:** Irvine CA; Denver CO; Atlanta GA; Alexandria VA. **Operations at this facility include:** Administration; Service. **Listed on:** Privately held. **Number of employees at this location:** 15. **Number of employees nationwide:** 200. **Number of employees worldwide:** 250.

FLUOR FEDERAL SERVICES
P.O. Box 1050, Richland WA 99352. 509/372-2000. **Contact:** Human Resources. **World Wide Web address:** http://www.fluor.com. **E-mail address:** ffshr@flour.com. **Description:** A full-service engineering and construction company serving the power, industrial, hydrocarbon, and process industries, as well as the federal government. **Parent company:** Fluor Corporation (Irvine CA) is engaged in engineering and construction, as well as the production of various natural resources. Fluor Corporation provides its services to energy, natural resource, industrial, commercial, utility, and government clients. Natural resources mined include gold, silver, lead, zinc, iron ore, coal, oil, and gas. The corporation also provides contract drilling services. **Listed on:** New York Stock Exchange. **Stock exchange symbol:** FLR. **Number of employees worldwide:** 20,000.

HUTTIG BUILDING PRODUCTS

P.O. Box 1049, Auburn WA 98071-1049. 253/941-2600. **Contact:** Director of Employee Relations. **World Wide Web address:** http://www.huttig.com. **Description:** A wholesale distributor of building materials. **Positions advertised include:** Branch Manager; Outside Sales Representative. **Corporate headquarters location:** Chesterfield MO.

JCV CONSTRUCTORS

P.O. Box 80346, Seattle WA 98108-0346. 206/762-4219. **Contact:** Personnel Department. **Description:** Engaged in general contract construction. Founded in 1991. **Annual sales/revenues:** $11 - $20 million. **Number of employees at this location:** 10.

KIEWIT COMPANIES

P.O. Box 1769, Vancouver WA 98668. 360/693-1478. **Contact:** Human Resources Manager. **E-mail address:** human.resources @kiewit.com. **World Wide Web address:** http://www.kiewit.com. **Description:** One of the largest construction companies in the country. Kiewit's primary markets are building, power, transportation, water resources, and mining. Types of projects include highways, bridges, high-rise buildings, office complexes, railroads, tunnels, subways, dams, airports, power plants, canals, water treatment facilities, offshore petroleum platforms, and other heavy civil projects. The company has district offices throughout North America. **Positions advertised include:** Engineer; Project Manager. **Corporate headquarters location:** Omaha NE.

LINDAL CEDAR HOMES INC.

4300 South 104th Place, Seattle WA 98178. 206/725-0900. **Fax:** 206/725-1615. **Contact:** Personnel Department. **E-mail address:** employment@lindal.com. **World Wide Web address:** http:/www.lindal.com. **Description:** Manufactures cedar homes and sunrooms. Lindal also provides wholesale lumber, building materials, and related services. **Positions advertised include:** Area Manager. **Corporate headquarters location:** This location.

LANCE MUELLER & ASSOCIATES

130 Lakeside Avenue, Suite 250, Seattle WA 98122. 206/325-2553. **Fax:** 206/328-0554. **Contact:** Personnel Department. **World Wide Web address:** http://www.lma-architects.com. **Description:** An architectural firm that specializes in commercial projects.

NBBJ ARCHITECTURE DESIGN PLANNING

111 South Jackson Street, Seattle WA 98104. 206/223-5555. **Contact:** Personnel. **World Wide Web address:** http://www.nbbj.com. **Description:** An architectural design firm. NBBJ specializes in commercial buildings, health facilities, sports and entertainment complexes, airports, retail centers, government buildings, and senior living facilities. The company is also heavily engaged in urban planning and design, campus planning, and graphic design services. **Positions advertised include:** Architect; Planner; Interior Designer; Graphic Designer. **Other U.S. locations:** Los Angeles CA; San Francisco CA; Research Triangle Park NC; New York NY; Columbus OH. **International locations:** Japan; Norway; Taiwan. **Operations at this facility include:** Service.

NORD COMPANY

P.O. Box 1187, Everett WA 98206. 425/259-9292. **Contact:** Personnel Department. **Description:** Produces wood-style and rail-panel doors, louver products, columns and posts, and arch spindles. **Corporate headquarters location:** Clamout Falls OR.

PARSONS BRINCKERHOFF INC.

999 Third Avenue, Suite 2200, Seattle WA 98104-4020. 206/382-5200. **Fax:** 206/382-5222. **Contact:** Personnel. **World Wide Web address:** http://www.pbworld.com. **Description:** An engineering and design firm engaged in the design of bridges, tunnels, rapid transit systems, hydroelectric facilities, water supply systems, and marine facilities worldwide. **Corporate headquarters location:** New York NY.

THE SIMPSON DOOR COMPANY

400 Simpson Avenue, McCleary WA 98557. 360/495-3291. **Fax:** 360/495-3295. **Contact:** Personnel. **World Wide Web address:** http://www.simpsondoor.com. **Description:** Manufactures doors. Founded in 1912. **Note:** Simpson Door does not accept unsolicited resumes, nor do they list openings on their Website. Positions are regularly listed in local papers for the following communities: Seattle; Shelton; Olympia; and Tacoma. **Corporate headquarters location:** This location.

STRAND HUNT CONSTRUCTION INC.

12015 115th Avenue NE, Kirkland WA 98034. 425/823-1954. **Fax:** 425/823-8635. **Contact:** Human Resources. **E-mail address:** hr@strandhunt.com. **World Wide Web address:** http://

www.strandhunt.com. **Description:** Engaged in general contract construction.

URS CORPORATION
Century Square, 1501 Fourth Avenue, Suite 1440, Seattle WA 98101-1616. 206/438-2700. **Contact:** Human Resources. **World Wide Web address:** http://www.urscorp.com. **Description:** An architectural, engineering, and environmental consulting firm that specializes in air transportation, environmental solutions, surface transportation, and industrial environmental and engineering concerns. **Positions advertised include:** Accounting Clerk; Assistant Project Administrator; Environmental Engineer; Program Assistant; Program Manager.

UTILX CORPORATION
P.O. Box 97009, Kent WA 98064-9709. 253/395-0200. **Fax:** 253/395-1040. **Contact:** Personnel. **World Wide Web address:** http://www.utilx.com. **Description:** Provides installation and maintenance services for underground utilities including electricity, water, gas, and telephone. UTILX's technologies include the FlowMole guided drilling system and the CableCure service for injecting silicon fluids into utility cables to repair damage from water. The company's services are marketed domestically while their products are sold primarily in international markets. **Corporate headquarters location:** This location. **Subsidiaries include:** Flow Mole Limited (UK). **Number of employees at this location:** 100. **Number of employees nationwide:** 500.

WEATHERVANE WINDOW COMPANY
P.O. Box 2424, Kirkland WA 98083. 425/827-9669. **Fax:** 425/822-9797. **Contact:** Human Resources. **World Wide Web address:** http://www.weathervanewindows.com. **Description:** Manufactures wood, aluminum-clad wood, and vinyl windows.

HOWARD S. WRIGHT CONSTRUCTION COMPANY
P.O. Box 3764, Seattle WA 98124. 206/447-7654. **Contact:** Personnel. **World Wide Web address:** http://www.hswright.com. **Description:** A general contracting company for nonresidential buildings.

ARTS, ENTERTAINMENT, SPORTS, AND RECREATION

You can expect to find the following types of companies in this chapter:

Botanical and Zoological Gardens
Entertainment Groups
Motion Picture and Video Tape Production and Distribution
Museums and Art Galleries
Physical Fitness Facilities
Professional Sports Clubs
Public Golf Courses
Racing and Track Operations
Sporting and Recreational Camps
Theatrical Producers

ACKERLEY PARTNERS

1301 Fifth Avenue, Suite 4000, Seattle WA 98101. 206/624-2888. **Contact:** Personnel Department. **World Wide Web address:** http://www.ackerleypartners.com. **Description:** Operates a group of media and entertainment companies. The Ackerley Group's national operations include an outdoor advertising agency, 14 television stations, three radio stations, and a sports/entertainment division that operates the NBA's Seattle SuperSonics and the WNBA's Seattle Storm. **Corporate headquarters location:** This location. **Listed on:** New York Stock Exchange. **Stock exchange symbol:** AK.

AMERICAN PRODUCTION SERVICES

2247 15th Avenue West, Seattle WA 98119. 206/282-1776. **Toll-free phone:** 888/282-1776. **Fax:** 206/282-3535. **Contact:** Human Resources. **World Wide Web address:** http://www.apsnw.com. **Description:** Provides video duplication, audio and editing services, and computer graphics services. **Corporate headquarters location:** This location. **Other U.S. locations:** North Hollywood CA. **Operations at this facility include:** Administration. **Annual sales/revenues:** $5 - $10 million. **Number of employees at this location:** 50. **Number of employees nationwide:** 75.

THE BURKE MUSEUM OF NATURAL HISTORY & CULTURE

University of Washington, P.O. Box 353010, Seattle WA 98195-3010. 206/543-5590. **Contact:** Department of Human Resources. **World Wide Web address:** http://www.washington.edu/burkemuseum. **Description:** A museum that explores the natural and cultural history of the Pacific Northwest region. The museum houses more than 3 million geological, anthropological, and zoological specimens.

CRYSTAL MOUNTAIN RESORT

33914 Crystal Mountain Boulevard, Crystal Mountain WA 98022. 360/663-2265. **Contact:** Human Resources. **World Wide Web address:** http://www.crystalmt.com. **Description:** A ski resort and lodge.

FUNTASIA FAMILY FUN PARK

7212 220th Street SW, Edmonds WA 98026. 425/774-4263. **Contact:** Human Resources. **World Wide Web address:** http://www.familyfunpark.com. **Description:** An amusement park offering a variety of recreational facilities including a go-cart track, a mini-golf course, bumper cars and boats, a video arcade, and batting cages.

SEATTLE ATHLETIC CLUB/DOWNTOWN

2020 Western Avenue, Seattle WA 98121. 206/443-1111. **Fax:** 206/443-2632. **Contact:** Human Resources. **World Wide Web address:** http://www.sacdt.com. **Description:** A full-service athletic club offering a variety of classes, personal training services, and extensive free weights and cardiovascular equipment. Other club amenities include a swimming pool, a whirlpool, saunas and steam rooms, and basketball and squash courts.

SEATTLE CENTER

305 Harrison Street, Seattle WA 98109-4645. 206/684-7202. **Fax:** 206/233-3932. **Contact:** Personnel. **World Wide Web address:** http://www.seattlecenter.com. **Description:** An entertainment complex. The Seattle Center is home to many cultural and athletic organizations including the Seattle Symphony, Seattle Opera, the NBA's Seattle SuperSonics, and the WNBA's Seattle Storm.

SEATTLE CHORAL COMPANY

1518 NE 143rd Street, Seattle WA 98125. 206/365-8765. **Fax:** 206/365-8714. **Contact:** Mr. Fred Coleman, Artistic Director. **World Wide Web address:** http://www.seattlechoralcompany.org. **Description:** An oratorio society performing symphonic and a cappella masterworks. Founded in 1980. **Corporate headquarters location:** This location.

THE SEATTLE MARINERS

P.O. Box 4100, Seattle WA 98104. 206/346-4000. **Fax:** 206/346-4050. **Contact:** Personnel Department. **World Wide Web address:** http://www.mariners.org. **Description:** A professional baseball team playing in Major League Baseball's American League West division. Founded in 1977.

THE SUMMIT AT SNOQUALMIE

P.O. Box 1068, 101 State Route 906, Snoqualmie Pass WA 98068. 425/434-7669. **Contact:** Manager of Human Resources Department. **World Wide Web address:** http://www.summitatsnoqualmie.com. **Description:** Operates four ski areas in the metropolitan Seattle area. This location also hires seasonally. **Corporate headquarters location:** This location. **Number of employees at this location:** 1,200.

WOODLAND PARK ZOO
601 North 59th Street, Seattle WA 98103. 206/684-4800. **Contact:** Personnel. **World Wide Web address:** http://www.zoo.org. **Description:** A zoo located on 92 acres of botanical gardens. Exhibits include over 300 different animal species, as well as the African Savannah, Elephant Forest, Northern Trail, and the Tropical Rain Forest. **Positions advertised include:** Classes/Camp Assistant; Cashier; Drafting and Design Specialist; Outreach and Education Coordinator; Security Officer.

AUTOMOTIVE

You can expect to find the following types of companies in this chapter:

Automotive Repair Shops
Automotive Stampings
Industrial Vehicles and Moving Equipment
Motor Vehicles and Equipment
Travel Trailers and Campers

CUMMINS NORTHWEST
P.O. Box 9811, Renton WA 98057. 425/235-3440. **Contact:** Human Resources. **World Wide Web address:** http://www.cummins.com. **Description:** One of the world's leading producers of diesel engines, engine parts, and power train systems for the mining, military, construction, transportation, agriculture, and industrial markets. **Positions advertised include:** Product Manager. **Corporate headquarters location:** Portland OR. **Listed on:** New York Stock Exchange. **Stock exchange symbol:** CUM.

KENWORTH TRUCK COMPANY
P.O. Box 1000, Kirkland WA 98038. 425/828-5000. **Physical address:** 10630 NE 38th Place, Kirkland WA 98033. **Fax:** 425/828-5054. **Contact:** Human Resources Department. **E-mail address:** kw.jobs@paccar.com. **World Wide Web address:** http://www.kenworth.com. **Description:** Manufactures Class 8 trucks. **Positions advertised include:** Senior Programmer/Analyst. **Special programs:** Internships. **Corporate headquarters location:** Bellevue WA. **Parent company:** PACCAR, Inc. **Operations at this facility include:** Administration; Divisional Headquarters; Sales; Service. **Listed on:** NASDAQ. **Stock exchange symbol:** PCAR. **Number of employees nationwide:** 2,500.

MAR LAC PARTS PLUS
P.O. Box 1896, Auburn WA 98071-1896. 206/322-2626. **Contact:** Human Resources. **Description:** A distributor of automotive parts. **Corporate headquarters location:** This location. **Parent company:** Mar Lac Distributing Company.

PACCAR INC.
P.O. Box 1518, Bellevue WA 98009. 425/468-7400. **Fax:** 425/468-8206. **Contact:** Human Resources. **World Wide Web address:** http://www.paccar.com. **Description:** Manufactures, leases, and finances heavy-duty on- and off-road trucks and industrial winches for industrial and commercial use. Brand names include Peterbilt, Foden, DAF, and Kenworth. **Special programs:** Internships. **Corporate headquarters location:** This location. **Other U.S. locations:** Nationwide. **International locations:** Australia; Canada; Mexico; the Netherlands; United Kingdom. **Annual sales/revenues:** More than $100 million. **Number of employees at this location:** 425. **Number of employees nationwide:** 10,000.

RED DOT CORPORATION
P.O. Box 58270, Seattle WA 98138-1270. 206/575-3840. **Fax:** 206/575-8267. **Contact:** Human Resources. **World Wide Web address:** http://www.reddotcorp.com. **Description:** A manufacturer and wholesaler of heating and air conditioning equipment for heavy vehicles such as semi-trucks and off-road vehicles. **Office hours:** Monday - Friday, 7:45 a.m. - 4:30 p.m. **Corporate headquarters location:** This location.

SIX STATES DISTRIBUTORS
3711 East Trent Avenue, Spokane WA 99202-4420. 509/535-7671. **Fax:** 509/535-9105. **Contact:** Rick Baird, Manager. **World Wide Web address:** http://www.sixstates.com. **Description:** Primarily engaged in the wholesaling of truck parts. The company also manufactures systems for trucks including transmissions and drive lines.

WESTERN RECREATIONAL VEHICLE INC.
P.O. Box 9547, Yakima WA 98909-0547. 509/457-4133. **Contact:** Human Resources. **World Wide Web address:** http://www.wrv.com. **Description:** Manufactures a variety of recreational vehicles including travel trailers and campers.

BANKING/SAVINGS AND LOANS

You can expect to find the following types of companies in this chapter:

Banks
Bank Holding Companies and Associations
Lending Firms/Financial Services Institutions

AMERICANWEST BANCORPORATION
9506 North Newport Highway, Spokane WA 99218. 509/467-6949. **Contact:** Human Resources. **World Wide Web address:** http://www.awbank.net. **Description:** A bank holding company. **Corporate headquarters location:** This location.

BANK OF AMERICA
800 Fifth Avenue, 33rd Floor, Seattle WA 98104. 206/461-0800. **Recorded jobline:** 800/587-JOBS. **Contact:** Human Resources Department. **World Wide Web address:** http://www.bankofamerica.com. **Description:** Bank of America is a full-service banking and financial institution. The company operates through four business segments: Global Corporate and Investment Banking, Principal Investing and Asset Management, Commercial Banking, and Consumer Banking. **Corporate headquarters location:** Charlotte NC. **Other U.S. locations:** Nationwide. **Operations at this facility include:** This location is a bank. **Listed on:** New York Stock Exchange. **Stock exchange symbol:** BAC.

COLUMBIA BANK
P.O. Box 2156, Mail Stop 2500, Tacoma WA 98401. 253/305-1900. **Recorded jobline:** 253/305-0717. **Contact:** Human Resources. **World Wide Web address:** http://www.columbiabank.com. **Description:** A full-service bank. **Corporate headquarters location:** This location. **Listed on:** NASDAQ. **Stock exchange symbol:** COLB.

FIRST MUTUAL BANK
P.O. Box 1647, Bellevue WA 98009. 425/455-7300. **Contact:** Paulette O'Connell, Vice President of Human Resources Department. **World Wide Web address:** http://www.firstmutual.com. **Description:** A savings bank primarily offering real estate loan services. The company also offers a variety of depository and banking services. Founded in 1953. **Positions advertised include:** Assistant Branch Manager; Consumer Loan Servicing Representative; Sales Finance Assistant; Wholesale Loan Representative; Workflow Analyst. **Corporate headquarters location:** This location. **Other area locations:** Issaquah WA; Ballard WA; Bellingham WA; Monroe WA; Redmond WA; Seattle WA.

THE IMAGE BANK, INC.
601 North 34th Street, Seattle WA 98103. 206/268-3714. **Toll-free phone:** 877/438-8966. **Contact:** Personnel. **World Wide Web address:** http://www.imagebank.com. **Description:** Stocks and sells

photographs, illustrations, and film obtained from photographers and artists. **Corporate headquarters location:** This location. **International locations:** Worldwide.

KEYBANK N.A.

P.O. Box 6, Bellingham WA 98227-0006. 360/676-6300. **Contact:** Human Resources. **World Wide Web address:** http://www.keybank.com. **Description:** A bank. **NOTE:** Please send resumes to KeyBank N.A., Human Resources, P.O. Box 92933, Cleveland OH 44101. **Positions advertised include:** Underwriting Officer; Portfolio Manager; Client Relations Representative; Sales and Service Associate. **Corporate headquarters location:** Cleveland OH. **Other U.S. locations:** Nationwide. **Parent company:** KeyCorp. **Listed on:** New York Stock Exchange. **Stock exchange symbol:** KEY. **Number of employees nationwide:** 33,000.

KEYBANK N.A.

1536 NW Market, Seattle WA 98107. 206/789-4000. **Toll-free phone:** 888/KEY2JOBS. **Contact:** Human Resources. **World Wide Web address:** http://www.keybank.com. **Description:** A bank. **NOTE:** Please send resumes to KeyBank N.A., Human Resources, P.O. Box 92933, Cleveland OH 44101. **Positions advertised include:** Underwriting Officer; Portfolio Manager; Client Relations Representative; Sales and Service Associate. **Corporate headquarters location:** Cleveland OH. **Other U.S. locations:** Nationwide. **Parent company:** KeyCorp. **Listed on:** New York Stock Exchange. **Stock exchange symbol:** KEY. **Number of employees nationwide:** 33,000.

KEYBANK N.A.

1119 Pacific Avenue, Mail Stop WA 31-03-0850, Tacoma WA 98402-5500. 253/305-7750. **Fax:** 253/305-7908. **Contact:** Personnel Director. **World Wide Web address:** http://www.keybank.com. **Description:** A bank. **NOTE:** Please send resumes to KeyBank N.A., Human Resources, P.O. Box 92933, Cleveland OH 44101. **Positions advertised include:** Underwriting Officer; Portfolio Manager; Client Relations Representative; Sales and Service Associate. **Special programs:** Internships. **Corporate headquarters location:** Cleveland OH. **Other U.S. locations:** Nationwide. **Parent company:** KeyCorp. **Operations at this facility include:** Administration; Sales; Service. **Listed on:** New York Stock Exchange. **Stock exchange symbol:** KEY. **Number of employees at this location:** 4,000. **Number of employees nationwide:** 33,000.

PACIFIC NORTHWEST BANK

P.O. Box 1649, Oak Harbor WA 98277. 360/679-4181. **Toll-free phone:** 800/321-8592. **Fax:** 360/675-8860. **Recorded jobline:** 800/321-8592x1605. **Contact:** Human Resources. **World Wide Web address:** http://www.pnwbank.com. **Description:** A full-service bank. **NOTE:** Entry-level positions and part-time jobs are offered. **Special programs:** Internships. **Corporate headquarters location:** This location.

PEMCO FINANCIAL SERVICES

P.O. Box 778, Seattle WA 98111. 206/628-4090. **Toll-free phone:** 800/552-7430. **Fax:** 206/628-6072. **Recorded jobline:** 206/628-8740. **Contact:** Human Resources. **E-mail address:** jobs@ pfcenter.com. **World Wide Web address:** http://www.pemco. com. **Description:** Provides insurance, banking, and credit union services through its subsidiaries. Founded in 1936. **NOTE:** Entry-level positions and second and third shifts are offered. **Positions advertised include:** Sales Supervisor; Individual Life Underwriter; Document Services Specialist; Training Consultant; Risk Management Representative. **Special programs:** Training. **Corporate headquarters location:** This location. **Subsidiaries include:** PEMCO Insurance Companies; PEMCO Life Insurance Company; Washington School Employees Credit Union; PEMCO Corporation; EvergreenBank. **Number of employees at this location:** 800. **Number of employees nationwide:** 1,030.

STERLING SAVINGS ASSOCIATION

111 North Wall Street, Spokane WA 99201. 509/458-2711. **Fax:** 509/358-6161. **Contact:** Human Resources. **Description:** Provides full-service banking services including deposits and originating consumer, business banking, commercial real estate, and residential construction loans. The company operates 77 branches. **Subsidiaries include:** Action Mortgage Company operates residential loan production offices; Harbor Financial Services provides nonbank investments including mutual funds, variable annuities, and tax-deferred annuities to clients through regional representatives; INTERVEST-Mortgage Investment Company provides commercial real estate lending. **Number of employees nationwide:** 860.

U.S. BANK OF WASHINGTON

1420 Fifth Avenue, Seattle WA 98101. 206/344-3619. **Contact:** Human Resources. **World Wide Web address:** http://www.usbank. com. **Description:** A commercial and consumer banking institution.

U.S. Bank provides a full range of commercial real estate products and services, cash management services and consultation, and merchant services and sales. The Homepartners family of mortgage loan products provides down payment assistance, flexible underwriting and repayment terms, and homebuyer education for first-time and low- to moderate-income buyers. **Corporate headquarters location:** Portland OR. **Parent company:** U.S. Bancorp. **Number of employees nationwide:** 3,500.

UNITED SAVINGS AND LOAN BANK
601 South Jackson Street, Seattle WA 98104. 206/624-7581. **Fax:** 206/624-2326. **Contact:** Personnel Department. **Description:** A full-service bank. **Corporate headquarters location:** This location. **Operations at this facility include:** Administration; Service. **Number of employees at this location:** 50.

WASHINGTON FEDERAL SAVINGS & LOAN ASSOCIATION
425 Pike Street, Seattle WA 98101. 206/624-7930. **Fax:** 206/624-2334. **Contact:** Human Resources. **World Wide Web address:** http://www.washingtonfederal.com. **Description:** Offers a full range of banking services through 85 branch offices. Subsidiaries of the company are also involved in real estate development and insurance brokerage operations. **Positions advertised include:** Customer Service Representative; Loan Coordinator. **Corporate headquarters location:** This location. **Other U.S. locations:** AZ; ID; OR; UT. **Listed on:** NASDAQ. **Stock exchange symbol:** WFSL.

WASHINGTON MUTUAL SAVINGS BANK
P.O. Box 834, SAS0108, Seattle WA 98101. 206/461-6400. **Contact:** Human Resources. **World Wide Web address:** http://www.wamu.com. **Description:** One of the largest independently-owned and locally-managed banks in Washington state. Washington Mutual offers a wide array of financial products and services through the bank and its affiliates including deposit accounts, loans, annuities, mutual funds, full-service securities brokerage, and travel services. **Positions advertised include:** Technology Analyst; Integration Engineer; Technical Project Manager. **Special programs:** Internships. **Corporate headquarters location:** This location. **Other U.S. locations:** CA; FL; ID; MT; OR; TX; UT. **Subsidiaries include:** Composite Research & Management Company; Murphey Favre; Mutual Travel; WM Insurance Services; WM Life Insurance. **Listed on:** American Stock Exchange; NASDAQ; New York Stock Exchange. **Annual sales/revenues:** More than $100 million.

BIOTECHNOLOGY, PHARMACEUTICALS, AND SCIENTIFIC R&D

You can expect to find the following types of companies in this chapter:

Clinical Labs
Lab Equipment Manufacturers
Pharmaceutical Manufacturers and Distributors

BIO-RAD LABORATORIES

6565 185th Avenue NE, Redmond WA 98052. 425/881-8300. **Contact:** Human Resources. **World Wide Web address:** http://www.bio-rad.com. **Description:** Engaged in the research and development of diagnostic test equipment used to detect blood viral disease.

CARDINAL DISTRIBUTION

P.O. Box 1589, Auburn WA 98001-1589. 253/939-5550. **Physical address:** 801 C Street NW, Auburn WA. **Fax:** 253/833-9402. **Contact:** Human Resources. **World Wide Web address:** http://www.cardinal.com. **Description:** A nationwide wholesale distributor of pharmaceuticals, medical and surgical products, and related health supplies. The company also distributes merchandise typically sold in retail drug stores, hospitals, and health care provider facilities. Cardinal Distribution also provides its clients with such specialized support services as order entry and confirmation, inventory control, monitoring pricing strategies, and financial reporting. The company has developed an in-pharmacy computer system that provides prices, patient profiles, financial data, and management services. **Corporate headquarters location:** Dublin OH. **Other U.S. locations:** Nationwide. **Operations at this facility include:** Regional Headquarters; Warehouse/Distribution; Wholesaling. **Number of employees at this location:** 175. **Number of employees nationwide:** 3,000.

CELL THERAPEUTICS, INC.

201 Elliott Avenue West, Seattle WA 98119. 206/282-7100. **Fax:** 206/272-4010. **Recorded jobline:** 800/656-2355. **Contact:** Human Resources. **E-mail address:** resume@ctiseattle.com. **World Wide Web address:** http://www.cticseattle.com. **Description:** Researches and develops oncology products designed to manage cancer and cancer treatment side effects. Founded in 1992. **Corporate headquarters location:** This location. **Listed on:** NASDAQ. **Annual sales/revenues:** $5 - $10 million. **Number of employees at this location:** 190.

DYNACARE LABORATORY

1229 Madison Street, Suite 500, Seattle WA 98104. 206/386-2672. **Fax:** 206/386-2991. **Contact:** Human Resources. **E-mail address:** jobsdnw@dynacare.com. **World Wide Web address:** http://www.dynacare.com. **Description:** A medical laboratory. **Positions advertised include:** Lab Assistant; Phlebotomist; Medical

Technologist; Assistant Supervisor of Specimen Processing; Route Representative. **Listed on:** NASDAQ. **Stock exchange symbol:** DNCR.

EPOCH PHARMACEUTICALS, INC.
P.O. Box 82554, Kenmore WA 98028. 425/481-0696. **Contact:** Human Resources. **World Wide Web address:** http://www.epochpharm.com. **Description:** A biomedical company focused on the development of oligonucleotides as new therapeutic compounds and for use in diagnostic testing. Utilizing proprietary and unique technology in the design, synthesis, and chemical modification of oligonucleotides, the company is developing gene blockers that act by specifically binding to and inactivating the DNA of disease-associated genes; protein blockers that act by selective inhibition of certain proteins that are central to the growth and reproduction of cells and viruses; and DNA probe-based diagnostic systems for the rapid identification of certain disease pathogens. **Listed on:** NASDAQ. **Stock exchange symbol:** EBIO.

HOLLISTER-STIER LABORATORIES, LLC
3525 North Regal Street, Spokane WA 99207. 509/489-5656. **Fax:** 509/482-1792. **Contact:** Human Resources. **E-mail address:** human_resources@hollister-stier.com. **World Wide Web address:** http://www.hollister-stier.com. **Description:** Engaged in the development and manufacture of allergy medication. **Positions advertised include:** Senior Validation Specialist; Accountant; Environmental Monitoring Technician; Warehouse Clerk; Pollen Collector.

ICOS CORPORATION
22021 20th Avenue SE, Bothell WA 98021. 425/485-1900. **Fax:** 425/489-0356. **Recorded jobline:** 425/485-1900x2032. **Contact:** Human Resources. **E-mail address:** hr@icos.com. **World Wide Web address:** http://www.icos.com. **Description:** Discovers and develops new pharmaceuticals by targeting early stages of the chronic inflammatory process and by seeking points of intervention that may lead to more specific and efficacious drugs. ICOS's signal transduction programs in PDE inhibitors and cell cycle checkpoint modulators have yielded additional approaches to treating inflammatory conditions, as well as male erectile dysfunction, cardiovascular diseases, and cancer. **Positions advertised include:** Building Facilities Coordinator; Clinical Pharmacist; Purchasing Assistant; Payroll Specialist; Senior Staff Scientist. **Corporate**

headquarters location: This location. **Number of employees at this location:** 200.

IMMUNEX CORPORATION
51 University Street, Seattle WA 98101-2936. 206/587-0430. **Fax:** 206/621-1399. **Contact:** Human Resources. **E-mail address:** immunexcareers@webhirepc.com. **World Wide Web address:** http://www.immunex.com. **Description:** A leading biopharmaceutical company focused on the discovery, manufacture, and marketing of products to treat immune system disorders. **Positions advertised include:** Business Analyst; Engineer; Facilities Maintenance Technician; Global Project Manager. **Corporate headquarters location:** This location. **Other area locations:** Bothell WA. **Operations at this facility include:** Administration; Manufacturing; Research and Development. **Listed on:** NASDAQ. **Stock exchange symbol:** IMNX. **Number of employees at this location:** 800.

IMMUNEX CORPORATION
21511 23rd Drive SE, Bothell WA 98021. 425/487-3659. **Contact:** Human Resources. **E-mail address:** immunexcareers@webhirepc.com. **World Wide Web address:** http://www.immunex.com. **Description:** Immunex Corporation is a leading biopharmaceutical company focused on the discovery, manufacture, and marketing of products to treat immune system disorders. **Corporate headquarters location:** Seattle WA. **Operations at this facility include:** This location is a manufacturing plant. **Listed on:** NASDAQ. **Stock exchange symbol:** IMNX.

LABORATORY CORPORATION OF AMERICA (LABCORP)
21903 68th Avenue South, Kent WA 98032-2427. 253/395-4000. **Contact:** Human Resources. **World Wide Web address:** http://www.labcorp.com. **Description:** One of the nation's leading clinical laboratory companies, providing services primarily to physicians, hospitals, clinics, nursing homes, and other clinical labs nationwide. LabCorp performs tests on blood, urine, and other body fluids and tissue, aiding the diagnosis of disease. **Positions advertised include:** Account Representative; Medical Laboratory Sales Representative. **Corporate headquarters location:** Burlington NC. **Listed on:** New York Stock Exchange. **Stock exchange symbol:** LH.

MDS PHARMA SERVICES
11804 North Creek Parkway South, Bothell WA 98011-8805. 425/487-8200. **Contact:** Human Resources. **World Wide Web**

address: http://www.mdsps.com. **Description:** Engaged in pharmaceutical research and development.

MERIDIAN VALLEY CLINICAL LAB, INC.
515 West Harrison Street, Suite 9, Kent WA 98032. 253/859-8700. **Contact:** Human Resources Department. **World Wide Web address:** http://www.meridianvalleylab.com. **Description:** Engaged in testing related to adrenal steroids and allergies. The lab also performs stool analyses. **Corporate headquarters location:** This location.

NEORX CORPORATION
410 West Harrison Street, Seattle WA 98119. 206/281-7001. **Fax:** 206/284-7112. **Contact:** Human Resources. **World Wide Web address:** http://www.neorx.com. **Description:** Develops treatments for cancer and cardiovascular disease. The company's focus is on targeting therapeutic agents on diseased or injured cells, while sparing normal tissues the full impact of these treatments. The company's cardiovascular program is focused primarily on reducing reclosure of coronary arteries following balloon angioplasty. **Corporate headquarters location:** This location. **Listed on:** NASDAQ. **Number of employees at this location:** 80.

PACIFIC NORTHWEST NATIONAL LABORATORY
P.O. Box 999, 902 Battelle Boulevard, Richland WA 99352. 509/375-2121. **Toll-free phone:** 888/375-PNNL. **Contact:** Human Resources. **World Wide Web address:** http://www.pnl.gov. **Description:** A national laboratory engaged in basic and applied research in energy, material and chemical sciences, earth and environmental engineering, waste technology, environmental restoration, and nuclear-related areas. **Positions advertised include:** Duty Forecaster; Senior Atmospheric Scientist; HR Generalist; Program Director. **Special programs:** Internships. **Corporate headquarters location:** Columbus OH. **Operations at this facility include:** Research and Development. **Number of employees at this location:** 4,800.

PATHOLOGY ASSOCIATES MEDICAL LABORATORIES
110 West Cliff Avenue, Spokane WA 99204. 509/926-2400. **Contact:** Human Resources. **E-mail address:** hr@paml.com. **World Wide Web address:** http://www.paml.com. **Description:** A laboratory that performs blood, tissue, and drug tests. **Corporate headquarters location:** This location.

QUEST DIAGNOSTICS INCORPORATED

1737 Airport Way South, Suite 200, Seattle WA 98134. 206/623-8100. **Fax:** 206/624-5488. **Contact:** Human Resources Department. **World Wide Web address:** http://www.questdiagnostics.com. **Description:** One of the largest clinical laboratories in North America, providing a broad range of clinical laboratory services to health care clients, which include physicians, hospitals, clinics, dialysis centers, pharmaceutical companies, and corporations. The company offers and performs tests on blood, urine, and other bodily fluids and tissues to provide information for health and well-being. **Positions advertised include:** Specimen Processor; Phlebotomy Services Representative; Pricing Manager.

TARGETED GENETICS CORPORATION

1100 Olive Way, Suite 100, Seattle WA 98101. 206/623-7612. **Fax:** 206/521-4782. **Recorded jobline:** 206/521-7300. **Contact:** Human Resources. **E-mail address:** careers@targen.com. **World Wide Web address:** http://www.targen.com. **Description:** Develops gene therapy products for the treatment of certain acquired and inherited diseases. The principal focus is on three product development programs that address high-risk diseases for which there are no known cures: cytoxic T lymphocyte, (CTL)-based, immunotherapy for infectious diseases and cancer; in vivo adeno-associated virus, (AAV)-based, therapy for cystic fibrosis and other diseases; and stem cell therapy. The company approaches gene therapy through multiple delivery systems including retroviral vector delivery, AAV vector delivery, and nonviral vector delivery. **NOTE:** Entry-level positions are offered. **Positions advertised include:** Quality Assurance Associate. **Special programs:** Internships. **Corporate headquarters location:** This location. **Operations at this facility include:** Research and Development. **Annual sales/revenues:** Less than $5 million. **Number of employees at this location:** 80.

TRIPATH IMAGING, INC.

8271 154th Avenue NE, Redmond WA 98052. 425/869-7284. **Fax:** 425/556-3052. **Contact:** Human Resources. **World Wide Web address:** http://www.tripathimaging.com. **Description:** Engaged in the research and development of technologies to automate the interpretation of medical images. The company's initial products are automated screening systems that are used to analyze and classify Pap smears. These screening systems use high-speed video microscopes, image interpretation software, and field-of-view computers to recognize, analyze, and classify individual cells within the complex images on a Pap smear. These products include the AutoPap QC and the AutoPap Screener. **Corporate headquarters location:** Burlington NC. **Number of employees at this location:** 100.

BUSINESS SERVICES AND NON-SCIENTIFIC RESEARCH

You can expect to find the following types of companies in this chapter:

Adjustment and Collection Services
Cleaning, Maintenance, and Pest Control Services
Credit Reporting
Detective, Guard, and Armored Car Services
Miscellaneous Equipment Rental and Leasing
Secretarial and Court Reporting Services

ADT SECURITY SERVICES

841 Powell Avenue SW, Suite 101, Renton WA 98055. 206/624-3103. **Contact:** Human Resources. **World Wide Web address:** http://www.adtsecurityservices.com. **Description:** Designs, installs, sells, and monitors fire and burglar alarm systems for commercial and industrial retail customers. The company also offers armed and unarmed security guards. **Corporate headquarters location:** Boca Raton FL. **Other U.S. locations:** Nationwide.

ADT SECURITY SERVICES

528 South Cannon Street, Spokane WA 99204-1717. 509/838-8283. **Contact:** Human Resources. **World Wide Web address:** http://www.adtsecurityservices.com. **Description:** Designs, installs, sells, and monitors fire and burglar alarm systems for commercial and industrial retail customers. The company also offers armed and unarmed security guards. **Corporate headquarters location:** Boca Raton FL. **Other U.S. locations:** Nationwide.

APS PINKERTON

9212 East Mission, Suite A, Spokane WA 99206. 509/927-2552. **Contact:** Human Resources. **World Wide Web address:** http://www.pinkertons.com. **Description:** One of the world's largest suppliers of global, total security solutions. The company provides a broad array of security-related services including business intelligence, investigations, security systems integration, and consulting. **Corporate headquarters location:** Salt Lake City UT. **International locations:** Asia; Canada; Europe; Mexico.

LABOR READY, INC.

P.O. Box 2910, Tacoma WA 98401. 253/383-9101. **Toll-free phone:** 800/610-8920. **Fax:** 800/850-9559. **Contact:** Human Resources. **World Wide Web address:** http://www.laborready.com. **Description:** Provides temporary employees, primarily to construction, warehousing, landscaping, and manufacturing businesses. Founded in 1989. **Corporate headquarters location:** This location. **Other U.S. locations:** Nationwide. **International locations:** Canada; Puerto Rico; United Kingdom. **Listed on:** New York Stock Exchange. **Stock exchange symbol:** LRW. **Annual sales/revenues:** More than $100 million.

LYNX MEDICAL SYSTEMS

15325 SE 30th Place, Suite 200, Bellevue WA 98007. 425/641-4451. **Contact:** Human Resources. **E-mail address:**

humanresources@lynxmed.com. **World Wide Web address:** http://www.lynxmed.com. **Description:** Offers coding, billing, transcription, and consulting services to professional medical groups, health care facilities and systems, and third-party payers. **Corporate headquarters location:** This location. **Other U.S. locations:** Waterloo IA.

MUZAK LLC

P.O. Box 80416, Seattle WA 98108. 206/763-2517. **Physical address:** 200 South Orcas Street, Seattle WA 98108. **Contact:** Personnel Department. **E-mail address:** corporate@nbbi.com. **World Wide Web address:** http://www.muzak.com. **Description:** Provides satellite delivered and on-site music services to commercial and retail establishments delivered both directly and through franchised dealers worldwide. Muzak serves approximately 300,000 locations worldwide through over 200 sales and service locations. **Corporate headquarters location:** Fort Mill SC.

NORTHWEST PROTECTIVE SERVICES, INC.

2700 Elliott Avenue, Seattle WA 98121. 206/448-4040. **Fax:** 206/448-2461. **Contact:** Human Resources. **World Wide Web address:** http://www.nwprotective.com. **Description:** Provides contract security services. **Positions advertised include:** Security Officer. **Corporate headquarters location:** This location. **Other area locations:** Spokane WA; Tacoma WA. **Other U.S. locations:** Portland OR. **Operations at this facility include:** Service. **Listed on:** Privately held. **Number of employees nationwide:** 700.

SIEMENS BUSINESS SERVICES, INC.

4500 150th Avenue NE, Overlake North, Building A, Redmond WA 98052. 425/895-2250. **Contact:** Personnel. **World Wide Web address:** http://www.siemens.com. **Description:** Provides systems integration, help desk, and PC repair services to *Fortune* 1000 companies and federal clients. **Corporate headquarters location:** Norwalk CT. **Other U.S. locations:** Nationwide. **Listed on:** New York Stock Exchange. **Stock exchange symbol:** SI.

VENTURI TECHNOLOGY PARTNERS

11255 Kirkland Way, Kirkland WA 98033. 425/814-8104. **Toll-free phone:** 888/878-1888. **Contact:** Human Resources Department. **World Wide Web address:** http://www.venturipartners.com. **Description:** Offers software consulting services. Venturi Technology Partners provides businesses with support for mainframes, personal computers, systems configurations, information systems, and software testing.

VERISIGN
P.O. Box 2909, Olympia WA 98501. 360/493-6000. **Physical address:** 4501 Intelco Loop SE, Olympia WA 98507. **Contact:** Human Resources. **World Wide Web address:** http://www.verisign.com. **Description:** Provides web presence services, security services, payment services, and telecommunications services. **Corporate headquarters location:** Mountain View CA. **Listed on:** NASDAQ. **Stock exchange symbol:** VRSN.

THE WACKENHUT CORPORATION
1035 Andover Park West, Suite 210, Tukwila WA 98188. 253/872-1555. **Contact:** Human Resources. **World Wide Web address:** http://www.wackenhut.com. **Description:** Provides physical security services, correction services, and related products to businesses, governments, and individuals from more than 150 offices worldwide. Specific services include security guard services; corrections staffing; private investigative services; the assembly and sale of electronic security equipment and systems; the training of security guards and fire and crash rescue personnel; providing fire protection and emergency ambulance service to municipalities; security consulting; planning, designing, and implementing integrated security systems; and providing specialized services to the nuclear power industry. **Corporate headquarters location:** Palm Beach Gardens FL. **Other U.S. locations:** Nationwide. **Number of employees nationwide:** 40,000.

CHARITIES AND SOCIAL SERVICES

You can expect to find the following types of organizations in this chapter:

Social and Human Service Agencies
Job Training and Vocational
Rehabilitation Services
Nonprofit Organizations

AMERICAN RED CROSS
1900 25th Avenue South, Seattle WA 98144-4708. 206/323-2345. **Contact:** Human Resources. **World Wide Web address:** http://www.redcross.org. **Description:** A humanitarian organization that aids disaster victims, gathers blood for crisis distribution, trains individuals to respond to emergencies, educates individuals on various diseases, and raises funds for other charitable establishments. **Corporate headquarters location:** Washington DC.

CHILDCARE INTERNATIONAL
P.O. Box W, Bellingham WA 98227-1582. 360/647-2283. **Physical address:** 3350 Airport Drive, Suite 200, Bellingham WA 98226. **Contact:** Human Resources. **World Wide Web address:** http://www.childcare-intl.org. **Description:** Dedicated to the global relief of children in need. The organization's programs include feeding and sponsorship of these children. Founded in 1981.

GOODWILL INDUSTRIES
307 West Columbia Street, Pasco WA 99301. 509/547-7717. **Contact:** Employment. **World Wide Web address:** http://www.goodwill.org. **Description:** Goodwill Industries is a nonprofit provider of employment training for the disabled and the poor, and operates 1,400 thrift stores nationwide. **Corporate headquarters location:** Bethesda MD. **Operations at this facility include:** This location houses the area administrative offices and a thrift store.

IAM CARES
9125 15th Place South, Seattle WA 98108. 206/764-0454. **Toll-free phone:** 800/763-1301. **Fax:** 206/764-0452. **Contact:** Steve Miller, Area Project Director. **World Wide Web address:** http://www.iamcareswa.org. **Description:** A nonprofit agency sponsored by the Machinist Union (IAM & AW). IAM Cares provides employment and training services to individuals with disabilities. Founded in 1980. **NOTE:** Entry-level positions are offered. **Special programs:** Internships. **Corporate headquarters location:** Upper Marlboro MD. **Other U.S. locations:** Nationwide. **International locations:** Canada. **Number of employees at this location:** 15. **Number of employees nationwide:** 150.

LIFELONG AIDS ALLIANCE
1002 East Seneca, Seattle WA 98122. 206/329-6923. **Fax:** 206/325-2689. **Contact:** Human Resources. **E-mail address:** jobs@lifelongaidsalliance.org. **World Wide Web address:**

http://www.lifelongaidsalliance.org. **Description:** Provides case management, financial advocacy, and housing assistance to individuals infected with the AIDS virus.

LUTHERAN COMMUNITY SERVICES
433 Minor Avenue North, Seattle WA 98109. 206/694-5700. **Contact:** Human Resources. **World Wide Web address:** http://www.lcsnw.org. **Description:** Provides a variety of social services including counseling, family support, grassroots, and foster care services. Annually, the organization serves more than 20,000 individuals.

OVERLAKE SERVICE LEAGUE
P.O. Box 53203, Bellevue WA 98015. 425/451-1175. **Fax:** 425/451-1088. **Contact:** Special Services. **World Wide Web address:** http://www.overlakeserviceleague.com. **Description:** A social services organization that provides emergency financial assistance, develops and offers several youth programs, and operates a thrift store. Founded in 1911.

TACOMA GOODWILL INDUSTRIES
REHABILITATION CENTER INC.
714 South 27th Street, Tacoma WA 98409. 253/272-5166. **Fax:** 253/428-4162. **Contact:** Laura Discus, Human Resources Director. **World Wide Web address:** http://www.tacomagoodwill.org. **Description:** Provides vocational rehabilitation programs. **Positions advertised include:** Loss Prevention Analyst; Custodian; Maintenance Worker. **Corporate headquarters location:** Bethesda MD. **Number of employees at this location:** 600.

THE WEST SEATTLE HELPLINE
4517 California Avenue SW, Suite A, Seattle WA 98116. 206/932-4357. **Contact:** Human Resources. **World Wide Web address:** http://www.scn.org/civic/wshelpline. **Description:** Provides financial assistance to families facing homelessness. The West Seattle Helpline also works closely with other community organizations to provide clothing and food for these families.

YMCA OF GREATER SEATTLE
909 Fourth Avenue, Seattle WA 98104. 206/382-5000. **Contact:** Personnel. **World Wide Web address:** http://www.ymca.com. **Description:** The YMCA provides health and fitness, social and personal development, sports and recreation, education and career

development, and camps and conferences to children, youths, adults, the elderly, families, the disabled, refugees and foreign nationals, YMCA residents, and community residents, through a broad range of specific programs. **Corporate headquarters location: Chicago IL. Other U.S. locations:** Nationwide.

CHEMICALS/RUBBER AND PLASTICS

You can expect to find the following types of companies in this chapter:

Adhesives, Detergents, Inks, Paints, Soaps, Varnishes
Agricultural Chemicals and Fertilizers
Carbon and Graphite Products
Chemical Engineering Firms
Industrial Gases

AIR LIQUIDE CORPORATION

4230 East Trent Avenue, Spokane WA 99202. 509/536-7484. **Contact:** Human Resources. **World Wide Web address:** http://www.airliquide.com. **Description:** Air Liquide Corporation is a diversified manufacturer engaged in the recovery and sale of atmospheric industrial gases, the manufacture and sale of oil field equipment and supplies, and the distribution of welding and industrial equipment and supplies. **Corporate headquarters location:** Houston TX. **International locations:** Worldwide. **Operations at this facility include:** This location processes and distributes industrial and medical gases.

ALCIDE CORPORATION

P.O. Box 89, Redmond WA 98073-0089. 425/882-2555. **Physical address:** 8561 154th Avenue NE, Redmond WA 98052. **Fax:** 425/861-0173. **Contact:** Human Resources. **World Wide Web address:** http://www.alcide.com. **Description:** Researches, develops, and markets antimicrobial products for industrial, human, and animal health uses and for direct application to food in order to control food-borne pathogens. Alcide has developed several disinfectants and a sterilant to kill microorganisms on surface areas and to reduce the threat of disease transmission in health care facilities. In the animal health field, the company has marketed technology to prevent mastitis in dairy cattle. **Positions advertised include:** Lab Chemist; Clerk/Receptionist. **Corporate headquarters location:** This location. **Listed on:** NASDAQ. **Stock exchange symbol:** ALCO.

ATOFINA CHEMICALS INCORPORATED

2901 Taylor Way, Tacoma WA 98421. 253/627-9101. **Contact:** Human Resources. **World Wide Web address:** http://www.atofina.com. **Description:** Atofina Chemicals is a diversified chemicals manufacturer. **Headquarters location:** Philadelphia PA. **Operations at this facility include:** This location manufactures chlorate.

BOC GASES

4715 NE 78th Street, Vancouver WA 98665. 360/695-1255. **Contact:** Human Resources. **E-mail address:** jobs@us.gases.boc.com. **World Wide Web address:** http://www.boc.com. **Description:** Manufactures and markets industrial gases and related products. BOC Gases also provides full engineering and technical services. **Listed on:** New York Stock Exchange. **Stock exchange symbol:** BOX.

BUNZL EXTRUSION

3110 70th Avenue East, Tacoma WA 98424-3608. 253/284-8000. **Contact:** Human Resources. **World Wide Web address:** http://www.bunzlextrusion.com. **Description:** Manufactures plastic extrusions specializing in core, fence, and highway products. **Corporate headquarters location:** Richmond VA.

FOAMEX INTERNATIONAL, INC.

19635 78th Avenue South, Kent WA 98032. 253/872-0170. **Contact:** Personnel Manager. **E-mail address:** careers@foamex.com. **World Wide Web address:** http://www.foamex.com. **Description:** One of the nation's largest manufacturers of flexible polyurethane foam products. Foamex products are classified into four groups: cushion foams, carpet cushion foams, automotive foams, and technical foams. Cushion foams are used for mattresses, quilting and borders, home and office furniture, computer and electronics packaging, and padding foams for health care. Foamex carpet cushion foams include prime, bonded, sponge rubber, felt carpet cushion, synthetic grass turf, and a variety of textured carpeting and wall coverings. Automotive foams include foams for cushioning and seating, acoustical foams, headliner foams, trim foams, and foams for door panel parts. Technical foams include those for filtration, reservoiring, sound absorption and transmission, carburetors, high-speed inkjet printers, speaker grilles, oxygenators, and EKG pads, as well as cosmetic applicators, mop heads, paint brushes, and diapers. **Corporate headquarters location:** Linwood PA. **Listed on:** NASDAQ. **Stock exchange symbol:** FMXI. **Annual sales/revenues:** More than $100 million. **Number of employees worldwide:** 3,600.

GACO WESTERN INC.

P.O. Box 88698, Seattle WA 98138-2698. 206/575-0450. **Contact:** Yolanda Sewell, Human Resources Manager. **E-mail address:** ysewell@gaco.com. **World Wide Web address:** http://www.gaco.com. **Description:** Manufactures elastomeric coatings. **Corporate headquarters location:** This location.

GENERAL CHEMICAL CORPORATION

8579 North Texas Road, Anacortes WA 98221. 360/293-2171. **Contact:** Human Resources. **E-mail address:** hrinfo@genchem.com. **World Wide Web address:** http://www.genchem.com. **Description:** Manufactures sulfuric acid and other inorganic chemicals. **Parent company:** The General Chemical Group, Inc.

HEXCEL CORPORATION
P.O. Box 97004, Kent WA 98064. 253/872-7500. **Contact:** Human Resources. **World Wide Web address:** http://www.hexcel.com. **Description:** Manufactures structural materials including aerospace products, nonaerospace honeycomb, resin-impregnated industrial fabrics, and nonimpregnated fabrics; and specialty chemicals including bulk pharmaceuticals, custom and special-purpose chemicals, specialty resins, and industrial maintenance chemicals. **Corporate headquarters location:** Stamford CT.

KELLY-MOORE PRESERVATIVE PAINTS
5400 Airport Way South, Seattle WA 98108. 206/763-0300. **Contact:** Personnel Department. **World Wide Web address:** http://www.kellymoore.com. **Description:** The Kelly-Moore Paint Company manufactures and sells paint through four manufacturing facilities and more than 150 retail locations in 10 states. **Corporate headquarters location:** San Carlos CA. **Other U.S. locations:** AZ; AR; CA; CO; ID; NV; OK; OR; TX; UT. **International locations:** Guam. **Operations at this facility include:** This location manufactures industrial paint coatings.

LAIRD PLASTICS
650 South Industrial Way, Seattle WA 98108. 206/623-4900. **Contact:** Human Resources. **World Wide Web address:** http://www.laird-plastics.com. **Description:** A distributor of a wide range of plastics and plastics materials including films, rods, sheets, tubes, and related products. **Corporate headquarters location:** West Palm Beach FL.

MIKRON INDUSTRIES
1034 Sixth Avenue North, Kent WA 98032. 253/854-8020. **Contact:** Amy Rhodes, Human Resources. **World Wide Web address:** http://www.mikronvinyl.com. **Description:** Engaged in the extrusion of custom vinyl profiles, primarily for windows and doors. **Corporate headquarters location:** This location.

PREMIER INDUSTRIES INC.
1019 Pacific Avenue, Suite 1501, Tacoma WA 98402. 253/572-5111. **Fax:** 253/383-7100. **Contact:** Human Resources. **World Wide Web address:** http://www.premier-industries.com. **Description:** Manufactures integrated plastic products.

UNIVAR USA

8201 South 212th Street, Kent WA 98032. 253/872-5000. **Fax:** 425/889-3671. **Contact:** Human Resources. **E-mail address:** iewar@univarusa.com. **World Wide Web address:** http://www.univarusa.com. **Description:** Manufactures and wholesales chemical pesticides and industrial chemicals. **Positions advertised include:** Administrative Assistant; Sales Engineer.

COMMUNICATIONS: TELECOMMUNICATIONS AND BROADCASTING

You can expect to find the following types of companies in this chapter:

Cable/Pay Television Services
Communications Equipment
Radio and Television Broadcasting Systems
Telephone, Telegraph, and other Message Communications

AT&T BROADBAND
900 132nd Street SW, Everett WA 98204. **Toll-free phone:** 877/824-2288. **Contact:** Human Resources. **E-mail address:** nwcareers@ broadband.att.com. **World Wide Web address:** http:// www.attbroadband.com. **Description:** One of the nation's largest cable television and broadband services companies. **Listed on:** New York Stock Exchange. **Stock exchange symbol:** T.

AT&T WIRELESS SERVICES
P.O. Box 97061, Redmond WA 98073. 206/624-5700. **Contact:** Human Resources. **World Wide Web address:** http://www.attws. com. **Description:** One of the nation's largest digital wireless networks providing wireless voice and data communication. **Other U.S. locations:** Nationwide. **Listed on:** New York Stock Exchange. **Stock exchange symbol:** AWC.

ACTIVE VOICE CORPORATION
2901 Third Avenue, Suite 500, Seattle WA 98121-9800. 206/441-4700. **Fax:** 206/441-4784. **Contact:** Human Resources. **E-mail address:** personnel@activevoice.com. **World Wide Web address:** http://www.activevoice.com. **Description:** A leading provider of PC-based voice processing systems and CTI solutions. The company's software products enable small to medium-sized businesses and offices to communicate more effectively by integrating their traditional office telephone systems with voicemail, automated attendant, and interactive voice response functions. The company's products are utilized by a broad variety of enterprises in manufacturing, retail, service, health care, governmental, and institutional settings. Founded in 1983. **Positions advertised include:** Senior Software Engineer. **Corporate headquarters location:** This location. **International locations:** Australia; Canada; China; France; India; South Africa; Sweden; the Netherlands; United Kingdom. **Subsidiaries include:** Pronexus, Inc., Ontario, Canada. **Listed on:** NASDAQ. **Stock exchange symbol:** ACVC. **Number of employees at this location:** 175.

ANIXTER-SEATTLE
21419 64th Avenue South, Kent WA 98032. 253/872-6200. **Contact:** Shelly Geiss, Operations Manager. **E-mail address:** jobs@anixter.com. **World Wide Web address:** http://www.anixter. com. **Description:** A value-added provider of industrial wire and cabling solutions that support voice and data applications. Solutions include customized pre- and postsale services, a wide range of

technology products from the world's leading manufacturers, and logistics management through a global distribution network. Founded in 1957. **Corporate headquarters location:** Skokie IL. **Parent company:** Anixter International. **Operations at this facility include:** Administration; Sales; Service. **Listed on:** New York Stock Exchange. **Stock exchange symbol:** AXE. **Annual sales/revenues:** More than $100 million. **Number of employees at this location:** 50. **Number of employees nationwide:** 3,500. **Number of employees worldwide:** 5,000.

CENTURYTEL
P.O. Box 9901, Vancouver WA 98668-8701. 360/696-0983. **Physical address:** 805 Broadway, Vancouver WA 98660. **Contact:** Manager of Employment and Administration. **E-mail address:** staffing@centurytel.com. **World Wide Web address:** http://www.centurytel.com. **Description:** A holding company providing administrative and other services to its subsidiaries, whose operations include providing telephone services. **Positions advertised include:** Customer Service Representative. **Other area locations:** Cheney WA; Gig Harbor WA. **Other U.S. locations:** Anchorage AK; Kalispell MT; Lebanon OR; Tomah WI. **Operations at this facility include:** Administration. **Listed on:** New York Stock Exchange. **Stock exchange symbol:** CTL. **Number of employees at this location:** 500. **Number of employees nationwide:** 3,000.

ITRON, INC.
P.O. Box 15288, Spokane WA 99215. 509/891-3903. **Physical address:** 2818 North Sullivan Road, Spokane WA 99216. **Toll-free phone:** 800/635-5461. **Fax:** 800/462-6119. **Contact:** Human Resources. **E-mail address:** itron@webhire.com. **World Wide Web address:** http://www.itron.com. **Description:** A leading supplier of data acquisition and wireless communications products for the remote data management needs of electric, gas, and water utilities worldwide. The company also designs, manufactures, markets, installs, and services hardware, software, and integrated systems for automatic meter reading and other related applications. **NOTE:** Resumes should be sent to Human Resources, P.O. Box 430, Burlington MA 01803. Entry-level positions are offered. **Company slogan:** Collect data, deliver information, enable innovation. **Positions advertised include:** Sales Order Planner; Marketing Manager; Quality Service Analyst; Principal Service Analyst. **Corporate headquarters location:** This location. **Other U.S. locations:** Waseca MN; Raleigh NC; Pittsburgh PA; Philadelphia PA.

Listed on: NASDAQ. **Stock exchange symbol:** ITRI. **Annual sales/revenues:** More than $100 million. **Number of employees nationwide:** 1,000.

KCTS-TV CHANNEL 9

401 Mercer Street, Seattle WA 98109. 206/728-6463. **Recorded jobline:** 206/443-4800. **Fax:** 206/443-6691. **Contact:** Human Resources Office. **E-mail address:** jobs@kcts.org. **World Wide Web address:** http://www.kcts.org. **Description:** A public television station. **Positions advertised include:** Network Administrator; Public Television Sponsorship Sales Representative. **Corporate headquarters location:** This location. **Other U.S. locations:** Washington DC. **Subsidiaries include:** Pacific Coast Public TV (Vancouver, Canada). **Listed on:** Privately held. **Number of employees at this location:** 300.

KIRO-TV

2807 Third Avenue, Seattle WA 98121. 206/728-7777. **Recorded jobline:** 206/728-5205. **Personnel phone:** 206/728-8285. **Contact:** Human Resources. **World Wide Web address:** http://www.kirotv.com. **Description:** A television broadcasting company. **NOTE:** Part-time jobs are offered. **Positions advertised include:** Audio Operator; Production Assistant; Promotion Writer; Producer; Reporter. **Special programs:** Internships. **Internship information:** Applicants for internships must be in their junior or senior years of college or be in their final year of community college or vocational school. Resumes and letters of interest are required. **Corporate headquarters location:** Atlanta GA. **Parent company:** Cox Broadcasting, Inc. **Facilities Manager:** LeRoy Gates. **Sales Manager:** Sandy Zogg. **Number of employees at this location:** 240.

KOMO-TV CHANNEL 4
FISHER BROADCASTING INC.

140 Fourth Avenue North, Seattle WA 98109. 206/404-4000. **Contact:** Human Resources. **World Wide Web address:** http://www.komotv.com. **Description:** An ABC-affiliated television station. Fisher Broadcasting (also at this location) is engaged in television and radio broadcasting. **Parent company:** Fisher Companies, Inc. **Listed on:** NASDAQ. **Stock exchange symbol:** FSCI.

KWJZ FM RADIO
KSRB AM RADIO

3650 131st Avenue SE, Suite 550, Bellevue WA 98006. 425/373-5536. **Contact:** Promotions Director. **World Wide Web address:** http://www.kwjz.com. **Description:** An FM radio station. KSRB (also at this location) is an AM radio station. **Parent company:** Sandusky Radio.

KING 5 TELEVISION

333 Dexter Avenue North, Seattle WA 98109. 206/448-5555. **Contact:** Human Resources Department. **E-mail address:** hr@king5.com. **World Wide Web address:** http://www.king5.com. **Description:** An NBC-affiliated television station. Programming includes daily newscasts, *Evening Magazine*, *Almost Live*, and *Watch This!* **Number of employees nationwide:** 225.

LEVITON VOICE & DATA

2222 222nd Street SE, Suite 100, Bothell WA 98021. 425/486-2222. **Contact:** Human Resources. **E-mail address:** hr@levitonvoicedata.com. **World Wide Web address:** http://www.levitonvoicedata.com. **Description:** Produces system solutions for network infrastructure. The company offers frame-to-station solutions; fiber and copper systems; horizontal and backbone infrastructure; and voice, data, and video connections. **Corporate headquarters location:** Littleneck NY.

MOTOROLA, INC.

24000 35th Avenue SE, Bothell WA 98021. 425/487-1234. **Contact:** Human Resources. **World Wide Web address:** http://www.motorola.com. **Description:** Provides applied research, development, manufacturing, and marketing of high-technology electronic systems and components for industry and government in the fields of communications, automotive, controls, semiconductor, information systems, and office information. Motorola manufactures communications equipment and electronic products including car radios, cellular phones, semiconductors, computer systems, cellular infrastructure equipment, pagers, cordless phones, and LAN systems. **Corporate headquarters location:** Schaumburg IL. **Listed on:** New York Stock Exchange. **Stock exchange symbol:** MOT. **Number of employees worldwide:** 107,000.

NORTHLAND COMMUNICATIONS CORPORATION

1201 Third Avenue, Suite 3600, Seattle WA 98101. 206/621-1351. **Toll-free phone:** 800/448-0273. **Fax:** 206/623-9015. **Contact:** Personnel. **World Wide Web address:** http://www.northlandtel.com. **Description:** Provides cable television services, local news production, and local advertising for small-market radio and cable systems. **Corporate headquarters location:** This location. **Other U.S. locations:** Nationwide. **Operations at this facility include:** Administration. **Listed on:** Privately held. **Number of employees at this location:** 50. **Number of employees nationwide:** 470.

TELECT, INC.

2111 North Molter Road, Liberty Lake WA 99019. 509/926-6000. **Fax:** 509/927-0852. **Contact:** Human Resources. **World Wide Web address:** http://www.telect.com. **Description:** An international designer and manufacturer of fiber-optic, digital, analog, professional audio/video, power, and electronic monitoring and control equipment. Founded in 1982. **NOTE:** Entry-level positions and second and third shifts are offered. **Positions advertised include:** Electronic Engineer; Mechanical Engineer; Senior Business Analyst. **Special programs:** Internships; Training. **Corporate headquarters location:** This location. **International locations:** Guadalajara, Mexico. **Listed on:** Privately held. **Annual sales/revenues:** More than $100 million. **Number of employees at this location:** 900. **Number of employees nationwide:** 950. **Number of employees worldwide:** 1,150.

TELTONE CORPORATION

22522 29th Drive SE, Canyon Business Park, Bothell WA 98021. 425/487-1515. **Fax:** 425/402-7222. **Contact:** Wendy Herzog, Human Resources Manager. **E-mail address:** hr@teltone.com. **World Wide Web address:** http://www.teltone.com. **Description:** Manufactures telecommunications equipment including testing equipment for the communications industry and telecommuting products. **Special programs:** Internships. **Corporate headquarters location:** This location. **Operations at this facility include:** Administration; Manufacturing; Research and Development; Sales; Service. **Number of employees at this location:** 75.

TONE COMMANDER SYSTEMS INC.

11609 49th Place West, Mukilteo WA 98275. 425/349-1000. **Fax:** 425/349-1010. **Contact:** Personnel. **World Wide Web address:** http://www.tonecommander.com. **Description:** Manufactures telecommunications equipment including Centrex attendant consoles and ISDN equipment. **Corporate headquarters location:** This location. **Listed on:** Privately held. **Annual sales/revenues:** $5 - $10 million. **Number of employees at this location:** 40.

VERIZON COMMUNICATIONS
1800 41st Street, Everett WA 98201. 425/261-5321. **Fax:** 425/258-5901. **Contact:** Human Resources. **World Wide Web address:** http://www.verizon.com. **Description:** Provides a wide variety of communications services ranging from local telephone services for the home and office to highly complex voice and data services for governments and commercial industries. **Other U.S. locations:** Nationwide.

COMPUTER HARDWARE, SOFTWARE, AND SERVICES

You can expect to find the following types of companies in this chapter:

Computer Components and Hardware Manufacturers
Consultants and Computer Training Companies
Internet and Online Service Providers
Networking and Systems Services
Repair Services/Rental and Leasing
Resellers, Wholesalers, and Distributors
Software Developers/Programming Services
Web Technologies

AVOCENT CORPORATION

9911 Willows Road NE, Redmond WA 98052. 425/402-9393. **Contact:** Human Resources Department. **E-mail address:** hr@avocent.com. **World Wide Web address:** http://www.avocent. com. **Description:** Manufactures a variety of computer components such as concentrated switches. **Positions advertised include:** Auditor; Quality Engineer; Business Analyst; Help Desk Technician; Product Manager; Web Developer. **Listed on:** NASDAQ. **Stock exchange symbol:** AVCT.

AVTECH CORPORATION

3400 Wallingford Avenue North, Seattle WA 98103. 206/634-2540. **Contact:** Personnel Director. **E-mail address:** hr@avtcorp.com. **World Wide Web address:** http://www.avtcorp.com. **Description:** Manufactures a variety of electronic equipment products including interior lighting and flight deck audio control panels. **Positions advertised include:** QA Supervisor. **Corporate headquarters location:** This location.

ADOBE SYSTEMS, INC.

801 North 34th Street, Seattle WA 98103. 206/470-7000. **Contact:** Personnel Department. **World Wide Web address:** http:// www.adobe.com. **Description:** Adobe Systems develops, markets, and supports computer software products and technologies for Macintosh, Windows, and OS/2 platforms that enable users to create, display, print, and communicate electronic documents. The company distributes its products through a network of original equipment manufacturer customers, distributors and dealers, and value-added resellers and system integrators. The company has operations in the Americas, Europe, and the Pacific Rim. **Corporate headquarters location:** San Jose CA. **Operations at this facility include:** This location develops several of the company's software products and provides sales and support services. **Listed on:** NASDAQ. **Stock exchange symbol:** ADBE.

ADVANCED BUSINESSLINK CORPORATION

5808 Lake Washington Boulevard NE, Suite 100, Kirkland WA 98033. 425/602-4777. **Contact:** Human Resources. **E-mail address:** jobs_via_web@businesslink.com. **World Wide Web address:** http:// www.businesslink.com. **Description:** Develops web-to-host and remote access software for IBM AS/400 servers. **Positions advertised include:** Account Executive; Outside Sales Representative; Marketing

Director; Media Relations Manager. **Corporate headquarters location:** San Jose CA.

ADVANCED DIGITAL INFORMATION CORPORATION
11431 Willows Road NE, Redmond WA 98052. 425/881-8004. **Fax:** 425/881-2296. **Contact:** Human Resources. **E-mail address:** jobs@adic.com. **World Wide Web address:** http://www.adic.com. **Description:** Designs, manufactures, and markets hardware and software products for data storage and protection. Founded in 1983. **Positions advertised include:** Mechanical Engineer; Product Test Engineer. **Corporate headquarters location:** This location. **Parent company:** Lockheed Martin Corporation. **Listed on:** NASDAQ. **Stock exchange symbol:** ADIC. **Annual sales/revenues:** $51 - $100 million.

ADVANCED HARDWARE ARCHITECTURE
2345 Northeast Hopkins Court, Pullman WA 99163-5601. 509/334-1000. **Fax:** 509/334-9000. **Contact:** Human Resources. **E-mail address:** hr@aha.com. **World Wide Web address:** http://www.aha.com. **Description:** Manufactures products for data storage, digital communications, and digital hard copy. **Corporate headquarters location:** This location.

AJILON CONSULTING
310 120th Avenue NE, Suite A200, Bellevue WA 98005. 425/455-1004. **Contact:** Human Resources. **World Wide Web address:** http://www.ajilonconsulting.com. **Description:** Offers computer consulting services, project support, and end user services. **Positions advertised include:** Seibel/Genesys Architect; Senior Reports Analyst. **Other U.S. locations:** Nationwide.

ANALYSTS INTERNATIONAL CORPORATION (AIC)
10655 NE Fourth Street, Suite 800, Bellevue WA 98004-5022. 425/454-2500. **Toll-free phone:** 800/698-9411. **Contact:** Human Resources Department. **E-mail address:** jobs@analysts.com. **World Wide Web address:** http://www.analysts.com. **Description:** An international computer consulting firm. The company assists clients in developing systems in a variety of industries using different programming languages and software. Founded in 1966. **Office hours:** Monday - Friday, 8:00 a.m. - 5:00 p.m. **Corporate headquarters location:** Minneapolis MN. **Other U.S. locations:** Nationwide. **International locations:** Cambridge, England; Toronto, Canada. **Listed on:** NASDAQ. **Stock exchange symbol:** ANLY.

Annual sales/revenues: More than $100 million. **Number of employees at this location:** 250.

APPLIED MICROSYSTEMS CORPORATION
P.O. Box 97002, Redmond WA 98073-9702. 425/882-2000. **Physical address:** 5020 148th Avenue NE, Redmond WA 98052. **Contact:** Human Resources. **World Wide Web address:** http://www.amc.com. **Description:** Manufactures and supplies software development tools and in-circuit emulators for embedded system development. **Corporate headquarters location:** This location. **Listed on:** NASDAQ. **Stock exchange symbol:** APMC.

ASIX
10900 NE Eighth Avenue, Suite 700, Bellevue WA 98004. 425/635-0709. **Toll-free phone:** 800/335-2525. **Contact:** Personnel. **E-mail address:** resumes@asix.com. **World Wide Web address:** http://www.asix.com. **Description:** Provides computer consulting services.

ATTACHMATE CORPORATION
P.O. Box 90026, Bellevue WA 98009-9026. 425/644-4010. **Toll-free phone:** 800/426-6283. **Contact:** Recruiter. **E-mail address:** cooljobs@attachmate.com. **World Wide Web address:** http://www.attachmate.com. **Description:** Designs, manufactures, and markets personal computer to mainframe data communications products worldwide. Products are marketed under the IRMA, Crosstalk, and Quickappbrand names. Founded in 1982. **NOTE:** Entry-level positions are offered. **Positions advertised include:** Software Test Engineer; Senior Database Engineer; Technical Architect; Senior Administrative Assistant; User Interface Developer. **Special programs:** Internships. **Office hours:** Monday - Friday, 9:00 a.m. - 5:00 p.m. **Corporate headquarters location:** This location. **Other U.S. locations:** Nationwide. **International locations:** Worldwide. **Listed on:** Privately held. **Number of employees nationwide:** 1,000.

CAMINUS CORPORATION
13513 NE 126th Place, Suite B, Kirkland WA 98034. 425/814-4000. **Contact:** Human Resources. **World Wide Web address:** http://www.caminus.com. **Description:** Develops schedule management software for electric utility companies. **Corporate headquarters location:** New York NY.

CAP GEMINI ERNST & YOUNG U.S. LLC
999 Third Avenue, Suite 3330, Seattle WA 98104. 206/624-4600. **Contact:** Human Resources. **World Wide Web address:** http://www.cgey.com. **Description:** A leading provider of information technology consulting services with over 40 branch offices worldwide. The company provides its clients with the solutions needed to achieve business and operational goals. Cap Gemini Ernst & Young U.S. focuses on three major activities: consultancy, implementation, and systems integration. **Corporate headquarters location:** This location. **Parent company:** The Cap Gemini Sogeti Group.

CAPTARIS
P.O. Box 97025, Kirkland WA 98083-9725. 425/820-6000. **Physical address:** 11410 NE 122nd Way, Kirkland WA 98034. **Contact:** Human Resources. **World Wide Web address:** http://www.captaris.com. **Description:** Develops, manufactures, markets, and supports a broad line of open systems-based, computer technology software products and systems that automate call answering. **Positions advertised include:** Financial Analyst; Configuration Management Engineer. **Corporate headquarters location:** This location. **Listed on:** NASDAQ. **Stock exchange symbol:** CAPA.

CELLULAR TECHNICAL SERVICES COMPANY (CTS)
2815 Second Avenue, Suite 100, Seattle WA 98121. 206/443-6400. **Fax:** 206/269-1404. **Contact:** Human Resources. **E-mail address:** hr@celtech.com. **World Wide Web address:** http://www.cellulartech.com. **Description:** Develops and markets real-time information management software systems used for fraud detection, billing, and customer service. Cellular Technical Services Company serves clients in the wireless communications industry. **Corporate headquarters location:** This location. **Listed on:** New York Stock Exchange. **Stock exchange symbol:** CTSC.

COMPUTER ASSOCIATES INTERNATIONAL, INC.
12131 113th Avenue NE, Suite 300, Kirkland WA 98034. 425/825-2600. **Contact:** Human Resources. **World Wide Web address:** http://www.cai.com. **Description:** Computer Associates International is one of the world's leading developers of client/server and distributed computing software. The company develops, markets, and supports enterprise management, database and applications development, business applications, and consumer software

products for a broad range of mainframe, midrange, and desktop computers. Computer Associates serves major business, government, research, and educational organizations. Founded in 1976. **Office hours:** Monday - Friday, 8:00 a.m. - 5:00 p.m. **Corporate headquarters location:** Islandia NY. **Other U.S. locations:** Nationwide. **Operations at this facility include:** This location develops software. **Listed on:** New York Stock Exchange. **Stock exchange symbol:** CA. **Annual sales/revenues:** More than $100 million. **Number of employees nationwide:** 4,000. **Number of employees worldwide:** 9,000.

CORBIS CORPORATION
15395 SE 30th Place, Suite 300, Bellevue WA 98007. 425/641-4505. **Recorded jobline:** 425/649-3431. **Contact:** Human Resources. **World Wide Web address:** http://www.corbis.com. **Description:** Develops and sells digital images to businesses. **Positions advertised include:** Assistant to General Counsel; Staff Accountant; Client Services Technician; Account Executive. **Corporate headquarters location:** This location.

CRAY INC.
Merrill Place, 411 First Avenue South, Suite 600, Seattle WA 98104-2860. 206/701-2000. **Contact:** Corporate Recruiter. **E-mail address:** resumes@cray.com. **World Wide Web address:** http://www.cray.com. **Description:** Develops high-end supercomputers. **Positions advertised include:** Floor Plan Engineer; Release Engineer; Platform Manager; Program Manager. **Corporate headquarters location:** This location. **Listed on:** NASDAQ. **Stock exchange symbol:** CRAY.

DEALER INFORMATION SYSTEMS CORPORATION (DIS)
1315 Cornwall Avenue, Bellingham WA 98225. 360/733-7610. **Contact:** Human Resources. **World Wide Web address:** http://www.discorp.com. **Description:** Develops management software for agricultural, construction, and automobile dealerships throughout the United State and Canada. DIS Corporation also offers its customers communications equipment and technical support. **Corporate headquarters location:** This location.

E-TERRA CORPORATION
1800 72nd Avenue South, Suite 160, Kent WA 98032. 425/401-1100. **Contact:** Human Resources. **E-mail address:** jobs@myeterra.com. **World Wide Web address:** http://www.ivocad.com.

Description: Resells CAD software, PC workstations and peripherals, and offers computer consulting services.

EDS (ELECTRONIC DATA SYSTEMS CORPORATION)

19351 Eighth Avenue NE, Suite B, Poulsbo WA 98370. 360/697-3330. **Contact:** Human Resources. **E-mail address:** careers@eds.com. **World Wide Web address:** http://www.eds.com. **Description:** Provides consulting, systems development, systems integration, and systems management services for large-scale and industry-specific applications. Founded in 1962. **Corporate headquarters location:** Plano TX. **Other U.S. locations:** Nationwide. **International locations:** Worldwide. **Listed on:** New York Stock Exchange. **Stock exchange symbol:** EDS. **Number of employees worldwide:** 115,000.

FILENET CORPORATION

720 Fourth Avenue, Suite 100, Kirkland WA 98033. 425/893-7000. **Contact:** Human Resources. **E-mail address:** cooljobs@filenet.com. **World Wide Web address:** http://www.filenet.com. **Description:** FileNET develops and markets electronic content management software and e-business solutions. Products and services are used to help corporations and organizations build intranets, create electronic portals to streamline information management, and to create, process, edit, organize, and store all forms of digital content for Internet applications. Founded in 1983. **Company slogan:** Putting documents to work. **Special programs:** Internships. **Corporate headquarters location:** Costa Mesa CA. **Other U.S. locations:** Nationwide. **International locations:** Worldwide. **Listed on:** NASDAQ. **Stock exchange symbol:** FILE. **Facilities Manager:** Jennifer Shepherel. **Number of employees nationwide:** 1,700.

GETRONICS

22425 East Appleway Road, Liberty Lake WA 99019. 509/927-5600. **Contact:** Human Resources. **World Wide Web address:** http://www.getronics.com. **Description:** Provides information and communication technology solutions and support services worldwide. Getronics conducts its business through two major sectors: Systems Integration and Networked Technology Services includes enterprise system integration, managed services and infrastructure outsourcing, and network integration; and Business Solutions and Consulting includes software services, consulting, industry business solutions, and financial business solutions.

Corporate headquarters location: Billerica MA. **International locations:** Worldwide.

HEWLETT-PACKARD COMPANY

3380 146th Place SE, Suite 200, Bellevue WA 98007. 425/643-4000. **Contact:** Human Resources. **World Wide Web address:** http://www.hp.com. **Description:** Hewlett-Packard is engaged in the design and manufacture of measurement and computation products and systems used in business, industry, engineering, science, health care, and education. Principal products are integrated instrument and computer systems including hardware and software, peripheral products, and medical electronic equipment and systems. **NOTE:** Jobseekers should send resumes to Employment Response Center, Hewlett-Packard Company, Mail Stop 20-APP, 3000 Hanover Street, Palo Alto CA 94304-1181. **Corporate headquarters location:** Palo Alto CA. **Other U.S. locations:** Nationwide. **Operations at this facility include:** This location is engaged in the sale of electronic measurement and computing products. **Listed on:** New York Stock Exchange. **Stock exchange symbol:** HPQ. **Number of employees at this location:** 225.

IBM CORPORATION

3600 Carillon Point, Kirkland WA 98033. 425/803-0600. **Toll-free phone:** 800/796-9876. **Contact:** Human Resources. **World Wide Web address:** http://www.ibm.com. **Description:** IBM is a developer, manufacturer, and marketer of advanced information processing products including computers and microelectronic technology, software, networking systems, and information technology-related services. **NOTE:** Jobseekers should send a resume to IBM Staffing Services, 1DPA/051, 3808 Six Forks Road, Raleigh NC 27609. **Corporate headquarters location:** Armonk NY. **Other U.S. locations:** Nationwide. **Operations at this facility include:** This location is a programming center. **Subsidiaries include:** IBM Credit Corporation; IBM Instruments, Inc.; IBM World Trade Corporation.

INFORMATION BUILDERS INC.

8644 154th Avenue NE, Redmond WA 98052. 425/861-9400. **Contact:** Human Resources. **E-mail address:** employment_opportunities@ibi.com. **World Wide Web address:** http://www.informationbuilders.com. **Description:** Develops software for client/server technology and application development. **Corporate headquarters location:** New York NY. **Other U.S. locations:** Nationwide. **Number of employees nationwide:** 1,500.

INTEGRATRAK
12600 SE 38th Street, Suite 250, Bellevue WA 98006. 425/401-1000. **Contact:** Harry Chesman, Human Resources. **E-mail address:** harry.chesman@mtsint.com. **World Wide Web address:** http://www.integratrak.com. **Description:** Develops software for the telecommunications industry. **Corporate headquarters location:** This location.

INTEL CORPORATION
2800 Center Drive, Du Pont WA 98327-5050. 253/371-8080. **Toll-free phone:** 800/628-8686. **Contact:** Human Resources. **E-mail address:** resumes@intel.com. **World Wide Web address:** http://www.intel.com. **Description:** Intel Corporation is a manufacturer of computer microprocessors and computer related parts. **NOTE:** Resumes should be sent to Intel Corporation, Staffing Department, P.O. Box 549263, Suite 281, Waltham MA 02454. **Corporate headquarters location:** Santa Clara CA.

INTERLINQ SOFTWARE CORPORATION
11980 NE 24th Street, Bellevue WA 98005. 425/827-1112. **Fax:** 425/827-0927. **Contact:** Human Resources. **E-mail address:** talent@interlinq.com. **World Wide Web address:** http:// www.interlinq.com. **Description:** A leading provider of PC-based software solutions for the residential mortgage lending industry. The company's MortgageWare Enterprise product line is sold to banks, savings institutions, mortgage banks, mortgage brokers, and credit unions. The MortgageWare Enterprise product line is a complete PC-based software system that automates all aspects of the loan origination and secondary marketing processes, from qualifying a borrower to processing, settling, closing, and selling loans. MortgageWare Enterprise also includes tools to help lenders track and manage loans in their system, as well as a proprietary electronic communications system that enables data to be transferred via modem between headquarters, branch offices, and laptop origination systems. **Corporate headquarters location:** This location. **Listed on:** NASDAQ. **Stock exchange symbol:** INLQ. **Number of employees at this location:** 180.

IOLINE CORPORATION
14140 200th Street NE, Woodinville WA 98072. 425/398-8282. **Fax:** 425/398-8383. **Contact:** Human Resources. **E-mail address:** resume@ioline.com. **World Wide Web address:** http://www.ioline. com. **Description:** Manufactures plotters for computers. **Positions**

advertised include: Apparel Systems Specialist; Sales/Marketing Director. **Corporate headquarters location:** This location.

IVOCAD WEST

1800 72nd Avenue South, Suite 160, Kent WA 98032. 425/401-1100. **Contact:** Human Resources. **E-mail address:** jobs@myeterra.com. **World Wide Web address:** http://www.ivocad.com. **Description:** Resells CAD software, PC workstations and peripherals, and offers computer consulting services.

KEANE, INC.

636 120th Avenue NE, Bellevue WA 98005. 425/451-8272. **Contact:** Human Resources. **E-mail address:** careers@keane.com. **World Wide Web address:** http://www.keane.com. **Description:** Keane offers businesses a variety of computer consulting services. Keane also develops, markets, and manages software for its clients and assists in project management. Founded in 1965. **Corporate headquarters location:** Boston MA. **Other U.S. locations:** Nationwide. **Operations at this facility include:** This location is an office of the healthcare solutions division. **Listed on:** American Stock Exchange. **Stock exchange symbol:** KEA. **Number of employees nationwide:** 4,500.

KEY TRONIC CORPORATION

P.O. Box 14687, Spokane WA 99214. 509/928-8000. **Physical address:** 4424 North Sullivan Road, Spokane WA 99216. **Fax:** 509/927-5307. **Contact:** Personnel. **E-mail address:** jobs@keytronic.com. **World Wide Web address:** http://www.keytronic.com. **Description:** One of the world's largest independent manufacturers of computer keyboards and input devices. Key Tronic designs, develops, and manufactures standard and custom keyboards for integration with personal computers, terminals, and word processors made by original equipment manufacturers. Founded in 1969. **NOTE:** Entry-level positions and second and third shifts are offered. **Positions advertised include:** Buyer/Planner. **Special programs:** Internships. **Internship information:** Internships are offered on an as needed basis. The company has year-round internships, but primarily has openings in the summer and recruits through local colleges. Please call this location for more information. **Corporate headquarters location:** This location. **Other U.S. locations:** Las Cruces NM; El Paso TX. **International locations:** Dundalk, Ireland; Juarez, Mexico. **Listed on:** NASDAQ. **Stock exchange symbol:** KTCC. **Annual sales/revenues:** More than $100 million. **Number of** employees at this location: 550. **Number of employees nationwide:** 650. **Number of employees worldwide:** 3,000.

LAPLINK.COM, INC.

98192 North Creek Parkway, Suite 100, Bothell WA 98011. 425/483-8088. **Contact:** Human Resources. **E-mail address:** hotjobs@laplink.com. **World Wide Web address:** http://www.laplink.com. **Description:** Develops software for businesses and individuals enabling access to private and public computer networks, the Internet, and individual PCs. Founded in 1982. **Company slogan:** The remote access champion. **Office hours:** Monday - Friday, 8:00 a.m. - 5:00 p.m. **Corporate headquarters location:** This location. **Listed on:** Privately held. **Annual sales/revenues:** $21 - $50 million. **Number of employees at this location:** 80. **Number of employees worldwide:** 90.

MICROSOFT CORPORATION

One Microsoft Way, Redmond WA 98052-6399. 425/882-8080. **Contact:** Recruiting Department. **World Wide Web address:** http://www.microsoft.com/jobs. **Description:** Designs, sells, and supports a product line of systems and applications software for business, home, and professional use. Microsoft also produces related books and hardware products. Software products include spreadsheet, desktop publishing, project management, graphics, word processing, and database applications, as well as operating systems and programming languages. **Corporate headquarters location:** This location. **Listed on:** NASDAQ. **Stock exchange symbol:** MSFT. **Annual sales/revenues:** More than $100 million.

MODIS, INC.

14535 Bel-Red Road, Suite 200, Bellevue WA 98007. 425/644-9500. **Contact:** Human Resources. **E-mail address:** resume@modisit.com. **World Wide Web address:** http://www.modisit.com. **Description:** An IT consulting firm. Founded in 1986. **Corporate headquarters location:** Jacksonville FL.

NETMANAGE, INC.

11332 NE 122nd Way, Kirkland WA 98034. 425/814-9255. **Contact:** Human Resources. **World Wide Web address:** http://www.netmanage.com. **Description:** Develops, markets, and supports Windows-based connectivity software and associated applications tools. The company's software products provide PC users easy access to computer applications and data residing on multiple host mainframes and minicomputers in enterprisewide information systems networks. **Corporate headquarters location:** Cupertino CA. **Listed on:** NASDAQ. **Stock exchange symbol:** NETM.

ONYX SOFTWARE CORPORATION
3180 139th Avenue SE, Suite 500, Bellevue WA 98005. 425/451-8060. **Fax:** 425/732-2415. **Contact:** Christa Vandivier, Human Resources Department. **E-mail address:** recruiting@onyxcorp.com. **World Wide Web address:** http://www.onyx.com. **Description:** Develops customer management software.

ORACLE CORPORATION
500 108th Avenue NE, Suite 1300, Bellevue WA 98004. 425/646-0200. **Contact:** Human Resources. **World Wide Web address:** http://www.oracle.com. **Description:** Oracle Corporation designs and manufactures database and information management software for business and provides consulting services. **NOTE:** For commercial consultant positions, address resumes to Tammy Yeager. For sales positions, address resumes to Virginia Wagner. **Corporate headquarters location:** Redwood Shores CA. **Other U.S. locations:** Nationwide. **International locations:** Worldwide. **Operations at this facility include:** Administration; Regional Headquarters; Sales. **Listed on:** NASDAQ. **Annual sales/revenues:** More than $100 million. **Number of employees at this location:** 230. **Number of employees nationwide:** 12,000.

OUTPUT TECHNOLOGY CORPORATION
3808 North Sullivan Road, Building 3, Spokane WA 99216. 509/536-0468. **Contact:** Personnel Administration. **Email address:** hr@output.com. **World Wide Web address:** http://www.output.com. **Description:** Manufactures and distributes printers and related products. **Corporate headquarters location:** This location. **Listed on:** Privately held. **Number of employees at this location:** 130.

PRECISION DIGITAL IMAGES CORPORATION
11715 North Creek Parkway South, Suite 110, Bothell WA 98011. 425/882-0218. **Fax:** 425/867-9177. **Contact:** Human Resources. **World Wide Web address:** http://www.precisionimages.com. **Description:** Designs image processing and image collection subsystems for computers. Products are sold to original equipment manufacturers primarily for such applications as machine vision, desktop video conferencing and medical imaging. Founded in 1992.

REALNETWORKS
2601 Eliot Avenue, Seattle WA 98121. 206/674-2700. **Fax:** 206/674-2699. **Contact:** Human Resources. **World Wide Web address:** http://www.real.com. **Description:** Develops software that allows users to listen to audio applications over the Internet. **Stock exchange symbol:** RNWK.

SHARP MICROELECTRONICS USA
5700 NW Pacific Rim Boulevard, Camas WA 98607. 360/834-8700. **Fax:** 360/817-7544. **Contact:** Human Resources. **World Wide Web address:** http://www.sharp-usa.com. **Description:** Sharp Corporation develops business products, consumer electronics, and electronic components. **Corporate headquarters location:** Mahwah NJ. **Operations at this facility include:** This location is a sales and marketing facility. **Parent company:** Sharp Corporation.

SIERRA, INC.
3060 139th Avenue SE, Suite 500, Bellevue WA 98005. 425/649-9800. **Fax:** 425/641-7617. **Contact:** Human Resources. **E-mail address:** recruit@sierra.com. **World Wide Web address:** http://www.sierra.com. **Description:** Develops and distributes entertainment and educational software. The company's products are designed for IBM compatible and Macintosh systems. Founded in 1979. **Positions advertised include:** Animator; Modeler; Principal Engineer. **Corporate headquarters location:** Oakhurst CA. **Other U.S. locations:** Nationwide. **International locations:** France; Germany. **Annual sales/revenues:** More than $100 million. **Number of employees at this location:** 450.

SOLUCIENT
411 108th Avenue NE, Suite 800, Bellevue WA 98004. 425/455-2652. **Contact:** Human Resources. **E-mail address:** becareers@solucient.com. **World Wide Web address:** http://www.solucient.com. **Description:** Provides data processing services and develops software for the health care industry. **Positions advertised include:** Quality Assurance Manager; Receptionist; Senior Program Manager; Senior Technical Writer. **Corporate headquarters location:** Evanston IL.

TALLY PRINTERS
P.O. Box 97018, Kent WA 98064-9718. 425/251-5500. **Fax:** 425/251-5520. **Toll-free phone:** 800/843-1347. **Contact:** Personnel. **E-mail address:** hrd@tally.com. **World Wide Web address:**

http://www.tally.com. **Description:** Manufactures laser, serial, and line matrix printers. **Office hours:** Monday - Friday, 7:45 a.m. - 4:15 p.m.

VANTEON CORPORATION
8700 148th Avenue NE, Redmond WA 98052. 425/250-0000. **Contact:** Ruth Lobe, Recruiter. **E-mail address:** resume@ vanteon.com. **World Wide Web address:** http:// www.vanteon.com. **Description:** Custom designs software solutions for clients engaged in e-commerce services.

WACOM TECHNOLOGY COMPANY
1311 SE Cardinal Court, Vancouver WA 98683. 360/896-9833. **Fax:** 360/896-9724. **Contact:** Human Resources. **World Wide Web address:** http://www.wacom.com. **Description:** Manufactures image-enhancing software, animation software, and graphic digitizing equipment.

EDUCATIONAL SERVICES

You can expect to find the following types of facilities in this chapter:

Business/Secretarial/Data Processing Schools
Colleges/Universities/Professional Schools
Community Colleges/Technical Schools/Vocational Schools
Elementary and Secondary Schools
Preschool and Child Daycare Services

BAINBRIDGE ISLAND SCHOOL DISTRICT

8489 Madison Avenue NE, Bainbridge Island WA 98110. 206/842-4714. **Contact:** Dixie Brown, Personnel Specialist. **E-mail address:** dbrown@bainbridge.wednet.edu. **World Wide Web address:** http://www.bainbridge.wednet.edu. **Description:** A public school district that is comprised of one high school, one middle school, three elementary schools, and an alternative learning program. **Operations at this facility include:** Administration. **Number of employees at this location:** 400.

BELLEVUE COMMUNITY COLLEGE

3000 Landerholm Circle SE, Bellevue WA 98007-6484. 425/564-1000. **Recorded jobline:** 425/564-2082. **Contact:** Human Resources. **World Wide Web address:** http://www.bcc.ctc.edu. **Description:** A community college operating as part of the Washington State Community College System. Over 18,000 students are enrolled each quarter.

CENTRAL KITSAP SCHOOL DISTRICT

P.O. Box 8, Silverdale WA 98383-3078-0008. 360/692-3118. **Physical address:** 9210 Silverdale Way NW, Silverdale WA 98383. **Fax:** 360/698-5499. **Recorded jobline:** 360/698-3470. **Contact:** Personnel Department. **World Wide Web address:** http://www.cksd.wednet.edu. **Description:** Administrative offices for the school district. **Positions advertised include:** Executive Director of Secondary Teaching & Learning; Assistant Superintendent of Human Resources; Director of Special Services. **Corporate headquarters location:** This location. **Number of employees at this location:** 1,500.

CENTRAL WASHINGTON UNIVERSITY

400 East Eighth Avenue, Ellensburg WA 98926. 509/963-1202. **Recorded jobline:** 509/963-1562. **Contact:** Human Resources. **E-mail address:** humanres@cwu.edu. **World Wide Web address:** http://www.cwu.edu. **Description:** A regional university offering baccalaureate and graduate degrees in more than 90 academic programs serving nearly 8,000 students. **NOTE:** Entry-level positions are offered. **Number of employees at this location:** 1,000.

CLOVER PARK SCHOOL DISTRICT

10903 Gravelly Lake Drive SW, Lakewood WA 98499. 253/583-5095. **Recorded jobline:** 253/583-5003. **Fax:** 253/589-7440. **Contact:** Lori Mortenson, Recruitment Coordinator. **E-mail address:**

lmorten@cloverpark.k12.wa.us. **World Wide Web address:** http://cpsd.cloverpark.k12.wa.us. **Description:** Administrative offices of the Clover Park school district. **Positions advertised include:** Counselor; Math Teacher; Science Teacher; English Teacher; Social Studies Teacher. **Number of employees at this location:** 1,800.

COMMUNITY COLLEGE OF SPOKANE
P.O. Box 6000, Spokane WA 99217-6000. 509/434-5040. **Physical address:** 501 North Riverpoint Boulevard, Spokane WA 99202. **Fax:** 509/434-5055. **Recorded jobline:** 509/533-2013. **Contact:** Manager of Human Resources Department. **E-mail address:** hro@dist.spokane.cc.wa.us. **World Wide Web address:** http://www.ccs.spokane.cc.wa.us. **Description:** Provides academic and vocational education and training to more than 22,000 full- and part-time students in six northeastern Washington counties. Community College of Spokane operates two colleges, Spokane Community College and Spokane Falls Community College, as well as the Institute for Extended Learning, which is responsible for a variety of off-campus programs and services. **Number of employees at this location:** 1,900.

EASTERN WASHINGTON UNIVERSITY
314 Showalter Hall, Cheney WA 99004-2431. 509/359-2381. **Fax:** 509/359-2874. **Recorded jobline:** 509/359-4390. **Contact:** Human Resources Department. **E-mail address:** hr@ewu.edu. **World Wide Web address:** http://www.ewu.edu. **Description:** A four-year university offering undergraduate and graduate degrees to approximately 8,500 students. **Corporate headquarters location:** This location. **Operations at this facility include:** Administration. **Number of employees at this location:** 1,100.

EDMONDS COMMUNITY COLLEGE
20000 68th Avenue West, Lynnwood WA 98036. 425/640-1400. **Recorded jobline:** 425/640-1510. **Contact:** Human Resources. **E-mail address:** jobs@edcc.edu. **World Wide Web address:** http://www.edcc.edu. **Description:** A community college that operates as part of the Washington State Public Higher Education System. **NOTE:** Please call the jobline for a listing of available positions. **Positions advertised include:** Media Maintenance Technician; ESL Instructor; Mathematics Instructor; Chemistry Instructor. **Number of employees at this location:** 1,000.

EVERETT COMMUNITY COLLEGE
2000 Tower Street, Everett WA 98201. 425/388-9100. **Recorded jobline:** 425/388-9229. **Contact:** Human Resources Department. **World Wide Web address:** http://www.evcc.ctc.edu. **Description:** A two-year, community college. **Positions advertised include:** Dean of Communication and Social Sciences; Nursing Instructor.

FRANKLIN PIERCE SCHOOL DISTRICT
315 129th Street South, Tacoma WA 98444. 253/537-0211. **Contact:** Mrs. Jamie Siegel, Executive Director of Personnel. **E-mail address:** jamies@fp.k12.wa.us. **World Wide Web address:** http://www.midland.fp.k12.wa.us. **Description:** Public school district for the Tacoma area. **Positions advertised include:** Special Education Teacher; Physical Therapist; Elementary School Counselor; Music/Movement Teacher. **Operations at this facility include:** Administration.

GONZAGA UNIVERSITY
AD Box 80, 502 East Boone Avenue, Spokane WA 99258. 509/328-4220. **Recorded jobline:** 509/323-5916. **Contact:** Ms. Tricia Burns, Manager of Employment and Training. **E-mail address:** burnst@gu.gonzaga.edu. **World Wide Web address:** http://www.gonzaga.edu. **Description:** A university offering coursework in a number of fields including arts and sciences, business administration, education, engineering, law, nursing, and military science. Gonzaga University enrolls approximately 3,000 undergraduate and 2,000 graduate students.

HIGHLINE COMMUNITY COLLEGE
P.O. Box 98000, Des Moines WA 98198-9800. 206/878-3710. **Physical address:** 2400 South 240th Street, Des Moines WA. **Contact:** Human Resources. **World Wide Web address:** http://www.highline.ctc.edu. **Description:** A community college with an enrollment of approximately 10,000 students. Founded in 1961.

KENT SCHOOL DISTRICT
12033 SE 256th Street, Kent WA 98031-6643. 253/373-7209. **Contact:** Human Resources. **World Wide Web address:** http://www.kent.wednet.edu. **Description:** Provides administrative support to the 36 schools in the Kent school system. **Operations at this facility include:** Administration. **Number of employees at this location:** 2,500.

OLYMPIC COLLEGE

1600 Chester Avenue, 5th Floor, College Service Center, Bremerton WA 98337-1699. 360/475-7300. **Fax:** 360/475-7302. **Contact:** Linda Yerger, Personnel Director. **E-mail:** jobs@oc.ctc.edu. **World Wide Web address:** http://www.oc.ctc.edu. **Description:** A two-year community college that offers associate degrees in arts and science, transfer programs, and various technical degrees. **Corporate headquarters location:** This location.

RENTON SCHOOL DISTRICT

300 SW Seventh Street, Renton WA 98055. 425/204-2350. **Fax:** 425/204-2383. **Recorded jobline:** 425/204-2305. **Contact:** Marcia Darchuk, Recruiting Coordinator. **E-mail address:** mdarchuk@ renton.wednet.edu. **World Wide Web address:** http://www. renton.wednet.edu. **Description:** Administrative offices for the Renton public school district. **Office hours:** Monday - Friday, 7:30 a.m. - 4:30 p.m. **Number of employees at this location:** 1,400.

RENTON TECHNICAL COLLEGE

3000 NE Fourth Street, Renton WA 98056. 425/235-2352. **Fax:** 425/235-7832. **Recorded jobline:** 425/235-2354. **Contact:** Human Resources. **World Wide Web address:** http://www.renton-tc.ctc.edu. **Description:** A technical college operated by the State Board for Community and Technical Colleges.

RIVERDEEP/THE LEARNING COMPANY

6727 185th Avenue NE, Building A, Redmond WA 98052. 425/556-8400. **Contact:** Human Resources. **World Wide Web address:** http://www.riverdeep.net. **Description:** Develops, publishes, and markets educational software and other products for the early childhood and special education markets. **Corporate headquarters location:** Cambridge MA. **Listed on:** NASDAQ. **Stock exchange symbol:** RVDP. **Number of employees at this location:** 150.

SEATTLE CENTRAL COMMUNITY COLLEGE

1500 Harvard Avenue, Seattle WA 98122. 206/587-4155. **Fax:** 206/587-4158. **Contact:** Human Resources. **E-mail address:** jobs@sccd.ctc.edu. **World Wide Web address:** http://www.sccd.ctc. edu. **Description:** A community college. **Number of employees at this location:** 800.

SEATTLE PACIFIC UNIVERSITY

3307 Third Avenue West, Seattle WA 98119. 206/281-2809. **Fax:** 206/281-2846. **Recorded jobline:** 206/281-2065. **Contact:** Human Resources. **World Wide Web address:** http://www.spu.edu. **Description:** A Christian university of arts and sciences with an enrollment of approximately 3,400. **Positions advertised include:** Assistant Professor of Accounting; Physical Education Instructor; Residence Life Coordinator; Senior Administrative Assistant.

SEDRO-WOOLLEY SCHOOL DISTRICT

801 Trail Road, Sedro-Woolley WA 98284. 360/856-0831. **Fax:** 360/855-3501. **Contact:** Personnel. **World Wide Web address:** http://www.swsd.wednet.edu. **Description:** Offices of the Sedro-Woolley school system.

SHORELINE COMMUNITY COLLEGE

16101 Greenwood Avenue North, Shoreline WA 98133. 206/546-4769. **Fax:** 206/546-5850. **Recorded jobline:** 206/546-5894 x3306. **Contact:** Human Resources. **E-mail address:** scchr@ctc.edu. **World Wide Web address:** http://www.shore.ctc.edu. **Description:** A community college with an enrollment of approximately 8,000. Founded in 1965. **Positions advertised include:** Geography Instructor. **Number of employees at this location:** 850.

SKAGIT VALLEY COLLEGE

2405 East College Way, Mount Vernon WA 98273. 360/416-7600. **Fax:** 360/416-7878. **Recorded jobline:** 360/416-7800. **Contact:** Lisa Miller, Director of Human Resources. **World Wide Web address:** http://www.svc.ctc.edu. **Description:** A community college offering degrees in more than 20 disciplines.

SOUTH KITSAP SCHOOL DISTRICT

1962 Hoover Avenue SE, Port Orchard WA 98366. 360/874-7377. **Fax:** 360/876-7698. **Recorded jobline:** 360/874-7389. **Contact:** Manager of Human Resources Department. **E-mail address:** skjobs@skitsap.wednet.edu. **World Wide Web address:** http://www.skitsap.wednet.edu. **Description:** Administrative offices of the South Kitsap area school district. **Positions advertised include:** Principal; Special Education Teacher; Nurse; Speech/Language Pathologist. **Number of employees at this location:** 1,100.

SOUTH PUGET SOUND COMMUNITY COLLEGE
2011 Mottman Road SW, Olympia WA 98512-6218. 360/754-7711. **Recorded jobline:** 360/754-7711. **Contact:** Human Resources. **World Wide Web address:** http://www.spscc.ctc.edu. **Description:** A two-year, community college with over 5,000 full- and part-time students enrolled.

UNIVERSITY OF PUGET SOUND
1500 North Warner Street, Tacoma WA 98416. 253/879-3100. **Recorded jobline:** 253/879-3368. **Contact:** Human Resources Department. **World Wide Web address:** http://www.ups.edu. **Description:** A four-year, liberal arts college.

WASHINGTON STATE UNIVERSITY
P.O. Box 641014, Pullman WA 99164-1014. 509/335-4521. **Fax:** 509/335-1259. **Recorded jobline:** 509/335-7637. **Contact:** Human Resources. **World Wide Web address:** http://www.wsu.edu. **Description:** A state university. Approximately 15,000 undergraduate and 2,000 graduate students are enrolled in almost 100 programs of study. **Special programs:** Summer Jobs. **Office hours:** Monday - Friday, 8:00 a.m. - 5:00 p.m. **President:** V. Lane Rawlins, President.

WESTERN WASHINGTON UNIVERSITY
Mail Stop 5221, Bellingham WA 98225. 360/650-3774. **Fax:** 360/650-2810. **Contact:** Human Resources. **World Wide Web address:** http://www.wwu.edu. **Description:** A four-year university.

WHITMAN COLLEGE
345 Boyer Avenue, Walla Walla WA 99362. 509/527-5172. **Fax:** 509/527-5859. **Contact:** Personnel Director. **World Wide Web address:** http://www.whitman.edu.

WHITWORTH COLLEGE
300 West Hawthorne Road, Spokane WA 99251. 509/777-1000. **Fax:** 509/777-3773. **Recorded jobline:** 509/777-3202. **Contact:** Human Resources. **World Wide Web address:** http://www.whitworth.edu. **Description:** A private, liberal arts college affiliated with the Presbyterian Church. Academic programs include majors in 17 departments, interdisciplinary areas of concentration, off-campus internships and foreign studies, graduate learning opportunities, and career preparation programs. **President:** Bill Robinson.

ELECTRONIC/INDUSTRIAL ELECTRICAL EQUIPMENT

You can expect to find the following types of companies in this chapter:

Electronic Machines and Systems
Semiconductor Manufacturers

ACI Communications, Inc.

23413 66th Avenue South, Kent WA 98032. 253/854-9802. **Fax:** 253/813-1001. **Contact:** Lan Mosher, Director of Human Resources. **E-mail address:** lmosher@acicomms.com. **World Wide Web address:** http://www.acicomms.com. **Description:** Designs and produces a broad range of electromechanical products used for the interconnection of circuits in electronic applications. The company manufactures interconnection hardware accessories including high-performance sockets, switches, connectors, and test and packaging systems for the computer, mobile communication, test, and consumer electronics markét. The wiring systems division manufactures products for automotive and related industries including automotive connectors, terminal blocks, power distribution centers, cables and specialty wiring harnesses, safety devices, audio systems, and built-in cellular phones. **Corporate headquarters location:** This location.

AGILENT TECHNOLOGIES

8600 Soper Hill Road, Everett WA 98205-1209. 425/335-2000. **Contact:** Staffing Department. **World Wide Web address:** http://www.agilent.com. **Description:** Operates through four business segments: chemical analysis, healthcare solutions, semiconductor products, and test and measurement. **Positions advertised include:** Senior Solution Architect. **Corporate headquarters location:** Palo Alto CA. **Listed on:** New York Stock Exchange. **Stock exchange symbol:** A.

AVTECH CORPORATION

3400 Wallingford Avenue North, Seattle WA 98103. 206/634-2540. **Contact:** Personnel Director. **E-mail address:** hr@avtcorp.com. **World Wide Web address:** http://www.avtcorp.com. **Description:** Manufactures a variety of electronic equipment products including interior lighting and flight deck audio control panels. **Positions advertised include:** QA Supervisor. **Corporate headquarters location:** This location.

BRANOM INSTRUMENT COMPANY

P.O. Box 80307, Seattle WA 98108-0307. 206/762-6050. **Toll-free phone:** 800/767-6051. **Fax:** 206/762-9351. **Contact:** Personnel Department. **World Wide Web address:** http://www.branom.com. **Description:** A wholesaler of electronic parts and equipment including timing and counting, temperature, pressure, flow, level, and AC/DC instruments. Founded in 1947. **NOTE:** Resumes may be sent to the above e-mail address). **Office hours:** Monday - Friday, 8:00 a.m. - 5:00 p.m. **Corporate headquarters location:** This location. **CEO:** William W. Branom. **Sales Manager:** Joanne Nunn. **Annual sales/revenues:** $5 - $10 million. **Number of employees at this location:** 40. **Number of employees nationwide:** 80.

CADET MANUFACTURING COMPANY
P.O. Box 1675, Vancouver WA 98660-1675. 360/693-2505. **Contact:** Personnel. **World Wide Web address:** http://www.cadetco. com. **Description:** Manufactures electric heaters, thermostats, and air cleaning systems. Founded in 1957. **Corporate headquarters location:** This location.

COLUMBIA LIGHTING INC.
P.O. Box 2787, Spokane WA 99220-2787. 509/924-7000. **Contact:** Human Resources. **E-mail address:** hresources@columbia-ltg.com. **World Wide Web address:** http://www.columbialighting.com. **Description:** Manufactures lighting equipment for commercial and industrial use. The company is also a wholesaler of lighting fixtures. **Parent company:** USI. **Operations at this facility include:** Administration; Manufacturing; Sales; Service. **Listed on:** New York Stock Exchange. **Stock exchange symbol:** USI. **Number of employees at this location:** 620.

CUTLER-HAMMER SENSORS
720 80th Street SW, Everett WA 98203. 425/513-5300. **Contact:** Human Resources. **World Wide Web address:** http://www.cutler-hammer.com. **Description:** A manufacturer of electrical control products and equipment. **Parent company:** Eaton Corporation. **Listed on:** New York Stock Exchange. **Stock exchange symbol:** ETN.

DATA I/O CORPORATION
P.O. Box 97046, Redmond WA 98073-9746. 425/881-6444. **Physical address:** 10525 Willows Road NE, Redmond WA 98052. **Recorded jobline:** 425/867-6963. **Contact:** Employment Department. **World Wide Web address:** http://www.data-io.com. **Description:** Manufactures programmable integrated circuit chips. **NOTE:** Entry-level positions are offered. **Special programs:** Internships. **Corporate headquarters location:** This location. **Other U.S. locations:** Nationwide. **Listed on:** NASDAQ. **Stock exchange symbol:** DAIO. **Annual sales/revenues:** $51 - $100 million. **Number of employees at this location:** 285. **Number of employees nationwide:** 320.

ELDEC CORPORATION
P.O. Box 97027, Lynnwood WA 98046-9727. 425/743-1313. **Fax:** 425/743-8148. **Contact:** Employment Department. **E-mail address:** staffing@eldec.com. **World Wide Web address:** http://www.eldec. com. **Description:** Custom designs precision electronic and electromechanical equipment. Eldec markets its products to commercial and military aircraft companies. **Corporate headquarters location:** This location.

ESTERLINE TECHNOLOGIES
10800 NE Eighth Street, Suite 600, Bellevue WA 98004. 425/453-9400. **Fax:** 425/453-2916. **Contact:** Personnel Department. **E-mail address:** hr@esterline.com. **World Wide Web address:** http:// www.esterline.com. **Description:** A manufacturing company serving several market areas including commercial aerospace, the defense industry, and the electronics industries. The company is divided into three business groups: Advanced Materials, Aerospace, and Automation. **Corporate headquarters location:** This location. **Subsidiaries include:** Armtec Defense Products Company, Coachella CA; Auxitrol S.A., France; Excellon Automation Company, Torrance CA; Kirkhill Rubber Company, Brea CA; Korry Electronics Company, Seattle WA; W.A. Whitney Company, Rockford IL. **Listed on:** New York Stock Exchange. **Stock exchange symbol:** ESL. **CEO:** Wendell P. Hurlbut.

FLUKE CORPORATION
P.O. Box 9090, Everett WA 98206-9090. 425/347-6100. **Physical address:** 6920 Seaway Boulevard, Everett WA 98203. **Contact:** Personnel Department. **E-mail address:** jobs@fluke.com. **World Wide Web address:** http://www.fluke.com. **Description:** A manufacturer of electronic instrumentation for test measurement and calibration. **Positions advertised include:** Engineering Manager; Accounts Payable/Payroll Manager; Test Engineer. **Corporate headquarters location:** This location. **Parent company:** Danaher Corporation. **Listed on:** New York Stock Exchange. **Stock exchange symbol:** DHR.

GRAYBAR ELECTRIC COMPANY
P.O. Box 3727, Seattle WA 98124. 206/292-4848. **Contact:** Personnel Manager. **E-mail address:** opportunities@graybaronline. com **World Wide Web address:** http://www.gbe.com. **Description:** Distributes electrical and telecommunications equipment including wire, transformers, lighting fixtures, power transmission equipment,

telephone station apparatus, and other hardware, primarily to independent telephone companies and public power utilities. Founded in 1869. **Corporate headquarters location:** St. Louis MO. **Number of employees nationwide:** 7,660.

HERAEUS SHIN-ETSU AMERICA INC.
4600 NW Pacific Rim Boulevard, Camas WA 98607. 360/834-4004. **Contact:** Office Administrator. **Description:** Manufactures quartz products for the semiconductor industry. **Office hours:** Monday - Friday, 8:00 a.m. - 5:00 p.m. **Corporate headquarters location:** Duluth GA. **Listed on:** Privately held. **Number of employees at this location:** 50.

HEWLETT-PACKARD COMPANY
3380 146th Place SE, Suite 200, Bellevue WA 98007. 425/643-4000. **Contact:** Human Resources. **World Wide Web address:** http://www.hp.com. **Description:** Hewlett-Packard is engaged in the design and manufacture of measurement and computation products and systems used in business, industry, engineering, science, health care, and education. Principal products are integrated instrument and computer systems including hardware and software, peripheral products, and medical electronic equipment and systems. **NOTE:** Jobseekers should send resumes to Employment Response Center, Hewlett-Packard Company, Mail Stop 20-APP, 3000 Hanover Street, Palo Alto CA 94304-1181. **Corporate headquarters location:** Palo Alto CA. **Other U.S. locations:** Nationwide. **Operations at this facility include:** This location is engaged in the sale of electronic measurement and computing products. **Listed on:** New York Stock Exchange. **Stock exchange symbol:** HPQ. **Number of employees at this location:** 225.

HEWLETT-PACKARD COMPANY
18110 SE 34th Street, Vancouver WA 98683. 360/254-8110. **Contact:** Personnel Manager. **World Wide Web address:** http://www.hp.com. **Description:** Hewlett-Packard is engaged in the design and manufacture of measurement and computation products and systems used in business, industry, engineering, science, health care, and education. Principal products are integrated instrument and computer systems including hardware and software, peripheral products, and medical electronic equipment and systems. **NOTE:** Jobseekers should send resumes to Employment Response Center, Hewlett-Packard Company, Mail Stop 20-APP, 3000 Hanover Street, Palo Alto CA 94304-1181. **Corporate headquarters location:** Palo

Alto CA. **Other U.S. locations:** Nationwide. **Operations at this facility include:** This location produces workstation printers including serial impact and serial ink-jet printers. **Listed on:** New York Stock Exchange. **Stock exchange symbol:** HPQ.

HONEYWELL

15128 East Euclid Avenue, Spokane WA 99216. 509/924-2200. **Contact:** Human Resources. **World Wide Web address:** http://www.honeywell.com. **Description:** Honeywell is engaged in the research, development, manufacture, and sale of advanced technology products and services in the fields of chemicals, electronics, automation, and controls. The company's major businesses are home and building automation and control, performance polymers and chemicals, industrial automation and control, space and aviation systems, and defense and marine systems. **Operations at this facility include:** This location is a manufacturer of components for the electronics industry.

INTERMEC CORPORATION

6001 36th Avenue West, Everett WA 98203. 425/348-2600. **Contact:** Human Resources. **World Wide Web address:** http://www.intermec.com. **Description:** Develops and manufactures automated data collection systems and mobile computing systems. Founded in 1966. **Parent company:** Unova Company. **Listed on:** New York Stock Exchange. **Stock exchange symbol:** UNA.

INTERWORLD ELECTRONICS & COMPUTER INDUSTRIES INC.

P.O. Box 1280, Point Roberts WA 98281. **Toll-free phone:** 877/902-2979. **Contact:** Human Resources Department. **World Wide Web address:** http://www.interwld.com. **Description:** Distributes industrial computer solutions including software, hardware, and electronics. Interworld Electronics & Computer Industries also provides tech-support and custom design services. **International locations:** Australia.

KORRY ELECTRONICS

901 Dexter Avenue North, Seattle WA 98109. 206/281-1300. **Fax:** 206/286-5545. **Contact:** Human Resources. **World Wide Web address:** http://www.korry.com. **Description:** A manufacturer of lighted push-button switches, annunciators, panels, keyboards, and accessories. **Positions advertised include:** Accounts Receivable Associate; Quality Engineer; Test/Environmental Technician; Business Development Manager. **Corporate headquarters location:**

Bellevue WA. **Parent company:** Esterline Technologies. **Listed on:** New York Stock Exchange. **Stock exchange symbol:** ESL. **Number of employees at this location:** 400.

NATIONAL MUSIC SERVICE
P.O. Box 5378, Spokane WA 99205. 509/327-7784. **Contact:** Human Resources. **World Wide Web address:** http://www.natlmusic.com. **Description:** Manufactures and distributes music and video systems for funeral homes, mausoleums, churches, and hospitals.

PAINE ELECTRONICS
2401 South Bayview Street, Seattle WA 98144. 206/329-8600. **Fax:** 206/329-1615. **Contact:** Human Resources. **World Wide Web address:** http://www.painecorp. com. **Description:** Engaged in the manufacture of pressure-measuring instruments and thick-film microcircuits.

PROCTOR & ASSOCIATES, INC.
15305 NE 95th Street, Redmond WA 98052. 425/881-7000. **Contact:** Personnel Administrator. **World Wide Web address:** http://www.proctorinc.com. **Description:** Manufactures electronic equipment for the telephone industry including range extenders, test equipment, and security equipment. The company is also a leading developer of 9-1-1 backup systems. Founded in 1957.

RAYTHEON SYSTEMS COMPANY
1050 NE Hostmark, Poulsbo WA 98370. 360/697-6600. **Contact:** Personnel. **World Wide Web address:** http://www.raytheon.com. **Description:** Manufactures defense and commercial electronics systems and business aviation and special mission aircraft. **Corporate headquarters location:** Lexington MA.

ROCKWELL AUTOMATION
15375 SE 30th Place, Suite 150, Bellevue WA 98007. 425/746-2840. **Contact:** Human Resources. **World Wide Web address:** http://www.automation.rockwell.com. **Description:** Engaged in the production of industrial control equipment, software-based control equipment, magnetic materials, and electronic components. Founded in 1904. **Corporate headquarters location:** Milwaukee WI.

SEA, INC.
7030 220th Street SW, Mountlake Terrace WA 98043. 425/771-2182. **Contact:** Human Resources. **World Wide Web address:** http://www.sea-dmi.com. **Description:** Manufactures and markets electronics including radio and telephone systems for land and ocean applications, and ocean depth sounders and related instrumentation. **Office hours:** Monday - Friday, 8:00 a.m. - 5:00 p.m. **Parent company:** Datamarine International, Inc.

TTM TECHNOLOGIES
17550 Northeast 67th Court, Redmond WA 98052. 425/883-7575. **Contact:** Human Resources. **World Wide Web address:** http://www.ttmtech.com. **Description:** Manufactures circuit boards and related electrical components. **Positions advertised include:** Mechanical Engineer. **Corporate headquarters location:** This location.

TEMPO TEXTRON
11001 31st Place West, Everett WA 98204. 425/355-0590. **Contact:** Personnel Department. **World Wide Web address:** http://www.tempo.textron.com. **Description:** Manufactures high-technology support equipment, digital test equipment, and related products. **Parent company:** Greenlee Textron. **Operations at this facility include:** Administration; Manufacturing; Research and Development; Sales; Service.

SEH AMERICA INC.
4111 Northeast 112th Avenue, Vancouver WA 98682. 360/883-7000. **Fax:** 360/883-7074. **Contact:** Human Resources. **E-mail address:** resume@sehamerica.com. **World Wide Web address:** http://sehamerica.com. **Description:** Manufactures silicon wafers used primarily for the semiconductor industry.

SHARP MICROELECTRONICS USA
5700 NW Pacific Rim Boulevard, Camas WA 98607. 360/834-8700. **Fax:** 360/817-7544. **Contact:** Human Resources. **World Wide Web address:** http://www.sharp-usa.com. **Description:** Sharp Corporation develops business products, consumer electronics, and electronic components. **Corporate headquarters location:** Mahwah NJ. **Operations at this facility include:** This location is a sales and marketing facility. **Parent company:** Sharp Corporation.

SPECTRUM CONTROLS, INC.

P.O. Box 5533, Bellevue WA 98006. 425/746-9481. **Physical address:** 2700 Richards Road, Suite 200, Bellevue WA 98005. **Fax:** 425/641-9473. **Contact:** Lynn Robbins, Personnel Manager. **World Wide Web address:** http://www.spectrumcontrols.com. **Description:** Designs and manufactures electronic industrial control products for the industrial automation market. Founded in 1983. **Company slogan:** We are a product leadership company. **Other U.S. locations:** GA; MI; TX. **President:** Bruce Wanta. **Annual sales/revenues:** $5 - $10 million. **Number of employees at this location:** 40.

SQUARE D COMPANY

7525 SE 24th Street, Suite 320, Mercer Island WA 98040. 206/232-9702. **Contact:** Human Resources. **World Wide Web address:** http://www.squared.com. **Description:** A manufacturer of electrical distribution products for the construction industry. Products are used in commercial and residential construction, industrial facilities, and machinery and original equipment manufacturers' products. **Corporate headquarters location:** Palatine IL. **Other U.S. locations:** AZ; CA; KY; MO; NE; OH; SC; TN. **Parent company:** Groupe Schneider possesses global expertise in electrical contracting, industrial engineering, and construction. Groupe Schneider has five major operating companies: Jeumont-Schneider Industrie, Merlin Gerin, Spie Batignolles, Square D, and Telemecanique.

ENVIRONMENTAL AND WASTE MANAGEMENT SERVICES

You can expect to find the following types of companies in this chapter:

Environmental Engineering Firms
Sanitary Services

BROWN & CALDWELL
999 Third Avenue, Suite 500, Seattle WA 98104-4012. 206/624-0100. **Contact:** Personnel. **E-mail address:** resumes@brwncald.com. **World Wide Web address:** http://www.brownandcaldwell.com. **Description:** An employee-owned environmental engineering and consulting firm specializing in the planning, engineering, and design of waste management systems. The company is also engaged in construction management and analytical environmental testing. **Positions advertised include:** Engineer; Office Support Associate. **Corporate headquarters location:** Walnut Creek CA.

CAMP DRESSER & McKEE INC. (CDM)
P.O. Box 3885, Bellevue WA 98009. 425/453-8383. **Physical address:** 1181 NE First Street, Suite 201, Bellevue WA 98005. **Fax:** 425/646-9523. **Contact:** Human Resources Department. **E-mail address:** hr@cdm.com. **World Wide Web address:** http://www.cdm.com. **Description:** A worldwide provider of environmental engineering, scientific, planning, and management services. The company focuses on professional activities for the management of water resources, hazardous and solid wastes, wastewater, infrastructure, and environmental systems for industry and government. **Positions advertised include:** Senior Wastewater Engineer; Senior O&M Technician; Assistant Project Manager. **Other U.S. locations:** Nationwide. **International locations:** Worldwide.

DOWL ENGINEERS
8320 154th Avenue NE, Redmond WA 98052. 425/869-2670. **Contact:** Linda Finch, Human Resources. **E-mail address:** finch@dowl.com. **World Wide Web address:** http://www.dowl.com. **Description:** Offers specialized environmental engineering services to a variety of clients in government and industry. The company also provides civil engineering and surveying services to municipal and private development clients. **Positions advertised include:** Civil Engineer; Transportation/Traffic Engineer; Auto CAD Technician; Construction Inspector; Licensed Surveyor; Geologist.

FOSTER WHEELER ENVIRONMENTAL CORPORATION
12100 NE 195th Street, Suite 200, Bothell WA 98011. 425/482-7600. **Contact:** Human Resources Manager. **World Wide Web address:** http://www.fwenc.com. **Description:** A worldwide environmental consulting and engineering firm. **Positions advertised include:** Design/Task Construction Order Manager; Field Construction Engineer; Quality Control Inspector; Senior Associate

Cost Engineer. **Corporate headquarters location:** Lyndhurst NJ. **Other U.S. locations:** Oak Ridge CA; Denver CO; Atlanta GA. **Parent company:** Foster Wheeler Corporation. **Listed on:** New York Stock Exchange. **Stock exchange symbol:** FWC. **Number of employees at this location:** 175. **Number of employees nationwide:** 1,500.

HART CROWSER
1910 Fairview Avenue East, Seattle WA 98102. 206/324-9530. **Contact:** Human Resources. **World Wide Web address:** http://www.hartcrowser.com. **Description:** An environmental consulting firm offering site development, remediation, and waste management services. Founded in 1974. **Corporate headquarters location:** This location. **Other U.S. locations:** AK; CA; CO; IL; NJ; OR.

INTERNATIONAL ABSORBENTS INC.
P.O. Box 1587, Bellingham WA 98227-1587. 360/734-7415. **Physical address:** 1051 Hilton Avenue, Bellingham WA 98225. **Fax:** 360/671-1588. **Contact:** Human Resources. **World Wide Web address:** http://www.absorbent.com. **Description:** Develops, produces, and markets absorbent products for use in the marine spill clean-up, general industrial, oil/water filtration, animal litter/bedding, and commercial markets. **Corporate headquarters location:** This location. **Subsidiaries include:** Absorption Corp. **Operations at this facility include:** Manufacturing; Sales.

PARAMETRIX, INC.
P.O. Box 460, Sumner WA 98390. 253/863-5128. **Contact:** Human Resources. **World Wide Web address:** http://www.parametrix.com. **Description:** An environmental and engineering consulting firm. The company is also engaged in environmental surveying. Founded in 1969. **Positions advertised include:** Structural Design Engineer; Bridge Design Engineer; Senior Word Processor; Marketing Database Coordinator. **Corporate headquarters location:** This location.

PHILIP SERVICES CORPORATION
20245 77th Avenue South, Kent WA 98032. 253/872-8030. **Contact:** Human Resources. **World Wide Web address:** http://www.contactpsc.com. **Description:** Philip Services Corporation is divided into three groups: Northwest By-Products Management; Metals Recovery; and Industrial Services. Founded in 1970. **Operations at this facility include:** This location is a hazardous-

waste treatment facility. **Annual sales/revenues:** More than $100 million.

SEVERN TRENT LABORATORIES, INC.
2800 George Washington Way, Richland WA 99352. 509/375-3131. **Fax:** 509/375-5590. **Contact:** Human Resources. **World Wide Web address:** http://www.stlinc.com. **Description:** Provides a complete range of environmental testing services to private industry, engineering consultants, and government agencies in support of federal and state environmental regulations.

SHANNON & WILSON, INC.
P.O. Box 300303, Seattle WA 98103. 206/632-8020. **Physical address:** 400 North 34th Street, Suite 100, Seattle WA 98103. **Fax:** 206/633-6777. **Contact:** Human Resources. **E-mail address:** jobs@shanwil.com. **World Wide Web address:** http://www.shannonwilson.com. **Description:** Provides geotechnical consulting services to a variety of industrial and government clients. Services include foundation engineering studies, waste management, and construction monitoring. **Positions advertised include:** Office Support Clerk. **Corporate headquarters location:** This location.

URS CORPORATION
Century Square, 1501 Fourth Avenue, Suite 1440, Seattle WA 98101-1616. 206/438-2700. **Contact:** Human Resources. **World Wide Web address:** http://www.urscorp.com. **Description:** An architectural, engineering, and environmental consulting firm that specializes in air transportation, environmental solutions, surface transportation, and industrial environmental and engineering concerns. **Positions advertised include:** Accounting Clerk; Assistant Project Administrator; Environmental Engineer; Program Assistant; Program Manager.

FABRICATED/PRIMARY METALS AND PRODUCTS

You can expect to find the following types of companies in this chapter:

Aluminum and Copper Foundries
Die-Castings
Iron and Steel Foundries
Steel Works, Blast Furnaces, and Rolling Mills

ALASKAN COPPER WORKS

P.O. Box 3546, Seattle WA 98124-3546. 206/623-5800. **Physical address:** 3223 Sixth Avenue South, Seattle WA 98134. **Recorded jobline:** 206/382-8221. **Contact:** Human Resources. **World Wide Web address:** http://www.alascop.com. **Description:** Produces fabricated pipe and other metal products including heat exchangers and process equipment. **Parent company:** Alaskan Copper Companies.

ATLAS FOUNDRY & MACHINERY COMPANY

3021 South Wilkeson Street, Tacoma WA 98409. 253/475-4600. **Fax:** 253/471-7037. **Contact:** Personnel. **World Wide Web address:** http://www.atlasfoundry.com. **Description:** Produces a diversified range of steel and stainless steel castings for the construction, transportation, maritime, oil, and nuclear industries. The firm also has fabrication and machining capabilities in large, complex weldings and castings. **Corporate headquarters location:** This location.

BIRMINGHAM STEEL CORPORATION

2424 SW Andover Street, Seattle WA 98106. 206/933-2222. **Toll-free phone:** 800/677-1012. **Contact:** Human Resources Department. **World Wide Web address:** http://www.birminghamsteel.com. **Description:** Birmingham Steel operates minimills in the United States that produce steel and steel products on a low-cost basis. Primary products are steel reinforced bar (rebar) used in the construction industry, and rounds, squares, flats, angles, channels, and strips (merchant products), which are sold to fabricators and other merchants. **Subsidiaries include:** B&M American Steel and Wire manufactures steel rod and wire from semi-finished billets. These products are marketed to the automotive, agricultural, industrial fastener, welding, appliance, and aerospace industries. **Corporate headquarters location:** Birmingham AL. **Operations at this facility include:** This location manufactures rebar. **Number of employees at this location:** 300.

COEUR D'ALENE COMPANY

P.O. Box 2610, Spokane WA 99220-2610. 509/924-6363. **Contact:** Human Resources. **World Wide Web address:** http://www.coeurdal.com. **Description:** Engaged in the distribution, processing, and fabrication of steel and related products. Operations consist of the custom production of finished metal structures or products in accordance with a customer's specifications. The fabrication and processing operations include activities such as cutting, bending, drilling, riveting, welding, assembling, and painting metals. Items produced have included liners for aluminum, magnesium, or other metal producers; structural metal components for the construction of buildings; and structural metal supports for highway signs. **Corporate headquarters location:** This location. **Listed on:** New York Stock Exchange. **Stock exchange symbol:** CDE. **Number of employees at this location:** 70.

CROWN CORK & SEAL COMPANY, INC.

1202 Fones Road SE, Olympia WA 98501. 360/491-4900. **Contact:** Human Resources. **World Wide Web address:** http://www.crowncork.com. **Description:** Crown Cork & Steel is a worldwide manufacturer and distributor of a wide range of crowns, seals, and aluminum and steel cans including aerosol and beverage cans. The company also manufactures bottling equipment. **Corporate headquarters location:** Philadelphia PA. **Operations at this facility include:** This location manufactures aluminum and steel beverage cans. **Listed on:** New York Stock Exchange. **Stock exchange symbol:** CCK.

DAVIS WIRE CORPORATION

19411 80th Avenue South, Kent WA 98032. 253/872-8910. **Fax:** 253/395-3729. **Contact:** Dan Kay, Manager of Human Resources. **World Wide Web address:** http://www.daviswire.com. **Description:** Manufactures steel wire and related products. **Corporate headquarters location:** San Ramon CA. **Other U.S. locations:** Hayward CA; Irwindale CA. **Operations at this facility include:** Divisional Headquarters. **Listed on:** Privately held. **Number of employees at this location:** 200. **Number of employees nationwide:** 600.

GM NAMEPLATE INC.
INTAQ KEY PANELS

2040 15th Avenue West, Seattle WA 98119. 206/284-5475. **Fax:** 206/284-3705. **Contact:** Human Resources. **E-mail address:** humanresources@gnnameplate.com. **World Wide Web address:** http://www.gmnameplate.com. **Description:** Involved in coating, engraving, allied services, paper coatings, and glazing. GM Nameplate is also a manufacturer of a variety of metal products. **Corporate headquarters location:** This location.

JORGENSEN FORGE CORPORATION

8531 East Marginal Way South, Seattle WA 98108-4018. 206/762-1100. **Fax:** 206/762-5414. **Contact:** Personnel. **E-mail address:** jobs@jorgensenforge.com. **World Wide Web address:** http://www.jorgensenforge.com. **Description:** Provides services including melting, forging, heat treating, and machining of steel and aluminum forgings. **Corporate headquarters location:** This location. **Operations at this facility include:** Administration; Manufacturing. **Listed on:** Privately held. **Number of employees at this location:** 200.

PIONEER INDUSTRIES

7440 West Marginal Way South, Seattle WA 98106. 206/768-1990. **Fax:** 206/768-8910. **Contact:** Human Resources Department. **World Wide Web address:** http://www.pioneerhumanserv.com. **Description:** A contract manufacturer of aircraft components and sheet metal products for a variety of industrial uses. Founded in 1966. **NOTE:** Second and third shifts are offered. **Positions advertised include:** Chemical Dependency Counselor; Residential Supervisor; Case Manager; Sheet Metal Instructor. **Special programs:** Training. **Corporate headquarters location:** This location. **Parent company:** Pioneer Human Services operates rehabilitation and job training programs for work-release prisoners and people recovering from addictions. **Listed on:** Privately held. **Annual sales/revenues:** $11 - $20 million. **Number of employees at this location:** 300.

SANDVIK SPECIAL METALS

P.O. Box 6027, Kennewick WA 99336. 509/586-4131. **Contact:** Human Resources. **World Wide Web address:** http://www.sandvik.com. **Description:** Manufactures nuclear and aerospace tubing and bicycle frames and tubing. **Number of employees at this location:** 300.

FINANCIAL SERVICES

You can expect to find the following types of companies in this chapter:

Consumer Finance and Credit Agencies
Investment Specialists
Mortgage Bankers and Loan Brokers
Security and Commodity Brokers, Dealers, and Exchanges

CORUM GROUP LTD.
10500 NE Eighth Street, Suite 1500, Bellevue WA 98004. 425/455-8281. **Fax:** 425/455-1415. **Contact:** Gina Stanhope, Human Resources. **World Wide Web address:** http://www.corumgroup.com. **Description:** Assists software companies to successfully execute company mergers and alliances. **Corporate headquarters location:** This location.

FARM CREDIT SERVICES
P.O. Box 2515, Spokane WA 99224. 509/340-5300. **Contact:** Human Resources. **E-mail address:** hrdept@farm-credit.com. **World Wide Web address:** http://www.farm-credit.com. **Description:** Provides long-, intermediate-, and short-term financing to agricultural producers, farm-related businesses, fisherman, part-time farmers, and country homeowners. The banks and related associations provide credit and credit-related services to eligible borrowers for qualified agricultural purposes. **Positions advertised include:** Mortgage Loan Officer. **Corporate headquarters location:** This location. **Other U.S. locations:** AK; ID; MT.

INTERPACIFIC INVESTORS SERVICES, INC.
2623 Second Avenue, Seattle WA 98121-1294. 206/269-5050. **Fax:** 206/269-5055. **Contact:** Human Resources. **World Wide Web address:** http://www.iisbonds.com. **Description:** A regional securities broker/dealer specializing in conservative investments such as corporate and municipal bonds, mutual funds, stocks, and life insurance. **Sales Manager:** Bill Shultheis.

MERRILL LYNCH
601 108th Avenue NE, Suite 2100, Bellevue WA 98004. 425/462-8158. **Contact:** Human Resources. **World Wide Web address:** http://www.ml.com. **Description:** One of the largest securities brokerage firms in the United States, Merrill Lynch provides financial services in the following areas: securities, extensive insurance, and real estate and related services. The company also brokers commodity futures, commodity options, and corporate and municipal securities. In addition, Merrill Lynch is engaged in investment banking activities. **Positions advertised include:** Senior Underwriter; Investment Officer; Cash Flow Associate. **Corporate headquarters location:** New York NY. **Listed on:** NASDAQ. **Stock exchange symbol:** MITT.

MERRILL LYNCH HOWARD JOHNSON

1700 Seventh Avenue, Suite 2200, Seattle WA 98101. 206/625-1040. **Contact:** Human Resources. **World Wide Web address:** http://www.ml.com. **Description:** An international benefits consulting company. The company works mainly with 401(k) plans and group benefits for corporations.

NATIONAL SECURITIES CORPORATION

1001 Fourth Avenue, Suite 2200, Seattle WA 98154. 206/622-7200. **Contact:** Human Resources Manager. **World Wide Web address:** http://www.nationalsecurities.com. **Description:** A securities brokerage providing services such as asset management, investment banking, and institutional sales and research. **Corporate headquarters location:** This location.

RAGEN MACKENZIE INCORPORATED

999 Third Avenue, Suite 4300, Seattle WA 98104. 206/343-5000. **Fax:** 206/389-8245. **Contact:** Personnel Department. **World Wide Web address:** http://www.ragen-mackenzie.com. **Description:** Engaged in investment banking. Founded in 1982.

FRANK RUSSELL COMPANY

909 A Street, Tacoma WA 98402. 253/596-3056. **Fax:** 253/594-1727. **Recorded jobline:** 253/596-5454. **Contact:** Personnel. **E-mail address:** empsvc@russell.com. **World Wide Web address:** http://www.russell.com. **Description:** Provides a variety of financial services such as investment management, mutual funds, and investment consulting. Founded in 1936. **Corporate headquarters location:** This location. **Other U.S. locations:** Boston MA; New York NY. **International locations:** Australia; Canada; France; Italy; New Zealand; Singapore; South Africa; United Kingdom. **Listed on:** Privately held. **Number of employees at this location:** 1,000. **Number of employees nationwide:** 1,200.

SALOMON SMITH BARNEY

999 Third Avenue, Suite 4500, Seattle WA 98104. 206/344-3500. **Contact:** Personnel Department. **World Wide Web address:** http://www.salomonsmithbarney.com. **Description:** An international investment banking, market making, and research firm serving corporations, state and local governments, sovereign and provincial governments and their agencies, central banks, and other financial institutions. **Corporate headquarters location:** New York NY.

SALOMON SMITH BARNEY
411 108th Avenue NE, Suite 1600, Bellevue WA 98004. 425/453-3450. **Contact:** Human Resources. **World Wide Web address:** http://www.salomonsmithbarney.com. **Description:** An international investment banking, market making, and research firm serving corporations, state and local governments, sovereign and provincial governments and their agencies, central banks, and other financial institutions. **Corporate headquarters location:** New York NY.

SIRACH CAPITAL MANAGEMENT INC.
520 Pike Street, Suite 2800, Seattle WA 98101-1389. 206/624-3800. **Fax:** 206/626-5410. **Contact:** Personnel. **World Wide Web address:** http://www.sirachcap.com. **Description:** An investment advisory firm specializing in managing the assets of institutions and high-worth individuals. Services include mutual funds, 401(k) plan, investment, and trust fund management. **Number of employees at this location:** 45.

FOOD AND BEVERAGES/ AGRICULTURE

You can expect to find the following types of companies in this chapter:

Crop Services and Farm Supplies
Dairy Farms
Food Manufacturers/Processors and Agricultural Producers
Tobacco Products

ADM MILLING COMPANY

P.O. Box 5434, Spokane WA 99205. 509/328-0300. **Contact:** Personnel. **World Wide Web address:** http://www.admworld.com. **Description:** Processes wheat, barley, corn, oats, and rice. The company specializes in milling wheat for flour, cakes, cookies, and pasta. **Corporate headquarters location:** Decatur IL.

AGRINORTHWEST

P.O. Box 2308, Tri-Cities WA 99302. 509/735-6461. **Physical address:** 2810 West Clearwater Street, Kennewick WA 99336. **Fax:** 509/734-5075. **Contact:** Mark Knight, Human Resources Manager. **Description:** One of the largest diversified agricultural operations in the western United States. Agrinorthwest is engaged in the production of a variety of food crops including potatoes, grain, corn, and apples. **Number of employees nationwide:** 700.

ASSOCIATED GROCERS, INC.

P.O. Box 3763, Seattle WA 98124-2263. 206/762-2100. **Fax:** 206/767-8785. **Recorded jobline:** 206/767-8788. **Contact:** Human Resources Department. **E-mail address:** jobs@agsea.com. **World Wide Web address:** http://www.agsea.com. **Description:** Provides general merchandise and grocery products to over 400 independently-owned retail markets in several western states. The company also offers a variety of related services including retail promotion, human resources, accounting, procurement, warehousing, and transportation. Founded in 1934. **Positions advertised include:** Meat Specialist; Order Selector. **NOTE:** Jobseekers interested in driver or warehouse positions must call the Human Resources Department to set up an application appointment. All driver and warehouse positions are part-time, on-call positions, and applicants must be at least 18 years old. **Company slogan:** The food people. **Office hours:** Monday - Friday, 8:00 a.m. - 5:00 p.m. **Corporate headquarters location:** This location. **Other area locations:** Kent WA. **Listed on:** Privately held. **Annual sales/revenues:** More than $100 million. **Number of employees nationwide:** 1,400.

BESTFOODS BAKING COMPANY

155 NE 100th Street, Suite 100, Seattle WA 98125. 206/522-9983. **Contact:** Human Resources. **World Wide Web address:** http://www.bestfoods.com. **Description:** Bestfoods Baking Company produces and distributes a line of cakes, cookies, doughnuts, and various baked products. **Corporate headquarters location:**

Englewood Cliffs NJ. **Operations at this facility include:** This location houses administrative offices.

BIRDSEYE FOODS

P.O. Box 11046, Tacoma WA 98411-0046. 253/383-1621. **Physical address:** 3303 South 35th Street, Tacoma WA 98409. **Contact:** Personnel. **World Wide Web address:** http://www.birdseyefoods. com. **Description:** A food manufacturing company with products that include pickles and peanut butter.

CHIQUITA PROCESSED FOODS

P.O. Box 458, Walla Walla WA 99362. 509/525-8390. **Contact:** Personnel Department. **E-mail address:** jobs@chiquita.com. **World Wide Web address:** http://www.chiquita.com. **Description:** Manufactures and processes canned peas, carrots, corn, asparagus, green beans, and spinach. **Positions advertised include:** Business Account Manager; Director of New Business Development; Distribution Center Supervisor; Operations Manager. **Corporate headquarters location:** New Richmond WI. **Listed on:** New York Stock Exchange. **Stock exchange symbol:** CQB. **Number of employees nationwide:** 1,500.

COCA-COLA BOTTLING COMPANY

3333 South 38th Street, Tacoma WA 98409. 253/474-9567. **Contact:** Human Resources. **World Wide Web address:** http://www.coca-cola.com. **Description:** A bottling company packaging Coca-Cola, Barq's and Dr. Pepper brand beverages. **Corporate headquarters location:** Bellevue WA. **Parent company:** Coca-Cola Company is one of the world's largest marketers, distributors, and producers of bottled and canned products. Coca-Cola Enterprises, part of the Coca-Cola Company, is in the liquid, nonalcoholic refreshment business, which includes traditional carbonated soft drinks, still and sparkling waters, juices, isotonics, and teas. The company operates in 38 states, the District of Columbia, the U.S. Virgin Islands, the Islands of Tortola and Grand Cayman, and the Netherlands. Coca-Cola Enterprises operates 268 facilities, approximately 24,000 vehicles, and over 860,000 vending machines, beverage dispensers, and coolers used to market, distribute, and produce the company's products. **Listed on:** New York Stock Exchange. **Stock exchange symbol:** COKE.

DAIRY FARMERS OF WASHINGTON

4201 198th Street SW, Suite 101, Lynnwood WA 98036-6751. 425/672-0687. **Contact:** Personnel Department. **World Wide Web address:** http://www.eatsmart.org. **Description:** A commission engaged in the promotion of Washington's milk and dairy products.

DEL MONTE FOODS

P.O. Box 1528, Yakima WA 98907. 509/575-6580. **Physical address:** 108 West Walnut Street, Yakima WA 98902. **Contact:** Personnel. **World Wide Web address:** http://www.delmonte.com. **Description:** Del Monte Foods is a producer of canned fruits and vegetables, tomato sauces, condiments, and dessert products for the consumer, institutional, and military markets. The company operates over 60 plants worldwide where it processes food and makes, labels, and packs its own cans. Brand names include Del Monte, Morton Munchwich, Snack Cups, Bonanza, Ortega, Sunkist Plus, and Summer Crisp. **Corporate headquarters location:** San Francisco CA. **Operations at this facility include:** This location processes canned fruits. **Listed on:** New York Stock Exchange. **Stock exchange symbol:** DLM.

FOOD SERVICES OF AMERICA

P.O. Box 3547, Seattle WA 98124. 425/251-9100. **Physical address:** 18430 East Valley Highway, Kent WA 98032. **Contact:** Human Resources. **World Wide Web address:** http://www.fsafood.com. **Description:** A food service company specializing in the distribution of fruit, fresh seafood, canned and frozen goods, and fresh meat. **Positions advertised include:** Associate Services Specialist; Day Delivery Driver; Order Selector. **Corporate headquarters location:** Seattle WA.

FRITO-LAY, INC.

4808 NW Fruit Valley Road, Vancouver WA 98660. 360/694-8478. **Contact:** Human Resources. **World Wide Web address:** http://www.fritolay.com. **Description:** A worldwide manufacturer and wholesaler of snack products including Fritos Corn Chips, Lays Potato Chips, and Doritos Tortilla Chips. **NOTE:** All job openings are posted with the Washington State Job Service. Call 360/735-5000 for more information. **Corporate headquarters location:** Plano TX. **Parent company:** PepsiCo, Inc. (Purchase NY). **Listed on:** New York Stock Exchange. **Stock exchange symbol:** PEP.

GAI'S NORTHWEST BAKERIES

P.O. Box 24327, Seattle WA 98124. 206/322-0931. **Contact:** Human Resources. **World Wide Web address:** http:// www.gaisbakery.com. **Description:** A regional wholesale baking company. **Listed on:** Privately held. **Annual sales/revenues:** $51 - $100 million.

ICICLE SEAFOODS INC.

P.O. Box 79003, Seattle WA 98119. 206/282-0988. **Contact:** Personnel. **World Wide Web address:** http://www.icicleseafoods. com. **Description:** Manufactures canned and frozen fish, shellfish, and shrimp products. **Positions advertised include:** Accounts Payable Representative; Inventory Control Specialist; Human Resources Manager.

INTERSTATE BRANDS CORPORATION

P.O. Box 98949, Lakewood WA 98498. 253/444-1000. **Contact:** Personnel Department. **Description:** Manufactures and distributes a line of bread and cake products under the Wonderbread and Hostess brand names. **Operations at this facility include:** Manufacturing. **Corporate headquarters location:** Kansas City MO.

LAMB WESTON, INC.

P.O. Box 1900, Tri-Cities WA 99302. 509/735-4651. **Contact:** Personnel Administrator. **E-mail address:** resume@lambweston.com. **World Wide Web address:** http://www.lamb-weston.com. **Description:** Processes a broad line of nationally distributed frozen potato products including french fries and potato wedges. **Corporate headquarters location:** This location. **Parent company:** ConAgra, Inc. is a diversified, international food company. Products range from prepared foods to supplies farmers need to grow their crops. ConAgra has major businesses in branded grocery products including shelf-stable and frozen foods, processed meats, chicken and turkey products, and cheeses, as well as major businesses in potato products, private-label grocery products, beef, pork, seafood, grain and pulse merchandising, grain processing, specialty trailing, crop protection chemicals, fertilizers, and animal feed. ConAgra is a family of independent operating companies. **Listed on:** New York Stock Exchange. **Stock exchange symbol:** CAG.

MILLER BREWING COMPANY

100 Custer Way, Tumwater WA 98501. 360/754-5000. **Contact:** Alice Riley, Personnel Manager. **E-mail address:** miller@webhire.

com (Please do not include any attachments). **World Wide Web address:** http://www.millerbrewing.com. **Description:** Produces and distributes beer and other malt beverages. Principal beer brands include Miller Lite, Lite Ice, Miller Genuine Draft, Miller Genuine Draft Light, Miller High Life, Miller Reserve, Lowenbrau, Milwaukee's Best, Meister Brau, as well as Red Dog and Icehouse brewed at the Plank Road Brewery. Miller also produces Sharp's, a nonalcoholic brew. **Corporate headquarters location:** Milwaukee WI.

NATIONAL FROZEN FOODS CORPORATION
P.O. Box 9366, Seattle WA 98109. 206/322-8900. **Contact:** Human Resources. **World Wide Web address:** http://www.nationalfrozenfoods.com. **Description:** Processes, packages, and distributes frozen fruits and vegetables. Founded in 1912. **Company slogan:** The Best of the Great Northwest. **Special programs:** Co-ops.

OCEAN SPRAY CRANBERRIES
1480 State Route 105, Aberdeen WA 98520. 360/648-2201. **Contact:** Human Resources. **World Wide Web address:** http://www.oceanspray.com. **Description:** Ocean Spray Cranberries is a nationally recognized food processor engaged in the packaging, processing, and marketing of fresh cranberries, cranberry sauces, and cranberry and grapefruit juices. **Corporate headquarters:** Lakeville-Middleboro MA. **Other U.S. locations:** Vero Beach FL; Bordenton NJ; Sulphur Springs TX; Kenosha WI. **Operations at this facility include:** This location processes cranberry juices and sauces.

PACIFIC SEASONINGS
21612 88th Avenue South, Kent WA 98031. 253/395-9400. **Fax:** 253/395-3330. **Contact:** Personnel Department. **Description:** Produces foods such as raw and salted nuts, spices, extracts, and seasoning mixes.

PEPSI-COLA COMPANY
2300 26th Avenue South, Seattle WA 98144. 206/323-2932. **Fax:** 206/326-7484. **Contact:** Human Resources. **World Wide Web address:** http://www.pepsico.com. **Description:** Bottles and distributes Pepsi-Cola. **Parent company:** PepsiCo, Inc. (Purchase NY) consists of Frito-Lay Company, Pepsi-Cola Company, Quaker Oats Company, and Tropicana Products, Inc. **Number of employees at this location:** 1,300.

REXAM BEVERAGE CAN COMPANY
1220 Second Avenue North, Kent WA 98032. 253/854-9950. **Contact:** Human Resources. **Description:** Manufactures a variety of container products. **Corporate headquarters location:** Chicago IL.

SNOKIST GROWERS
P.O. Box 1587, Yakima WA 98907-1587. 509/453-5631. **Physical address:** 18 West Mead Avenue, Yakima WA 98902. **Contact:** Personnel. **World Wide Web address:** http://www.snokist.com. **Description:** A processor of fruit including plums, apples, and cherries. **Number of employees at this location:** 400.

SYSCO FOOD SERVICES OF SEATTLE, INC.
P.O. Box 97054, Kent WA 98064. 206/622-2261. **Physical address:** 22820 54th Avenue South, Kent WA 98032. **Fax:** 206/721-1559. **Recorded jobline:** 206/721-5484. **Contact:** Human Resources. **E-mail address:** jobs@syscoseattle.com. **World Wide Web address:** http://www.syscoseattle.com. **Description:** Engaged in the wholesale distribution of food and related products and services to other businesses such as hotels and schools. **Positions advertised include:** Outside Sales Representative. **Corporate headquarters location:** Houston TX.

P.J. TAGGARES COMPANY
850 North Broadway, Othello WA 99344. 509/488-3356. **Contact:** Personnel. **Description:** A farmer-owned agribusiness firm. The farmers raise vegetables that are then sold to processing plants and grain distributors for local consumption.

TREE TOP, INC.
P.O. Box 248, Selah WA 98942. 509/697-7251. **Contact:** Personnel Department. **E-mail address:** jobs@treetop.com. **World Wide Web address:** http://www.treetop.com. **Description:** An agricultural cooperative owned by 2,500 apple and pear growers in Washington, Oregon, and Idaho. The cooperative was formed to process and market its members' processor-grade fruit. Tree Top also produces and sells an array of dried, frozen, and concentrated fruit products in bulk as ingredients used in the food industry. Founded in 1960. **Number of employees nationwide:** 1,000.

UNISEA
P.O. Box 97019, Redmond WA 98073. 425/881-8181. **Physical address:** 15400 NE 90th Street, Redmond WA 98053. **Fax:** 425/861-

5276. **Contact:** Human Resources. **World Wide Web address:** http://www.unisea.com. **Description:** Processes seafood and related products. **Subsidiaries include:** Dutch Harbor Seafoods, Ltd. (also at this location) manufactures seafood products for sale at retail grocery stores.

WARDS COVE PACKING COMPANY INC.

88 East Hamlin Street, Seattle WA 98102. 206/323-3200. **Fax:** 206/323-9165. **Recorded jobline:** 206/325-4621. **Contact:** Personnel Department. **Description:** Operates seasonal salmon canneries in Alaska. Founded in 1912. **Corporate headquarters location:** This location. **Other U.S. locations:** AK. **Parent company:** Wards Cove Packing. **Listed on:** Privately held. **Number of employees at this location:** 150. **Number of employees nationwide:** 7,000.

WESTFARM FOODS

P.O. Box 79007, Seattle WA 98119. 206/284-7220. **Toll-free phone:** 800/333-MILK. **Fax:** 206/216-2871. **Contact:** Human Resources. **E-mail address:** jobs@wffoods.com. **World Wide Web address:** http://www.westfarm.com. **Description:** Manufactures, sells, and distributes dairy products. WestFarm Foods is divided into two groups: Consumer Products and Manufactured Products. The Consumer Products division produces and markets dairy-based products for the wholesale, retail market, and foodservice markets. The Manufactured Products division produces butter, whey powder, cheeses, and dry milk powder in bulk quantities and then markets its products to institutions, food brokers, and food processing companies. **Positions advertised include:** Director of Bulk Milk Sales; Director of Communications; Creative Services Manager. **Corporate headquarters location:** This location. **Other area locations:** Chehalis WA; Issaquah WA; Lynden WA; Spokane WA; Sunnyside WA; Yakima WA. **Other U.S. locations:** Los Angeles CA; San Jose CA; Boise ID; Caldwell ID; Eugene OR; Medford OR; Portland OR. **Number of employees at this location:** 660. **Number of employees nationwide:** 1,800.

GOVERNMENT

You can expect to find the following types of agencies in this chapter:

Courts
Executive, Legislative, and General Government
Public Agencies (Firefighters, Military, Police)
United States Postal Service

EVERETT, CITY OF
2930 Wetmore Avenue, Suite 6A, Everett WA 98201. 425/257-8700. **Recorded jobline:** 425/257-8768. **Fax:** 425/257-8754. **Contact:** Personnel. **E-mail address:** hr@ci.everett.wa.us. **World Wide Web address:** http://www.ci.everett.wa.us. **Description:** Houses the city of Everett's administrative offices and city hall. The city's population is approximately 84,000. **Office hours:** Monday - Friday, 8:00 a.m. - 5:00 p.m. **Corporate headquarters location:** This location.

MERCER ISLAND, CITY OF
9611 SE 36th Street, Mercer Island WA 98040. 206/236-5300. **Fax:** 206/236-3645. **Contact:** Human Resources Manager. **E-mail address:** hr@ci.mercer-island.wa.us. **World Wide Web address:** http://www.ci.mercer-island.wa.us. **Description:** City government offices for Mercer Island, a suburb of Seattle with over 21,000 residents. **Positions advertised include:** Development Engineer; Parks Maintenance Manager; Recreation Leader. **Special programs:** Internships. **Corporate headquarters location:** This location. **Operations at this facility include:** Administration. **Annual sales/revenues:** $11 - $20 million. **Number of employees at this location:** 170.

NATIONAL ASIAN PACIFIC CENTER ON AGING
Melborne Tower, 1511 Third Avenue, Suite 914, Seattle WA 98101. **Toll-free phone:** 800/336-2722. **Contact:** Director. **World Wide Web address:** http://www.napca. org. **Description:** A nonprofit, private organization that operates in conjunction with the Older Americans Act. National Asian Pacific Center on Aging maintains a national network of service agencies, compiles statistics on the Asian Pacific population, provides technical assistance to local Asian Pacific community groups so they may be better able to meet the needs of older people, conducts workshops and training programs to educate health care and social service professionals, disseminates information on support groups, and finds employment for older people through its Seniors' Community Service Employment Program. **Corporate headquarters location:** This location. **Other U.S. locations:** Los Angeles CA. **Parent company:** Administration on Aging.

OLYMPIC NATIONAL PARK
NATIONAL PARK SERVICE

600 East Park Avenue, Port Angeles WA 98362-6798. 360/452-4501. **Contact:** Human Resources Department. **World Wide Web address:** http://www.olympic.national-park.com. **Description:** A national park that includes glacier-capped mountains, over 60 miles of Pacific coastline, and parts of old growth and temperate rain forests. **Special programs:** Internships. **Corporate headquarters location:** Washington DC. **Parent company:** Department of the Interior. **Operations at this facility include:** Administration; Research and Development; Service. **Number of employees at this location:** 300.

RENTON, CITY OF

1055 South Grady Way, Renton WA 98055. 425/430-7650. **Fax:** 425/430-7665. **Contact:** Mike Webby, Human Resources. **World Wide Web address:** http://www.ci.renton.wa.us. **Description:** The administrative offices for the city of Renton. **Number of employees at this location:** 560.

SEATTLE POLICE DEPARTMENT

610 Third Avenue, 15th Floor, Seattle WA 98104-1886. 206/684-5464. **Fax:** 206/386-9022. **Contact:** Personnel. **World Wide Web address:** http://www.ci.seattle.wa.us. **Description:** Seattle's police department. **NOTE:** To obtain an application for an entry-level police officer position, call the City of Seattle Civil Service Commission at 206/386-1303. **Corporate headquarters location:** This location. **Number of employees at this location:** 1,200.

TACOMA, CITY OF

747 Market Street, Room 1336, Tacoma WA 98402-3764. 253/591-5400. **Recorded jobline:** 253/591-5795. **Contact:** Human Resources. **World Wide Web address:** http://www.cityoftacoma.org. **Description:** Government offices for the city of Tacoma. **Positions advertised include:** Convention Center Manager; Senior Financial Analyst; Water Control Plant Supervisor; Civil Engineer. **Special programs:** Internships. **Corporate headquarters location:** This location. **Number of employees nationwide:** 3,000.

U.S. ARMY CIVILIAN RECRUITING OFFICE

P.O. Box 3957, Seattle WA 98124-3957. 206/764-3592. **Contact:** Human Resources. **Description:** Recruits civilians as support staff for the Eighth U.S. Army in Korea. **Number of employees worldwide:** 3,200.

U.S. ARMY CORPS OF ENGINEERS
201 North Third Street, Walla Walla WA 99362-9265. 509/527-7424. **Contact:** Recruitment/Placement. **World Wide Web address:** http://www.nww.usace.army.mil. **Description:** A federal government agency engaged in water resource engineering.

U.S. ENVIRONMENTAL PROTECTION AGENCY (EPA)
1200 Sixth Avenue, OMP-077, Seattle WA 98101. 206/553-4973. **Contact:** Human Resources. **World Wide Web address:** http://www.epa.gov. **Description:** The EPA is dedicated to improving and preserving the quality of the environment, both nationally and globally, and protecting human health and the productivity of natural resources. The agency is committed to ensuring that federal environmental laws are implemented and enforced effectively; U.S. policy, both foreign and domestic, encourages the integration of economic development and environmental protection so that economic growth can be sustained over the long term; and public and private decisions affecting energy, transportation, agriculture, industry, international trade, and natural resources fully integrate considerations of environmental quality. Founded in 1970. **Special programs:** Internships. **Corporate headquarters location:** Washington DC. **Other U.S. locations:** San Francisco CA; Denver CO; Atlanta GA; Chicago IL; Kansas City KS; Boston MA; New York NY; Philadelphia PA; Dallas TX. **Number of employees nationwide:** 19,000.

WASHINGTON, STATE OF
DEPARTMENT OF PERSONNEL
521 Capital Way South, P.O. Box 47500, Olympia WA 98504-7500. 360/664-1960. **Recorded jobline:** 360/664-6226. **Contact:** Personnel. **World Wide Web address:** http://www.wa.gov/dop. **Description:** Engaged in the recruitment and examination of candidates for the purpose of establishing a register of qualified personnel for all state agencies and all job classifications. TDD: 360/664-0389. **NOTE:** This firm does not accept unsolicited resumes. Please only respond to advertised openings. **Special programs:** Internships; Summer Jobs. **Internship information:** Both resident and nonresident students are eligible to apply for state internships. Undergraduate internships are offered to students who have completed one full term or semester of undergraduate work

and are currently enrolled in an undergraduate program. Application materials should be submitted to the recruiting agency and contact person noted on the job bulletin. Executive fellowships, lasting either one or two years, are offered to students who have completed one academic year of graduate school, and who are pursuing a graduate degree. Students must be currently enrolled to be eligible. Permanent Washington State employees are eligible for fellowships regardless of academic status, though a recommendation letter from the appropriate agency director is required. Please contact the Department of Personnel for more information. **Office hours:** Monday - Friday, 8:00 a.m. - 5:00 p.m. **Corporate headquarters location:** This location.

WASHINGTON STATE APPLE COMMISSION
P.O. Box 18, Wenatchee WA 98807. 509/663-9600. **Contact:** Personnel. **World Wide Web address:** http://www.bestapples.com. **Description:** A commission engaged in the promotion of Washington's apple industry.

WASHINGTON STATE DEPARTMENT OF REVENUE
2409 Pacific Avenue NE, P.O. Box 47463, Olympia WA 98504-7463. 360/570-6183. **Contact:** Human Resources Manager. **World Wide Web address:** http://dor.wa.gov. **Description:** Administers state tax laws; acts as revenue advisor to the Governor, the Legislature, and other state and local agencies; and oversees the administration of property tax laws. **Number of employees at this location:** 500.

HEALTH CARE: SERVICES, EQUIPMENT, AND PRODUCTS

You can expect to find the following types of companies in this chapter:

Dental Labs and Equipment
Home Health Care Agencies
Hospitals and Medical Centers
Medical Equipment Manufacturers and Wholesalers
Offices and Clinics of Health Practitioners
Residential Treatment Centers/Nursing Homes
Veterinary Services

ADDUS HEALTHCARE, INC.

1010 North Normandie Street, Suite 303, Spokane WA 99202. 509/326-1090. **Fax:** 847/303-5376. **Contact:** Human Resources. **E-mail address:** personnel@addus.com. **World Wide Web address:** http://www.addus.com. **Description:** Provides home health care servic es for the elderly and disabled. Services include skilled nursing, respiratory therapy, rehabilitation, and home medical equipment.

AFFILIATED HEALTH SERVICES

P.O. Box 1376, Mount Vernon WA 98273-1376. 360/428-2174. **Fax:** 360/428-2482. **Recorded jobline:** 360/416-8345. **Contact:** Human Resources. **World Wide Web address:** http://www.affiliatedhealth.org. **Description:** A nonprofit, regional health system offering a full line of medical services. Affiliated Health Services is comprised of Skagit Home Health, Skagit Valley Hospital, Skagit Valley Kidney Center, Stanwood Camano Medical Center, United General Hospital, Whatcom Hospice, and Whatcom Visiting Nurses Home Health. **NOTE:** Part-time jobs and second and third shifts are offered. **Positions advertised include:** Patient Services Secretary; Monitor Telemetry Technician; Unit Assistant; Imaging Manager; Certified Nursing Assistant; Registered Nurse. **Corporate headquarters location:** This location. **Operations at this facility include:** Administration. **Number of employees at this location:** 1,200.

APRIA HEALTHCARE GROUP INC.

P.O. Box 3039, Redmond WA 98073-3039. 425/881-8500. **Physical address:** 14945 NE 87th Street, Redmond WA 98052. **Contact:** Human Resources. **World Wide Web address:** http://www.apria. com. **Description:** One of the largest national providers of home health care products and services including a broad range of respiratory therapy services, home medical equipment, and infusion therapy services. Apria's home health care services are provided to patients who have been discharged from hospitals, skilled nursing facilities, or convalescent homes and are being treated at home. In conjunction with medical professionals, Apria personnel deliver, install, and service medical equipment, as well as provide appropriate therapies and coordinate plans of care for their patients. Apria personnel also instruct patients and caregivers in the correct use of equipment and monitor the equipment's effectiveness. **Positions advertised include:** Staff Pharmacist; Branch Pharmacy Manager; Regional Respiratory Therapy Manager. **Corporate**

headquarters location: Costa Mesa CA. **Listed on:** New York Stock Exchange. **Stock exchange symbol:** AHG.

BOSTON SCIENTIFIC CORPORATION
15340 NE 92nd Street, Building B, Redmond WA 98052. 425/556-1540. **Contact:** Human Resources. **World Wide Web address:** http://www.bsci.com. **Description:** Develops noninvasive surgical products and procedures. **Corporate headquarters location:** Natick MA. **Listed on:** New York Stock Exchange. **Stock exchange symbol:** BSX.

CARE CENTER AT KELSEY CREEK
2210 132nd Avenue SE, Bellevue WA 98005. 425/957-2400. **Contact:** Human Resources. **E-mail address:** recruiters.i@ghc.org. **World Wide Web address:** http://www.ghc.org. **Description:** A skilled nursing home that offers hospice care and general long-term care. **Positions advertised include:** Visiting Nurse Hospice Case Manager; Pharmacy Technician; Physical Therapy Assistant; Occupational Therapist; Physical Therapist. **Parent company:** Group Health Cooperative.

CHILDREN'S HOSPITAL AND MEDICAL CENTER
4800 Sand Point Way NE, Seattle WA 98105-0371. 206/987-2000. **Recorded jobline:** 206/987-2230. **Contact:** Human Resources. **E-mail address:** jobs@chmc.org. **World Wide Web address:** http://www.chmc.org. **Description:** A tertiary pediatric hospital and medical center that serves Washington, Alaska, Idaho, and Montana. Children's Hospital also provides research and educational facilities. **Positions advertised include:** Lab Aide; Equipment and Logistics Technician; Food Service Worker; Nurse Technician. **Operations at this facility include:** Service. **Number of employees at this location:** 2,400.

EVERETT CLINIC
3901 Hoyt Avenue, Everett WA 98201. 425/259-0966. **Contact:** Human Resources Department. **E-mail address:** hr@everettclinic.com. **World Wide Web address:** http://www.everettclinic.com. **Description:** A multispecialty group medical clinic operating through eight sites in Snohomish County. **Positions advertised include:** Behavioral Health Technician; Staff Registered Nurse; Nursing Supervisor.

EVERGREEN COMMUNITY HOME HEALTH CARE

12910 Totem Lake Boulevard, Suite 3204, Kirkland WA 98034. 425/899-3300. **Contact:** Human Resources Department. **World Wide Web address:** http://www.evergreenhealthcare.com. **Description:** Offers health services including nursing care, physical therapy, speech therapy, occupational therapy, home health aides, and social work, with specializations in oncology, pediatrics, and diabetic management. Evergreen Community Home Health Care staff help with the transition from the hospital or nursing home back to the primary residence. **Positions advertised include:** Registered Nurse; Licensed Practical Nurse; Certified Nursing Assistant; Housekeeper.

EVERGREEN HOSPITAL MEDICAL CENTER

12040 NE 128th Street, Kirkland WA 98034. 425/899-1000. **Fax:** 425/899-2510. **Contact:** Human Resources. **E-mail address:** jobs@evergreenhealthcare.org. **World Wide Web address:** http://www.evergreenhealthcare.org. **Description:** A medical center housing an acute care hospital, a surgery center, a hospice center, a head injury rehabilitation center, a telemarketing center, and a home health department. **Positions advertised include:** Clinical Nurse Specialist. **Operations at this facility include:** Administration. **Number of employees at this location:** 1,500.

FOSS HOME & VILLAGE

13023 Greenwood Avenue North, Seattle WA 98133. 206/364-1300. **Contact:** Human Resources. **World Wide Web address:** http://www.fosscare.org. **Description:** A long-term care facility that offers skilled nursing and assisted living services.

GROUP HEALTH EASTSIDE HOSPITAL

2700 152nd Avenue NE, Redmond WA 98052. 425/883-5151. **Contact:** Human Resources. **E-mail address:** recruiters.i@ghc.org. **World Wide Web address:** http://www.ghc.org. **Description:** An acute care hospital that also offers physical therapy and pediatric care.

GUIDANT CORPORATION

6645 185th Avenue NE, Suite 100, Redmond WA 98052-6734. 425/376-1300. **Contact:** Human Resources. **World Wide Web address:** http://www.guidant.com. **Description:** Guidant Corporation designs, develops, manufactures, and markets a wide range of products for use in cardiac rhythm management, coronary artery disease intervention, and other forms of minimally invasive surgery. **Corporate headquarters location:** Indianapolis IN. **Operations at this facility include:** This location is engaged in research and development. **Listed on:** New York Stock Exchange. **Stock exchange symbol:** GDT. **Annual sales/revenues:** More than $100 million.

HARBORVIEW MEDICAL CENTER
325 Ninth Avenue, Seattle WA 98104. 206/223-3000. **Contact:** Human Resources. **World Wide Web address:** http:// www.washington.edu/medical. **Description:** A unit of the University of Washington Academic Medical Center. The Harborview Medical Center contains an adult and pediatric trauma center and a regional burn center.

HARRISON MEMORIAL HOSPITAL
2520 Cherry Avenue, Bremerton WA 98310. 360/377-3911. **Recorded jobline:** 360/792-6729. **Contact:** Sue Scriven, Recruiter. **E-mail address:** suescriven@hmh.westsound.net. **World Wide Web address:** http://www.harrisonhospital.org. **Description:** A 297-bed, full-service hospital specializing in cardiology care, diagnostic imaging, emergency and urgent care, oncology, radiation therapy, and retinal and laparoscopic surgery. Founded in 1918. **Positions advertised include:** Radiologic Technologist; Medical Imaging Aide; Surgical Technician; Supply Support Technician; Speech Language Pathologist; Physical Therapist; Occupational Therapist. **Number of employees at this location:** 1,400.

HOLY FAMILY HOSPITAL
5633 North Lidgerwood Street, Spokane WA 99207. 509/482-2111. **Fax:** 509/482-2178. **Recorded jobline:** 509/482-2104. **Contact:** Human Resources. **World Wide Web address:** http:// www.holy-family.org. **Description:** A 272-bed acute care hospital that offers a full range of medical, outpatient, and surgical care. **Positions advertised include:** Registered Nurse; Speech Pathologist; Pharmacist; Social Worker; Lab Assistant.

LAKELAND VILLAGE
P.O. Box 200, Medical Lake WA 99022. 509/299-1800. **Contact:** Human Resources. **Description:** A state residential habilitation facility for individuals with developmental disabilities.

MARTHA & MARY NURSING HOME
P.O. Box 127, Poulsbo WA 98370. 360/779-7500. **Physical address:** 19160 Front Street NE, Poulsbo WA 98370. **Contact:** Human Resources. **World Wide Web address:** http://www.marthaandmary. org. **Description:** A 180-bed nursing home that provides activities, horticulture therapy, intergenerational programs, pet therapy, and rehabilitation. **Positions advertised include:** Licensed Practical Nurse; Registered Nurse; Certified Nursing Assistant.

VIRGINIA MASON MEDICAL CENTER
P.O. Box 900, Seattle WA 98111. 206/223-6600. **Contact:** Human Resources. **World Wide Web address:** http://www.vmmc.org. **Description:** A complete health care system that operates a 336-bed, acute care hospital, 16 regional clinics, an AIDS facility, and research laboratories. Founded in 1920. **Positions advertised include:** Administrative Assistant; Biomedical Equipment Technician; Clinic Service Representative; Orthopedics Coordinator; File Clerk; Customer Service Representative. **Special programs:** Internships.

MEDICAL CENTER OF TACOMA
P.O. Box 34586, Seattle WA 98124. 253/596-3300. **Physical address:** 209 Martin Luther King Jr. Way, Tacoma WA 98405. **Contact:** Human Resources. **World Wide Web address:** http:// www.ghc.org. **Description:** A full-service medical center that also offers optometry and women's health care services.

MEDTRONIC PHYSIO-CONTROL INC.
P.O. Box 97006, Redmond WA 98073-9706. 425/867-4000. **Physical address:** 11811 Willows Road NE, Redmond WA 98052. **Contact:** Human Resources. **World Wide Web address:** http:// www.physiocontrol.com. **Description:** Manufactures, sells, and services defibrillators, monitors, and pacemakers. **Positions advertised include:** Administrative Assistant; Business Director; Commercial Sales Consultant; Commercial Segment Manager; Data Communications Systems Manager. **Parent company:** Medtronic, Inc. **Operations at this facility include:** Administration; Manufacturing; Research and Development; Sales; Service. **Listed on:** New York Stock Exchange. **Stock exchange symbol:** MDT.

NORTHWEST HOSPITAL
1550 North 115th Street, Suite 1, Seattle WA 98133. 206/368-1785. **Recorded jobline:** 206/368-1791. **Contact:** Human Resources Department. **World Wide Web address:** http://www.nwhospital.org.

Description: A full-service nonprofit hospital that specializes in brain, breast, and prostate cancer; treatment and rehabilitation for diabetes and vascular disease; radioactive seed implantation; neurological disorders; and rehabilitation therapy. Founded in 1960. **Positions advertised include:** Authorization Referral Representative; Nursing Assistant; Exercise Specialist; Inventory Coordinator; Lab Assistant; EKG Technician.

OVERLAKE HOSPITAL MEDICAL CENTER
1035 116th Avenue NE, Bellevue WA 98004. 425/688-5201. **Fax:** 425/688-5758. **Recorded jobline:** 425/688-5150. **Contact:** Human Resources Department. **World Wide Web address:** http://www.overlakehospital.org. **Description:** A 227-bed, nonprofit, acute care medical center. Overlake Hospital specializes in open-heart surgery and offers a comprehensive cardiac program. **NOTE:** Entry-level positions, part-time jobs, and second and third shifts are offered. **Special programs:** Internships. **Annual sales/revenues:** $5 - $10 million. **Number of employees at this location:** 1,900.

PACMED CLINIC
1200 12th Avenue South, Seattle WA 98144. 206/621-4111. **Fax:** 206/621-4031. **Contact:** Human Resources. **World Wide Web address:** http://www.pacmed.org. **Description:** A nonprofit medical center operating clinics throughout the Seattle area. **NOTE:** Entry-level positions and second and third shifts are offered. **Positions advertised include:** Coding Manager; Senior Supervisor of Health Data Services; Clinical RN; Medical Assistant; Physical Therapist; Healthcare Application Analyst. **Office hours:** Monday - Friday, 8:00 a.m. - 4:00 p.m. **Number of employees at this location:** 1,200.

PHILIPS MEDICAL SYSTEMS
P.O. Box 3003, Bothell WA 98041-3003. 425/487-7000. **Physical address:** 22100 Bothell Everett Highway, Bothell WA 98021. **Contact:** Personnel. **World Wide Web address:** http://www.medical.philips.com. **Description:** Engaged in the development and manufacture of medical diagnostic ultrasound systems. These systems serve a variety of uses in radiology, cardiology, obstetrics/gynecology, vascular, musculoskeletal, and intraoperative applications. Founded in 1969. **NOTE:** Second and third shifts are offered. Please call the jobline to obtain the specific job number before applying. **Company slogan:** We are ultrasound. **Special programs:** Internships; Training. **Corporate headquarters location:** This location.

PROCYTE CORPORATION
8511 154th Avenue NE, Building A, Redmond WA 98052. 425/869-1239. **Contact:** Human Resources. **World Wide Web address:** http://www.procyte.com. **Description:** Develops copper peptide complex-based products designed for hair care, skin care, and tissue repair. The company also offers contract manufacturing services to biotech and pharmaceutical companies. **Corporate headquarters location:** This location.

PROVIDENCE EVERETT MEDICAL CENTER
P.O. Box 1147, Everett WA 98206. 425/261-2000. **Fax:** 425/261-4470. **Contact:** Human Resources. **World Wide Web address:** http://www.providence.org. **Description:** A full-service, acute care hospital. The Center also specializes in advanced cancer treatment and heart surgery.

PROVIDENCE HOME SERVICES
425 Pontius Avenue North, Suite 300, Seattle WA 98109-5452. 206/320-4000. **Fax:** 206/320-2280. **Contact:** Human Resources. **Description:** Provides skilled nursing and other home and hospice services.

PROVIDENCE MOTHER JOSEPH CARE CENTER
3333 Ensign Road NE, Olympia WA 98506. 360/493-4900. **Fax:** 360/493-4000. **Contact:** Human Resources. **World Wide Web address:** http://www.providence.org. **Description:** A 152-bed skilled nursing home that also operates a special care facility for Alzheimer's residents.

PROVIDENCE MOUNT ST. VINCENT
4831 35th Avenue SW, Seattle WA 98126. 206/937-3700. **Fax:** 206/938-8999. **Contact:** Human Resources. **World Wide Web address:** http://www.providence.org. **Description:** A long-term care facility that offers assisted living and skilled nursing services, an intergenerational learning center, and rehabilitation programs.

QUINTON, INC.
3303 Monte Villa Parkway, Bothell WA 98021-8906. 425/402-2000. **Fax:** 425/402-2015. **Contact:** Human Resources. **E-mail address:** employment@quinton.com. **World Wide Web address:** http://www.quinton.com. **Description:** Manufactures, markets, and distributes cardiopulmonary instrumentation and devices such as cardiac stress test systems, electrocardiographs, and treadmills.

Positions advertised include: Accounts Payable Clerk; Contract Administrator. **Corporate headquarters location:** This location. **Listed on:** NASDAQ. **Stock exchange symbol:** QUIN.

ST. JOSEPH HOSPITAL
2901 Squalicum Parkway, Bellingham WA 98225. 360/734-5400. **Contact:** Personnel Office. **World Wide Web address:** http://www.peacehealth.org. **Description:** A 253-bed medical center and trauma center that provides a full range of inpatient and outpatient care including cancer care, emergency and trauma care, heart surgery, and neurosurgery. **Positions advertised include:** Registered Nurse; Certified Nurse Manger; Clinical Manager; Coder; Database System Administrator; Internal Auditor; Medical Technologist; Pharmacist; Speech Pathologist; Surgical Technologist.

SIEMENS ULTRASOUND
P.O. Box 7002, Issaquah WA 98027-7002. 425/392-9180. **Physical address:** 22010 SE 51st Street, Issaquah WA 98029. **Contact:** Human Resources. **World Wide Web address:** http://www.siemensultrasound.com. **Description:** Develops and manufactures ultrasound systems. **Positions advertised include:** Technical Instructor. **Corporate headquarters location:** This location.

SPACELABS MEDICAL, INC.
P.O. Box 7018, Issaquah WA 98027-7018. 425/882-3700. **Fax:** 425/657-7211. **Contact:** Human Resources Department. **E-mail address:** resumes@slmd.com. **World Wide Web address:** http://www.spacelabs.com. **Description:** Manufactures patient monitoring equipment, clinical information systems, ambulatory monitoring products, and monitoring supplies. **Positions advertised include:** Product Evaluation Specialist; CV Technologist. **Corporate headquarters location:** This location. **Other U.S. locations:** AZ; CA; CO; FL; NY; NC; OR. **Operations at this facility include:** Administration; Manufacturing; Research and Development. **Number of employees at this location:** 1,200. **Number of employees nationwide:** 1,700.

STEVENS MEMORIAL HOSPITAL
21727 76th Avenue West, #102, Edmonds WA 98026. 425/640-4190. **Fax:** 425/640-4449. **Contact:** Human Resources Department. **World Wide Web address:** http://www.stevenshealthcare.org. **Description:** A 217-bed, acute care medical center offering a full

range of health care services including emergency care, critical care, surgery, a birthing center, orthopedic care, comprehensive cancer care, mental health services, diagnostic imaging, and outpatient services. Founded in 1964.

SWEDISH MEDICAL CENTER
601 Broadway, Seattle WA 98122. 206/386-2141. **Recorded jobline:** 206/386-2888. **Fax:** 206/386-2145. **Contact:** Human Resources. **World Wide Web address:** http://www.swedish.org. **Description:** An 860-bed, full-service, acute care medical center that also provides a wide range of specialty services. **Positions advertised include:** Administrative Assistant; Medical Records Clerk; Nurse Manager; Registered Nurse; Accountant; Revenue Analyst. **Number of employees at this location:** 4,000.

TACOMA LUTHERAN HOME
1301 North Highlands Parkway, Tacoma WA 98406. 253/752-7112. **Contact:** Human Resources. **World Wide Web address:** http://www.tacomalutheran.com. **Description:** A retirement community providing skilled nursing, assisted living, and independent living services.

U.S. DEPARTMENT OF VETERANS AFFAIRS
VETERANS ADMINISTRATION PUGET SOUND HEALTHCARE SYSTEM
1660 South Columbian Way, Seattle WA 98108. 206/764-2135. **Contact:** Human Resources. **Description:** A 488-bed, critical care hospital affiliated with the University of Washington. The VA health care system includes 171 medical centers; more than 364 outpatient, community, and outreach clinics; 130 nursing home care units; and 37 domiciliary residences nationwide. **NOTE:** This firm does not accept unsolicited resumes. Please only respond to advertised openings. **Office hours:** Monday - Friday, 8:00 a.m. - 4:30 p.m. **Parent company:** U.S. Department of Veterans Affairs. **Number of employees at this location:** 1,800.

VISITING NURSE PERSONAL SERVICES
600 Birchwood Avenue, Suite 100, Bellingham WA 98225. 360/734-9662. **Contact:** Human Resources. **World Wide Web address:** http://www.visitingnurseservices.com. **Description:** Provides home health care and hospice services.

U.S. DEPARTMEN OF VETERANS AFFAIRS
WASHINGTON VETERANS HOME
P.O. Box 698, Retsil WA 98378. 360/895-4700. **Contact:** Human Resources. **Description:** A domiciliary with assisted-living and skilled nursing services for veterans and their spouses.

HOTELS AND RESTAURANTS

You can expect to find the following types of companies in this chapter:

Casinos
Dinner Theaters
Hotel/Motel Operators
Resorts
Restaurants

AZTECA RESTAURANTS
133 SW 158th Street, Seattle WA 98166. 206/243-7021. **Contact:** Human Resources. **World Wide Web address:** http://www.aztecamex.com. **Description:** Owns and operates a chain of Mexican restaurants. **Corporate headquarters location:** This location.

BEST WESTERN BELLEVUE INN
11211 Main Street, Bellevue WA 98004. 425/455-5240. **Fax:** 425/455-0654. **Contact:** Human Resources. **World Wide Web address:** http://www.bestwestern.com. **Description:** A 180-room hotel franchise offering rental car services, restaurants, and meeting facilities. **Corporate headquarters location:** Phoenix AZ.

CRYSTAL MOUNTAIN RESORT
33914 Crystal Mountain Boulevard, Crystal Mountain WA 98022. 360/663-2265. **Contact:** Human Resources. **World Wide Web address:** http://www.crystalmt.com. **Description:** A ski resort and lodge.

FOUR SEASONS OLYMPIC HOTEL
411 University Street, Seattle WA 98101. 206/621-1700. **Recorded jobline:** 206/287-4047. **Contact:** Personnel. **World Wide Web address:** http://www.fourseasons.com. **Description:** A 450-room hotel with 20,000 square feet of meeting and function space, three restaurants, a health club, and a retail arcade with 14 international shops. Four Seasons Hotels & Resorts operates approximately 50 luxury hotels and resorts in 22 countries. **NOTE:** Entry-level positions are offered. **Corporate headquarters location:** Ontario, Canada. **Other U.S. locations:** Nationwide. **International locations:** Worldwide. **Listed on:** New York Stock Exchange. **Stock exchange symbol:** FS. **Number of employees at this location:** 585.

HOTEL LUSSO
One North Post Street, Spokane WA 99201. 509/747-9750. **Fax:** 509/363-2389. **Contact:** Personnel. **World Wide Web address:** http://www.westcoasthotels.com. **Description:** A boutique-style, luxury hotel offering reception and conference rooms. **Parent company:** Westcoast Hotels.

THE PARAMOUNT HOTEL
724 Pine Street, Seattle WA 98101. 206/292-9500. **Fax:** 206/292-8610. **Contact:** Human Resources. **World Wide Web address:** http://

www.westcoasthotels.com. **Description:** A 146-room, chateau-style hotel featuring the Blowfish Asian Cafe and two meeting rooms. **Parent company:** Westcoast Hotels.

RESTAURANTS UNLIMITED INC.

1818 North Northlake Way, Seattle WA 98103. 206/634-0550. **Fax:** 206/634-1904. **Contact:** Director of Staffing. **World Wide Web address:** http://www.restaurants-unlimited.com. **Description:** Owns and operates a chain of full-service dinner houses. Founded in 1969. **Corporate headquarters location:** This location. **Operations at this facility include:** Administration.

S&W/CENTERFOODS MANAGEMENT COMPANY

20062 19th Avenue NE, Seattle WA 98155. 206/362-2255. **Fax:** 206/362-8850. **Contact:** Bret Stewart, Vice President of Operations. **E-mail address:** bstewart@centerfoods.com. **World Wide Web address:** http://www.centerfoods.com. **Description:** Owns and operates several fast-food restaurants located in malls, which are part of the national chains Orange Julius, A&W, Dairy Queen, and Auntie Anne's. Founded in 1971. **NOTE:** Entry-level positions are offered. **Special programs:** Internships; Training. **Internship information:** The company has a paid internship program for hotel/restaurant or business management students. To apply, submit a letter of application and include goals, schedule, and time frame. Call for more information. **Corporate headquarters location:** This location. **Listed on:** Privately held. **Number of employees at this location:** 300.

SEA-TAC MARRIOTT

3201 South 176th Street, Seattle WA 98188. 206/241-2000. **Fax:** 206/241-2235. **Contact:** Personnel Office. **World Wide Web address:** http://www.marriott.com. **Description:** A 465-room, full-service hotel featuring convention and banquet facilities and a restaurant. **Other U.S. locations:** Nationwide.

SEATTLE DAYS INN TOWN CENTER

2205 Seventh Avenue, Seattle WA 98121. 206/448-3434. **Contact:** Personnel. **World Wide Web address:** http://www.daysinn.com. **Description:** A 91-room hotel. This location also houses a restaurant and lounge.

STARBUCKS COFFEE CORPORATION

P.O. Box 34067, Seattle WA 98124. 206/447-1575. **Physical address:** 2401 Utah Avenue South, Seattle WA 98134. **Recorded jobline:** 206/447-4123. **Contact:** Human Resources. **World Wide Web address:** http://www.starbucks.com. **Description:** Sells whole-bean coffees, along with hot coffees and Italian-style espresso beverages through more than 2,500 retail stores worldwide. The company purchases green coffee beans for its coffee varieties from coffee-producing regions throughout the world and custom roasts them. In addition to coffee beans and beverages, the company's stores offer a selection of coffee-making equipment, accessories, pastries, and confections. Also, the company sells whole-bean coffees through specialty sales groups, a national mail-order operation, and supermarkets. **Corporate headquarters location:** This location. **Other U.S. locations:** Nationwide. **International locations:** Worldwide. **Number of employees worldwide:** 37,000.

UNIVERSAL SODEXHO

520 Pike Street, Suite 2230, Seattle WA 98101. 253/383-9200. **Contact:** Personnel Department. **World Wide Web address:** http://www.universalservices.com. **Description:** A catering service specializing in providing services to remote locations.

WESTCOAST VANCE HOTEL

620 Stewart Street, Seattle WA 98101. 206/441-4200. **Fax:** 206/441-8612. **Contact:** Human Resources. **World Wide Web address:** http://www.westcoasthotels.com. **Description:** A 165-room, boutique style, luxury hotel featuring the Yakima Grill Restaurant. **Parent company:** Westcoast Hotels.

INSURANCE

You can expect to find the following types of companies in this chapter:

Commercial and Industrial Property/Casualty Insurers
Health Maintenance Organizations (HMOs)
Medical/Life Insurance Companies

ALLSTATE INSURANCE COMPANY

18911 North Creek Parkway, Suite 301, Bothell WA 98011. 425/489-9000. **Contact:** Human Resources. **World Wide Web address:** http://www.allstate.com. **Description:** Provides a full line of property, liability, life, reinsurance, and commercial lines of insurance. **Positions advertised include:** Claims Associate; Claims Service Adjuster. **Corporate headquarters location:** Northbrook IL. **Parent company:** Sears, Roebuck & Company. **Operations at this facility include:** Administration; Regional Headquarters; Sales; Service. **Listed on:** New York Stock Exchange. **Stock exchange symbol:** S. **Number of employees at this location:** 1,500. **Number of employees nationwide:** 53,000.

AMERICAN GENERAL FINANCE

10740 Meridian Avenue North, Suite 105, Seattle WA 98133. 206/362-4566. **Contact:** Human Resources. **World Wide Web address:** http://www.agfinance.com. **Description:** One of the country's largest public insurance companies. American General Finance also provides financial services including mortgage loans, real estate investment and development, investment counseling, and management and distribution of mutual funds. **Corporate headquarters location:** New York NY. **Parent company:** American General Corporation. **Listed on:** New York Stock Exchange. **Stock exchange symbol:** AGC.

CHUBB GROUP INSURANCE

601 Union Street, Suite 3800, Seattle WA 98101. 206/624-2100. **Contact:** Human Resources. **World Wide Web address:** http:// www.chubb.com. **Description:** One of the largest property and casualty insurers in the United States, with more than 110 offices in 30 countries worldwide. The company offers a broad range of specialty insurance products and services designed for individuals and businesses, including high-technology, financial institutions, and general manufacturers. **Corporate headquarters location:** Warren NJ. **Other U.S. locations:** Nationwide. **Listed on:** New York Stock Exchange. **Stock exchange symbol:** CB.

FIC INSURANCE GROUP

2101 Fourth Avenue, Suite 700, Seattle WA 98121. 206/441-1942. **Contact:** Personnel Department. **E-mail address:** hr@ficgroup.com. **World Wide Web address:** http://www.ficgroup.com. **Description:** Sells life and disability insurance. **Corporate headquarters location:**

Austin TX. **Parent company:** Merrill Lynch & Co., Inc. **Number of employees at this location:** 420.

FIREMAN'S FUND INSURANCE COMPANY
2101 Fourth Avenue, Suite 1100, Seattle WA 98121. 206/728-5100. **Contact:** Human Resources. **World Wide Web address:** http:// www.the-fund.com. **Description:** Offers a variety of commercial insurance products and services. **Corporate headquarters location:** Novato CA. **Parent company:** Allianz AG. **Operations at this facility include:** Administration; Service.

GRANGE INSURANCE GROUP
ROCKY MOUNTAIN FIRE & CASUALTY
200 Cedar Street, Seattle WA 98121. 206/448-4911. **Fax:** 206/448-0942. **Contact:** Human Resources Department. **E-mail address:** hr@grange.com. **World Wide Web address:** http://www.grange.com. **Description:** A property and casualty insurance firm. Founded in 1894. **Corporate headquarters location:** This location.

GREAT REPUBLIC LIFE INSURANCE
1900 West Nickerson Street, Suite 200, Seattle WA 98119. 206/285-1422. **Contact:** Personnel Department. **World Wide Web address:** http://www.grlins.com. **Description:** A health insurance underwriting company.

GROUP HEALTH COOPERATIVE
P.O. Box 34586Y, Seattle WA 98124. 206/448-2748. **Physical address:** 12501 East Marginal Way, Tukwila WA 98168. **Contact:** Human Resources. **World Wide Web address:** http://www.ghc.org. **Description:** A health maintenance organization and hospital operator. **Corporate headquarters location:** This location. **Number of employees at this location:** 9,000.

MARSH ADVANTAGE OF AMERICA
1215 Fourth Avenue, Suite 600, Seattle WA 98161. 206/441-5900. **Contact:** Human Resources. **E-mail address:** hr.maa@seabury.com. **World Wide Web address:** http://www.marshadvantage.com. **Description:** An insurance brokerage. Marsh Advantage of America is an international insurance broker engaged in insurance booking, risk management, and benefits consulting.

PARKER, SMITH & FEEK
2233 112th Avenue NE, Bellevue WA 98004. **Fax:** 800/457-0220. **Contact:** Employee Relations. **World Wide Web address:** http://www.psfinc.com. **Description:** Provides a variety of insurance services including commercial property/casualty, health, life, and personal lines. Founded in 1937. **Corporate headquarters location:** This location. **Other U.S. locations:** Anchorage AK. **Listed on:** Privately held. **Annual sales/revenues:** $11 - $20 million.

PEMCO FINANCIAL SERVICES
P.O. Box 778, Seattle WA 98111. 206/628-4090. **Toll-free phone:** 800/552-7430. **Fax:** 206/628-6072. **Recorded jobline:** 206/628-8740. **Contact:** Human Resources. **E-mail address:** jobs@pfcenter.com. **World Wide Web address:** http://www.pemco.com. **Description:** Provides insurance, banking, and credit union services through its subsidiaries. Founded in 1936. **NOTE:** Entry-level positions and second and third shifts are offered. **Positions advertised include:** Sales Supervisor; Individual Life Underwriter; Document Services Specialist; Training Consultant; Risk Management Representative. **Special programs:** Training. **Corporate headquarters location:** This location. **Subsidiaries include:** PEMCO Insurance Companies; PEMCO Life Insurance Company; Washington School Employees Credit Union; PEMCO Corporation; EvergreenBank. **Number of employees at this location:** 800. **Number of employees nationwide:** 1,030.

PREMERA BLUE CROSS
P.O. Box 327, Mail Stop 314, Seattle WA 98111-0327. 425/670-4000. **Fax:** 425/670-4791. **Recorded jobline:** 888/647-3628. **Contact:** Human Resources. **World Wide Web address:** http://www.premera.com. **Description:** A nonprofit health care insurance provider. **NOTE:** Entry-level positions are offered.

SAFECO INSURANCE CORPORATION
Safeco Plaza, Seattle WA 98185. 206/545-5000. **Contact:** Personnel Director. **World Wide Web address:** http://www.safeco.com. **Description:** A diversified financial services company with operations including property and liability, life and health insurance, pension plans, mutual funds, commercial credit, and real estate development. **Positions advertised include:** Actuarial Assistant; Agency Incentive Compensation Manager; Analyst; Application Developer; Business Recovery Developer. **Special programs:** Internships. **Corporate headquarters location:** This location. **Other**

area locations: Redmond WA. **Other U.S. locations:** Nationwide. **Annual sales/revenues:** More than $100 million.

SAFECO LIFE INSURANCE COMPANY
P.O. Box 34690, Seattle WA 98124. 425/376-8000. **Contact:** Human Resources. **World Wide Web address:** http://www.safeco. com. **Description:** Provides life and health insurance. **Parent company:** Safeco Insurance Corporation. **Positions advertised include:** Actuarial Assistant; Agency Incentive Compensation Manager; Analyst; Application Developer; Business Recovery Developer.

TRANSNATION TITLE INSURANCE COMPANY
1206 Sixth Avenue, Suite 100, Seattle WA 98101. 206/628-3540. **Contact:** Louise Condon, Personnel Administrator. **World Wide Web address:** http://www.ttic-nw.com. **Description:** One of the nation's leading providers of title insurance. **Office hours:** Monday - Friday, 8:00 a.m. - 5:00 p.m.

UNIGARD INSURANCE COMPANY
15805 NE 24th Street, Bellevue WA 98008-2409. 425/644-5236. **Fax:** 425/671-0109. **Contact:** Personnel. **World Wide Web address:** http://www.unigard.com. **Description:** An insurance company specializing in property and casualty insurance. **Positions advertised include:** Administrative Services Representative; Agency Relations Manager. **Other U.S. locations:** AZ; CA; ID; NY; NC; UT. **Parent company:** Winterthur Group. **Number of employees at this location:** 500. **Number of employees nationwide:** 630.

WESTERN NATIONAL INSURANCE GROUP
P.O. Box 75189, Northgate Station, Seattle WA 98125. 206/526-5900. **Contact:** Personnel. **World Wide Web address:** http://www.wnins.com. **Description:** An insurance brokerage company.

WILLIS
P.O. Box 34201, Seattle WA 98124. 206/386-7400. **Contact:** Human Resources. **World Wide Web address:** http://www.willis. com. **Description:** An international insurance broker engaged in commercial property, liability, fidelity, security, and life insurance, as well as group benefits. **Positions advertised include:** Client Services Manager. **Special programs:** Internships. **Listed on:** New York Stock Exchange. **Stock exchange symbol:** WSH.

LEGAL SERVICES

You can expect to find the following types of companies in this chapter:

Law Firms
Legal Service Agencies

AIKEN, ST. LOUIS & SILJEG, P.S.
801 Second Avenue, Suite 1200, Seattle WA 98104. 206/624-2650.
Contact: Personnel. **World Wide Web address:** http://www.aiken.
com. **Description:** A law firm specializing in corporate, tax,
insurance, and environmental law. **Corporate headquarters
location:** This location.

FOSTER PEPPER & SHEFELMAN PLLC
1111 Third Avenue, Suite 3400, Seattle WA 98101. 206/447-4400.
Contact: Human Resources. **World Wide Web address:** http://
www.foster.com. **Description:** A law firm specializing in corporate
and environmental law. Founded in 1904. **Other area locations:**
Bellevue WA; Spokane WA. **Other U.S. locations:** Anchorage AK;
Portland OR. **Number of employees at this location:** 350.

McNAUL, EBEL, NAWROT, HELGREN & VANCE
600 University Street, One Union Square, Suite 2700, Seattle WA
98101. 206/624-7141. **Fax:** 206/624-5128. **Contact:** Human
Resources. **World Wide Web address:** http://www.mcnaul.com.
Description: A law firm specializing in the areas of real estate,
litigation, and business.

SCHWABE, WILLIAMSON & WYATT, P.C.
1420 Fifth Avenue, Suite 3010, Seattle WA 98101-2339. 206/622-
1711. **Contact:** Recruitment. **World Wide Web address:** http://
www.schwabe.com. **Description:** A law firm operating through two
departments: Transactions and Litigation. The Transactions
Department provides a wide range of legal services to area
businesses, specializing in general business, corporate tax, energy,
environment, natural resources, and real estate. The Litigation
Department specializes in admiralty, commercial litigation,
intellectual property, product liability, workers' compensation, and
insurance. Founded in 1892. **Corporate headquarters location:**
Portland OR. **Other area locations:** Vancouver WA.

SCHWABE, WILLIAMSON & WYATT, P.C.
1111 Main Street, Suite 410, Vancouver WA 98660. 360/694-7551.
Contact: Recruitment. **World Wide Web address:** http://
www.schwabe.com. **Description:** A law firm operating through two
departments: Transactions and Litigation. The Transactions
Department provides a wide range of legal services to area
businesses, specializing in general business, corporate tax, energy,
environment, natural resources, and real estate. The Litigation

Department specializes in admiralty, commercial litigation, intellectual property, product liability, workers' compensation, and insurance. Founded in 1892. **Corporate headquarters location:** Portland OR. **Other area locations:** Seattle WA.

STANISLAW ASHBAUGH, LLP
4400 Bank of America Tower, 701 Fifth Avenue, Seattle WA 98104-7012. 206/386-5900. **Contact:** Francine Wright, Administrator. **World Wide Web address:** http://www.stanislaw.com. **Description:** A law firm specializing in business, construction, employment, and insurance law. **Number of employees at this location:** 40.

WELLS, ST. JOHN, ROBERTS, GREGORY & MATKIN P.S.
601 West First Avenue, Suite 1300, Spokane WA 99201. 509/624-4276. **Contact:** Recruitment. **World Wide Web address:** http://www.wellsstjohn.com. **Description:** A law firm specializing in copyrights, patents, and trademarks.

MANUFACTURING: MISCELLANEOUS CONSUMER

You can expect to find the following types of companies in this chapter:

Art Supplies
Batteries
Cosmetics and Related Products
Household Appliances and Audio/Video Equipment
Jewelry, Silverware, and Plated Ware
Miscellaneous Household Furniture and Fixtures
Musical Instruments
Tools
Toys and Sporting Goods

BRANDRUD FURNITURE, INC.
1502 20th Street NW, Auburn WA 98001-3428. 253/922-6167. **Contact:** Personnel. **World Wide Web address:** http://www.brandrud.com. **Description:** Manufactures furniture for office, health care, and institutional settings. **Corporate headquarters location:** This location.

CONNELLY SKIS INC.
P.O. Box 716, Lynnwood WA 98046. 425/775-5416. **Physical address:** 20621 52nd Avenue West, Lynnwood WA 98036. **Contact:** Human Resources. **World Wide Web address:** http://www.connellyskis.com. **Description:** Manufactures water skis, tubes, wet suits, and related accessories. **Corporate headquarters location:** This location.

H.O. SPORTS
17622 NE 67th Court, Redmond WA 98052. 425/885-3505. **Contact:** Human Resources. **World Wide Web address:** http://www.hosports.com. **Description:** Manufactures a variety of outdoor recreation equipment including water skis and snowboards. **Corporate headquarters location:** This location.

HUNTER DOUGLAS NORTHWEST
1905 Raymond Avenue SW, Renton WA 98055. 425/430-6110. **Contact:** Human Resources. **World Wide Web address:** http://www.hunterdouglas.com. **Description:** Manufactures Venetian blinds. **Office hours:** Monday - Friday, 8:00 a.m. - 4:30 p.m.

INTERPOINT CORPORATION
P.O. Box 97005, Redmond WA 98073-9705. 425/882-3100. **Fax:** 425/556-5061. **Recorded jobline:** 425/895-5005. **Contact:** Human Resources Department. **E-mail address:** careers@intp.com. **World Wide Web address:** http://www.interpoint.com. **Description:** Manufactures microelectronic power-conversion products for the aerospace, space, military, medical, industrial, and commercial markets. Products include DC-DC converters, EMI Filters, and custom-designed microcircuits. **Corporate headquarters location:** This location.

KING ELECTRICAL MANUFACTURING COMPANY
9131 10th Avenue South, Seattle WA 98108. 206/762-0400. **Fax:** 206/763-7738. **Contact:** Human Resources. **World Wide Web address:** http://www.king-electric.com. **Description:** Manufactures a

wide range of electric heating equipment for the home. **Corporate headquarters location:** This location.

K2 CORPORATION
19215 Vashon Highway SW, Vashon WA 98070. 206/463- 3631. **Contact:** Personnel Director. **E-mail address:** employment@ k2snowboarding.com. **World Wide Web address:** http:// www.k2sports.com. **Description:** Manufactures outdoor recreation equipment. **Corporate headquarters location:** This location. **Listed on:** New York Stock Exchange. **Stock exchange symbol:** KTO. **Number of employees nationwide:** 800.

MATSUSHITA KOTOBUKI ELECTRONICS INDUSTRIES OF AMERICA, INC.
2001 Kotobuki Way, Vancouver WA 98660. 360/695-1338. **Fax:** 360/695-3155. **Contact:** Human Resources. **Description:** Manufactures combination TV/VCR units. **Listed on:** New York Stock Exchange. **Stock exchange symbol:** MC. **President:** Kenzo Hayashi.

NINTENDO OF AMERICA
P.O. Box 957, Redmond WA 98073. 425/882-2040. **Contact:** Human Resources. **World Wide Web address:** http:// www.nintendo.com. **Description:** An importer, wholesaler, and manufacturer of electronic games, home video systems, home video games, and watches. **Corporate headquarters location:** This location.

PACIFIC COAST FEATHER COMPANY INC.
P.O. Box 80385, Seattle WA 98134. 206/624-1057. **Contact:** Personnel Department. **World Wide Web address:** http:// www.pacificcoast.com. **Description:** Manufactures pillows, comforters, and featherbeds.

PRECOR, INC.
20031 142nd Avenue, Woodinville WA 98072. 425/486-9292. **Fax:** 425/398-3005. **Contact:** Human Resources. **E-mail address:** hr@ precor.com. **World Wide Web address:** http://www.precor.com. **Description:** One of the world's leading designers, manufacturers, and marketers of fitness equipment for home and commercial use. Products include treadmills, stairclimbers, cyclers, and elliptical crosstrainers. **Corporate headquarters location:** This location. **International locations:** England; Germany; Singapore. **Subsidiaries**

include: Pacific Fitness. **Parent company:** Premark International (Deerfield IL) is a *Fortune* 500 company. **President:** Bill Potts.

RIDE SNOWBOARD COMPANY
19215 Vashon Highway SW, Vashon WA 98070. 206/463-3631. **Toll-free phone:** 800/757-5806. **Fax:** 206/463-2861. **Contact:** Human Resources. **World Wide Web address:** http://www.ridesnowboards.com. **Description:** A leading designer, manufacturer, and marketer of snowboards, clothing, and related products under the Ride, Liquid, Preston, Cappel, and SMP brand names. Founded in 1992. **Special programs:** Internships. **Corporate headquarters location:** This location. **Subsidiaries include:** Ride - Canada, Toronto, Canada; Ride Manufacturing, Corona CA; SMP, Chula Vista CA. **Parent company:** Ride Inc. **Listed on:** NASDAQ. **Stock exchange symbol:** RIDE. **Annual sales/revenues:** $51 - $100 million. **Number of employees at this location:** 90. **Number of employees nationwide:** 250.

TACOMA GUITARS
4615 East 192 2nd Street, Tacoma WA 98446. 253/847-6508. **Contact:** Human Resources. **World Wide Web address:** http://www.tacomaguitars.com. **Description:** Manufactures a line of guitars and related accessories.

U.S. MARINE
BAYLINER MARINE CORPORATION
P.O. Box 9029, Everett WA 98206. 360/435-5571. **Fax:** 360/403-4249. **Contact:** Claudia Walker, Human Resources and Benefits Manager. **World Wide Web address:** http://www.baylinerboats.com. **Description:** Builds pleasure boats. **Corporate headquarters location:** Arlington WA. **Other U.S. locations:** Nationwide. **Parent company:** Brunswick Corporation. **Operations at this facility include:** Divisional Headquarters. **Number of employees at this location:** 900. **Number of employees nationwide:** 3,600.

MANUFACTURING: MISCELLANEOUS INDUSTRIAL

You can expect to find the following types of companies in this chapter:

Ball and Roller Bearings
Commercial Furniture and Fixtures
Fans, Blowers, and Purification Equipment
Industrial Machinery and Equipment
Motors and Generators/Compressors and Engine Parts
Vending Machines

BRANDRUD FURNITURE, INC.
1502 20th Street NW, Auburn WA 98001-3428. 253/922-6167. **Contact:** Personnel. **World Wide Web address:** http://www.brandrud.com. **Description:** Manufactures furniture for office, health care, and institutional settings. **Corporate headquarters location:** This location.

CONNELLY SKIS INC.
P.O. Box 716, Lynnwood WA 98046. 425/775-5416. **Physical address:** 20621 52nd Avenue West, Lynnwood WA 98036. **Contact:** Human Resources. **World Wide Web address:** http://www.connellyskis.com. **Description:** Manufactures water skis, tubes, wet suits, and related accessories. **Corporate headquarters location:** This location.

H.O. SPORTS
17622 NE 67th Court, Redmond WA 98052. 425/885-3505. **Contact:** Human Resources. **World Wide Web address:** http://www.hosports.com. **Description:** Manufactures a variety of outdoor recreation equipment including water skis and snowboards. **Corporate headquarters location:** This location.

HUNTER DOUGLAS NORTHWEST
1905 Raymond Avenue SW, Renton WA 98055. 425/430-6110. **Contact:** Human Resources. **World Wide Web address:** http://www.hunterdouglas.com. **Description:** Manufactures Venetian blinds. **Office hours:** Monday - Friday, 8:00 a.m. - 4:30 p.m.

KING ELECTRICAL MANUFACTURING COMPANY
9131 10th Avenue South, Seattle WA 98108. 206/762-0400. **Fax:** 206/763-7738. **Contact:** Human Resources. **World Wide Web address:** http://www.king-electric.com. **Description:** Manufactures a wide range of electric heating equipment for the home. **Corporate headquarters location:** This location.

K2 CORPORATION
19215 Vashon Highway SW, Vashon WA 98070. 206/463-3631. **Contact:** Personnel Director. **E-mail address:** employment@k2snowboarding.com. **World Wide Web address:** http://www.k2sports.com. **Description:** Manufactures outdoor recreation equipment. **Corporate headquarters location:** This location. **Listed on:** New York Stock Exchange. **Stock exchange symbol:** KTO. **Number of employees nationwide:** 800.

MATSUSHITA KOTOBUKI ELECTRONICS INDUSTRIES OF AMERICA, INC.
2001 Kotobuki Way, Vancouver WA 98660. 360/695-1338. **Fax:** 360/695-3155. **Contact:** Human Resources. **Description:** Manufactures combination TV/VCR units. **Listed on:** New York Stock Exchange. **Stock exchange symbol:** MC. **President:** Kenzo Hayashi.

NINTENDO OF AMERICA
P.O. Box 957, Redmond WA 98073. 425/882-2040. **Contact:** Human Resources. **World Wide Web address:** http://www.nintendo. com. **Description:** An importer, wholesaler, and manufacturer of electronic games, home video systems, home video games, and watches. **Corporate headquarters location:** This location.

PACIFIC COAST FEATHER COMPANY INC.
P.O. Box 80385, Seattle WA 98134. 206/624-1057. **Contact:** Personnel Department. **World Wide Web address:** http:// www.pacificcoast.com. **Description:** Manufactures pillows, comforters, and featherbeds.

PRECOR, INC.
20031 142nd Avenue, Woodinville WA 98072. 425/486-9292. **Fax:** 425/398-3005. **Contact:** Human Resources. **E-mail address:** hr@precor.com. **World Wide Web address:** http://www.precor.com. **Description:** One of the world's leading designers, manufacturers, and marketers of fitness equipment for home and commercial use. Products include treadmills, stairclimbers, cyclers, and elliptical crosstrainers. **Corporate headquarters location:** This location. **International locations:** England; Germany; Singapore. **Subsidiaries include:** Pacific Fitness. **Parent company:** Premark International (Deerfield IL) is a *Fortune* 500 company. **President:** Bill Potts.

RIDE SNOWBOARD COMPANY
19215 Vashon Highway SW, Vashon WA 98070. 206/463-3631. **Toll-free phone:** 800/757-5806. **Fax:** 206/463-2861. **Contact:** Human Resources. **World Wide Web address:** http:// www.ridesnowboards.com. **Description:** A leading designer, manufacturer, and marketer of snowboards, clothing, and related products under the Ride, Liquid, Preston, Cappel, and SMP brand names. Founded in 1992. **Special programs:** Internships. **Corporate headquarters location:** This location. **Subsidiaries include:** Ride - Canada, Toronto, Canada; Ride Manufacturing, Corona CA; SMP, Chula Vista CA. **Parent company:** Ride Inc. **Listed on:** NASDAQ.

Stock exchange symbol: RIDE. **Annual sales/revenues:** $51 - $100 million. **Number of employees at this location:** 90. **Number of employees nationwide:** 250.

VALIN NORTHWEST
1850 130th Avenue NE, Suite 1, Bellevue WA 98005-2244. 425/885-0372. **Contact:** Human Resources. **E-mail address:** resumes@valin.com. **World Wide Web address:** http://www.valinonline.com. **Description:** A supplier of fluid handling, measurement and control products for a wide range of industrial process applications. **Corporate headquarters location:** Sunnyvale CA.

MINING/GAS/PETROLEUM/ENERGY RELATED

You can expect to find the following types of companies in this chapter:

Anthracite, Coal, and Ore Mining
Mining Machinery and Equipment
Oil and Gas Field Services
Petroleum and Natural Gas

Gold Reserve Inc.
926 West Sprague Avenue, Suite 200, Spokane WA 99201. 509/623-1500. **Toll-free phone:** 800/625-9550. **Fax:** 509/623-1634. **Contact:** Human Resources. **World Wide Web address:** http://www.goldreserveinc.com. **Description:** A mining company engaged, through foreign subsidiaries, in the acquisition and exploration of gold and other mineral properties. Gold Reserve has focused its attention on mining opportunities in Venezuela due to the enormous mineral resources believed to be contained within the country. **Corporate headquarters location:** This location.

PHILLIPS PETROLEUM
3901 Unick Road, Ferndale WA 98248. 360/384-1011. **Fax:** 360/384-8344. **Contact:** Human Resources. **World Wide Web address:** http://www.phillips66.com. **Description:** Refines petroleum and related products. **Special programs:** Internships. **Corporate headquarters location:** Seattle WA. **Other U.S. locations:** Martinez CA; Lynden NJ. **Parent company:** ConocoPhillips. **Listed on:** New York Stock Exchange. **Stock exchange symbol:** P. **Number of employees at this location:** 300. **Number of employees nationwide:** 2,000.

THE ROBBINS COMPANY
22445 76th Avenue South, Kent WA 98032. 253/872-0500. **Contact:** Human Resources Department. **World Wide Web address:** http://www.robbinstbm.com. **Description:** Designs and manufactures mining machinery and equipment. **Corporate headquarters location:** Solon OH.

TESORO PETROLEUM
P.O. Box 700, Anacortes WA 98221. 360/293-9119. **Contact:** Personnel Director. **World Wide Web address:** http://www.tesoropetroleum.com. **Description:** A refinery engaged in the production of automobile and airplane fuels, kerosene, and diesel products. **Corporate headquarters location:** Houston TX.

TIME OIL COMPANY
P.O. 24447, Seattle WA 98124. 206/285-2400. **Physical address:** 2737 West Commodore Way, Seattle WA 98199. **Contact:** Personnel Department. **World Wide Web address:** http://www.timeoil.com. **Description:** Operates retail gasoline service stations, wholesales petroleum products, and retails fuel oil heaters.

U.S. OIL & REFINING COMPANY
3001 Marshall Avenue, Tacoma WA 98421. 253/383-1651. **Fax:** 253/383-9970. **Contact:** Marcia E. Nielsen, Administration Services Manager. **E-mail address:** men@usor.com. **World Wide Web address:** http://www.usor.com. **Description:** A petroleum refinery. **Special programs:** Summer Jobs. **Listed on:** Privately held. **Number of employees at this location:** 155.

PAPER AND WOOD PRODUCTS

You can expect to find the following types of companies in this chapter:

Forest and Wood Products and Services
Lumber and Wood Wholesale
Millwork, Plywood, and Structural Members
Paper and Wood Mills

A.P.A. - THE ENGINEERED WOOD ASSOCIATION

P.O. Box 11700, Tacoma WA 98411-0700. 253/565-6600. **Fax:** 253/565-7265. **Contact:** Human Resources. **E-mail address:** hr@ apawood.org. **World Wide Web address:** http://www.apawood.org. **Description:** A nonprofit trade association providing research, quality testing, and marketing services for its member mills. Members of the A.P.A. produce plywood, OSB, and I-joists. Founded in 1936. **NOTE:** Entry-level positions are offered. **Special programs:** Training. **Corporate headquarters location:** This location. **Other U.S. locations:** Nationwide. **Number of employees at this location:** 170.

ACRO-WOOD CORPORATION

P.O. Box 1028, Everett WA 98206. 425/258-3555. **Fax:** 425/252-7622. **Contact:** Controller. **World Wide Web address:** http://www.acrowood.com. **Description:** Operates a pulp and paper mill offering such products as plywood, particleboard, and machinery for the lumber industry. **Corporate headquarters location:** New York NY.

ALLPAK CONTAINER, INC.

1100 SW 27th Street, Renton WA 98055. 425/227-0400. **Fax:** 425/227-0197. **Contact:** Human Resources Manager. **E-mail address:** humanresources@allpak.com. **World Wide Web address:** http://www.allpak.com. **Description:** Produces recycled paperboard and paper packaging products including corrugated containers, specialty corrugated products, and folding cartons. **Corporate headquarters location:** This location.

BOISE CASCADE CORPORATION

P.O. Box 51, Yakima WA 98907-0051. 509/453-3131. **Contact:** Human Resources. **World Wide Web address:** http://www.bc.com. **Description:** An integrated paper and forest products company with operations located throughout the United States. The company manufactures and distributes paper and paper products, office products, and building products and owns and manages timberland to support these operations. Boise Cascade is one of the largest pulp and paper producers in the United States. Founded in 1957. **Corporate headquarters location:** Boise ID. **Other U.S. locations:** Emmett ID. **Listed on:** New York Stock Exchange. **Stock exchange symbol:** BCC.

BUFFELEN WOODWORKING COMPANY
P.O. Box 1383, Tacoma WA 98401-1383. 253/627-1191. **Contact:** Human Resources Department. **Description:** A large millwork manufacturing company. **Corporate headquarters location:** This location. **Operations at this facility include:** Administration; Manufacturing; Sales; Service.

DAISHOWA AMERICA COMPANY, LTD.
P.O. Box 271, Port Angeles WA 98362. 360/457-4474. **Fax:** 360/452-9004. **Contact:** David Flodstrom, Human Resources Manager. **Description:** Manufactures telephone directory paper. The company also operates pulp and de-ink facilities. **Corporate headquarters location:** This location. **Listed on:** Privately held. **Annual sales/revenues:** More than $100 million. **Number of employees at this location:** 300.

EKONO INC.
11061 NE Second Street, Suite 107, Bellevue WA 98004. 425/455-5969. **Contact:** Heikki Mannisto, President. **E-mail address:** mannisto.heikki@ekono.com. **World Wide Web address:** http://www.ekono.com. **Description:** An engineering consulting firm serving the pulp and paper industry. **Corporate headquarters location:** This location. **Parent company:** Duoplan Oy.

GEORGIA-PACIFIC CORPORATION
300 West Laurel Street, Bellingham WA 98225. 360/733-4410. **Contact:** Human Resources Manager. **World Wide Web address:** http://www.gp.com. **Description:** Manufactures, wholesales, and distributes building products, industrial wood products, pulp, paper, packaging, and related chemicals. **Other U.S. locations:** Nationwide. **Listed on:** New York Stock Exchange. **Stock exchange symbol:** GP.

GEORGIA-PACIFIC CORPORATION
401 NE Adams Street, Camas WA 98607. 360/834-3021. **Contact:** Kurt Christianson, Personnel Director. **World Wide Web address:** http://www.gp.com. **Description:** Manufactures, wholesales, and distributes building products, industrial wood products, pulp, paper, packaging, and related chemicals. **Other U.S. locations:** Nationwide. **Listed on:** New York Stock Exchange. **Stock exchange symbol:** GP.

K-PLY INC.
439 Marine Drive, Port Angeles WA 98363. 360/457-4421. **Contact:** Pam Anderson, Human Resources Director. **World Wide Web**

address: http://www.kplyinc.com. **Description:** A manufacturer of lumber products for use in home applications including exterior siding. **Corporate headquarters location:** This location. **Parent company:** Klukwan Inc. **Number of employees nationwide:** 300.

KIMBERLY-CLARK
2600 Federal Avenue, Everett WA 98201. 425/259-7333. **Contact:** Staffing and Compensation Manager. **World Wide Web address:** http://www.kimberly-clark.com. **Description:** Processes pulp and paper used in making tissues. **Corporate headquarters location:** Neenah WI. **Listed on:** New York Stock Exchange. **Stock exchange symbol:** KMB.

LONGVIEW FIBRE COMPANY
P.O. Box 639, Longview WA 98632. 360/425-1550. **Contact:** Human Resources. **World Wide Web address:** http://www.longviewfibre.com. **Description:** Owns and operates tree farms in Oregon and Washington and is a major pulp, wood, and paper products manufacturer. The company also produces shipping containers, merchandise, and grocery bags. **Listed on:** New York Stock Exchange. **Stock exchange symbol:** LFB.

MAIL-WELL ENVELOPE
6520 South 190th Street, Suite 100, Kent WA 98032. 206/576-4300. **Toll-free phone:** 800/347-6989. **Contact:** Human Resources Department. **World Wide Web address:** http://www.mailwellenvelope.com. **Description:** Manufactures envelopes and related paper products. Founded in 1921. **Corporate headquarters location:** Englewood CO. **Listed on:** New York Stock Exchange. **Stock exchange symbol:** MWL.

NORTHWEST HARDWOODS
P.O. Box 7, Arlington WA 98223. 360/435-8502. **Contact:** Personnel. **Description:** Produces maple and alder woods used in furniture construction.

OLYMPIC RESOURCE MANAGEMENT
P.O. Box 1780, Poulsbo WA 98370. 206/292-0517. **Physical address:** 19245 10th Avenue NE, Poulsbo WA 98370. **Contact:** Human Resources. **World Wide Web address:** http://www.orm.com. **Description:** Plants and harvests trees sold as timber to the domestic market. This company is also engaged in real estate development.

PACIFIC LUMBER & SHIPPING COMPANY

P.O. Box 21785, Seattle WA 98111. 206/682-7262. **Physical address:** 1301 Fifth Avenue, Suite 3131, Seattle WA 98101. **Fax:** 206/682-5887. **Contact:** Personnel. **World Wide Web address:** http://www.pls-lumber.com. **Description:** A worldwide lumber wholesaler providing both hardwoods and softwoods. **Corporate headquarters location:** This location. **Other area locations:** Everett WA; Longview WA. **Number of employees at this location:** 30.

PLUM CREEK TIMBER COMPANY, INC.

999 Third Avenue, Suite 2300, Seattle WA 98104. 206/467-3600. **Toll-free phone:** 800/858-5347. **Fax:** 206/467-3786. **Contact:** Personnel Department. **World Wide Web address:** http://www.plumcreek.com. **Description:** Manufactures softwood, hardwood, lumber, plywood, fiber bands, and laminates.

POTLATCH CORPORATION

601 West Riverside Avenue, Suite 1100, Spokane WA 99201. 509/835-1500. **Fax:** 509/835-1562. **Contact:** Employee Relations Administrator. **World Wide Web address:** http://www.potlatchcorp.com. **Description:** A fully-integrated manufacturer of forest products including lumber, plywood, paper, bleached paperboard, and consumer products. Wood products are produced at plants in Arkansas, Idaho, and Minnesota and are marketed through company sales representatives to wholesalers for distribution nationwide. Coated papers for magazines, catalogs, and direct-mail advertising are produced in Minnesota and sold mostly to merchants. **Corporate headquarters location:** Lewiston ID. **Listed on:** New York Stock Exchange. **Stock exchange symbol:** PCH. **Number of employees worldwide:** 7,000.

RSG FOREST PRODUCTS, INC.

985 NW Second Street, Kalama WA 98625. 360/673-2825. **Contact:** Human Resources. **World Wide Web address:** http://www.rsgfp.com. **Description:** A lumber company producing primarily cedar fencing, dougfir, and hemfir. **Corporate headquarters location:** This location. **Other U.S. locations:** OR.

RAYONIER INC.

3033 Ingram Street, Hoquiam, WA 98158. 360/533-7000. **Contact:** Human Resources. **World Wide Web address:** http://www.rayonier.com. **Description:** Rayonier is a leading international forest products company engaged in the trading, merchandising, and manufacturing of logs, timber, and wood products, and in the production and sale of high-value specialty pulps. Rayonier owns, buys, and harvests timber stumpage and purchases delivered logs, primarily in North America and New Zealand, for subsequent sale into export markets (primarily Japan, Korea, and China), as well as to domestic lumber and pulp mills. Rayonier also produces dimension and specialty products for residential construction and industrial uses. **Positions advertised include:** Timber Resource Manager; International Wood Products Controller. **Corporate headquarters location:** Jacksonville FL. **Operations at this facility include:** This location markets logs, lumber products, and pulp. **Listed on:** New York Stock Exchange. **Stock exchange symbol:** RYN.

SHAKERTOWN CORPORATION

P.O. Box 400, Winlock WA 98596. 360/785-3501. **Fax:** 360/785-3076. **Contact:** Personnel Department. **World Wide Web address:** http://www.shakertown.com. **Description:** Manufactures cedar shingle siding and roofing panels.

SIMPSON TACOMA KRAFT COMPANY

P.O. Box 2133, Tacoma WA 98401-2133. 253/572-2150. **Contact:** Human Resources. **Description:** Manufactures bleached and unbleached kraft pulp and liverboard.

SIMPSON TIMBER COMPANY

P.O. Box 460, Shelton WA 98584. 360/426-3381. **Contact:** Human Resources. **World Wide Web address:** http://www.simpson.com. **Description:** Produces and markets lumber, plywood, and wood chips for the lumber and paper industries. **Corporate headquarters location:** Seattle WA. **Number of employees at this location:** 1,200.

SMURFIT-STONE CONTAINER CORPORATION

P.O. Box 479, Renton WA 98057. 425/235-3300. **Contact:** Human Resources Department. **World Wide Web address:** http://www.smurfit-stone.com. **Description:** Smurfit-Stone Container Corporation is one of the world's leading paper-based packaging companies. The company's main products include corrugated containers, folding cartons, and multiwall industrial bags. The company is also one of the world's largest collectors and processors of recycled products that are then sold to a worldwide customer base. Smurfit-Stone Container Corporation also operates several paper tube, market pulp, and newsprint production facilities. **Corporate headquarters location:** Chicago IL. **Other U.S. locations:**

Nationwide. **Operations at this facility include:** This location manufactures folding cartons. **Listed on:** NASDAQ. **Stock exchange symbol:** SSCC.

SMURFIT-STONE CONTAINER CORPORATION
817 East 27th Street, Tacoma WA 98421. 253/627-1197. **Contact:** Human Resources. **World Wide Web address:** http://www.smurfit-stone.com. **Description:** Smurfit-Stone Container Corporation is one of the world's leading paper-based packaging companies. The company's main products include corrugated containers, folding cartons, and multiwall industrial bags. The company is also one of the world's largest collectors and processors of recycled products that are then sold to a worldwide customer base. Smurfit-Stone Container Corporation also operates several paper tube, market pulp, and newsprint production facilities. **Corporate headquarters location:** Chicago IL. **Other U.S. locations:** Nationwide. **Operations at this facility include:** This location is a paper mill that produces containerboard. **Listed on:** NASDAQ. **Stock exchange symbol:** SSCC.

VAAGEN BROTHERS LUMBER INC.
565 West Fifth Street, Colville WA 99114. 509/684-5071. **Fax:** 509/684-2168. **Contact:** Personnel. **World Wide Web address:** http://www.vaagenbros.com. **Description:** A lumber producer. **Number of employees at this location:** 480.

PRINTING AND PUBLISHING

You can expect to find the following types of companies in this chapter:

Book, Newspaper, and Periodical Publishers
Commercial Photographers
Commercial Printing Services
Graphic Designers

THE BELLINGHAM HERALD
P.O. Box 1277, Bellingham WA 98227-1277. 360/676-2600. **Contact:** Personnel. **World Wide Web address:** http://www.bellinghamherald.com. **Description:** Publishes a local evening newspaper.

THE CHRONICLE
P.O. Box 580, Centralia WA 98531. 360/736-3311. **Contact:** Human Resources. **World Wide Web address:** http://www.chronline.com. **Description:** Publishes a daily newspaper with a circulation of approximately 15,500. **Corporate headquarters location:** This location. **Number of employees at this location:** 100.

THE COLUMBIAN PUBLISHING COMPANY
P.O. Box 180, Vancouver WA 98666-0180. 360/694-3391. **Physical address:** 701 West Eighth Street, Vancouver WA 98660. **Contact:** Personnel. **E-mail address:** jobs@columbian.com. **World Wide Web address:** http://www.columbian.com. **Description:** Publishes the *Columbian*, a daily newspaper. **Corporate headquarters location:** This location. **Operations at this facility include:** Manufacturing; Sales; Service. **Number of employees at this location:** 350.

DAILY RECORD
PIONEER PUBLISHING
401 North Main Street, Ellensburg WA 98926. 509/925-1414. **Toll-free phone:** 800/676-4850. **Fax:** 509/925-5696. **Contact:** Managing Editor. **E-mail address:** dailyrecord@kvnews.com. **World Wide Web address:** http://www.kvnews.com. **Description:** Publishes a daily regional/community newspaper with a circulation of 6,000. Founded in 1899. **NOTE:** Part-time positions are offered. **Special programs:** Internships. **Corporate headquarters location:** Seattle WA. **Publisher:** Bill Kunerth. **Information Systems Manager:** Joe Johnson. **Number of employees at this location:** 40.

DAILY SUN NEWS
P.O. Box 878, Sunnyside WA 98944. 509/837-4500. **Contact:** Human Resources. **World Wide Web address:** http://www.sunnyside.net. **Description:** Publishes a daily newspaper. **Parent company:** Eagle Newspapers, Inc.

THE DAILY HERALD COMPANY
P.O. Box 930, Everett WA 98206. **Physical address:** 1213 California Street, Everett WA 98201. 425/339-3434. **Recorded jobline:**

425/339-3009. **Contact:** Human Resources. **E-mail address:** jobs@ heraldnet.com. **World Wide Web address:** http://www.heraldnet. com. **Description:** Publishes one daily newspaper and five weekly newspapers. The daily circulation of the *Herald* is approximately 55,000. **NOTE:** Entry-level positions and part-time jobs are offered. This firm does not accept unsolicited resumes. Please call the jobline for a list of openings. **Positions advertised include:** Inside Sales Representative. **Special programs:** Internships. **Internship information:** Summer internships in news, photography, and advertising are sometimes offered. **Corporate headquarters location:** This location. **Number of employees at this location:** 375.

THE DAILY WORLD
P.O. Box 269, Aberdeen WA 98520. 360/532-4000. **Contact:** Human Resources. **World Wide Web address:** http://www. thedailyworld.com. **Description:** Publishes a newspaper with a circulation of approximately 15,000.

EASTSIDE JOURNAL
P.O. Box 90130, Bellevue WA 98009-9230. 425/455-2222. **Physical address:** 1705 132nd Avenue NE, Bellevue WA 98005. **Contact:** Human Resources. **E-mail address:** hr@eastsidejournal.com. **World Wide Web address:** http://www.eastsidejournal.com. **Description:** Publishes a daily newspaper with a circulation of approximately 30,000. **NOTE:** Entry-level positions and second and third shifts are offered. **Parent company:** Horvitz Newspapers Group.

ELTON-WOLF PUBLISHING
2505 Second Avenue, Suite 515, Seattle WA 98121. 206/748-0345. **Fax:** 206/748-0343. **Contact:** Human Resources. **World Wide Web address:** http://www.elton-wolf.com. **Description:** Publishes author-subsidized cookbooks, autobiographies, fiction, poetry, computer manuals and business manuals. **Other U.S. locations:** Denver CO; Portland OR. **International locations:** Vancouver, British Columbia.

EMERALD CITY GRAPHICS
23328 66th Avenue South, Kent WA 98032. 253/520-2600. **Toll-free phone:** 877/631-5178. **Contact:** Human Resources Department. **World Wide Web address:** http://www.emeraldcg.com. **Description:** Prints manuals, manufactures custom binders, and offers electronic publishing services. **Parent company:** Consolidated Graphics. **Listed on:** New York Stock Exchange. **Stock exchange symbol:** CGX.

K.P. CORPORATION
2001 22nd Avenue South, Seattle WA 98144. 206/328-2770. **Contact:** Human Resources. **E-mail address:** jobs@kpcorp.com. **World Wide Web address:** http://www.kpcorp.com. **Description:** A commercial lithographic printer. **Corporate headquarters location:** San Ramon CA.

KING COUNTY JOURNAL
P.O. Box 130, Kent WA 98035-0130. 253/872-6600. **Contact:** Human Resources. **E-mail address:** hr-kent@kingcountyjournal. **World Wide Web address:** http://www.kingcountyjournal.com. **Description:** A daily newspaper. **Positions advertised include:** Delivery Assistant; Customer Calling Representative; Inside Sales Representative. **Special programs:** Internships. **Number of employees at this location:** 200.

MARTINGALE & CO.
20205 144th Avenue NE, Woodinville WA 98072. 425/483-3313. **Contact:** Human Resources. **World Wide Web address:** http://www.patchwork.com. **Description:** Publishes instructional quilt-making books and home decoration gift books.

THE OLYMPIAN
P.O. Box 407, Olympia WA 98507. 360/754-5490. **Physical address:** 111 Bethel Street NE, Olympia WA 98506. **Contact:** Carol Achatz, Director of Human Resources Department. **E-mail address:** cachatz@theolympian.com. **World Wide Web address:** http://www.theolympian.com. **Description:** Publishes a daily newspaper with a circulation of approximately 40,000 weekdays, and a Sunday circulation of approximately 50,000. **Positions advertised include:** Retail Sales Kiosk Representative; Health Care Account Executive; Strategic Marketing and Development Coordinator; Health/Social Services Reporter; Customer Services Representative. **Parent company:** Gannett Newspapers. **Listed on:** New York Stock Exchange. **Stock exchange symbol:** GCI.

OUTDOOR EMPIRE PUBLISHING
P.O. Box 19000, Seattle WA 98109. 206/624-3845. **Fax:** 206/695-8512. **Contact:** Patricia Waterhouse, Human Resources Department. **World Wide Web address:** http://www.fhnews.com. **Description:** Publishes *Fishing and Hunting News*, a semimonthly magazine.

PENINSULA DAILY NEWS

P.O. Box 1330, Port Angeles WA 98362. 360/452-2345. **Contact:** Publisher. **World Wide Web address:** http://www.peninsuladailynews.com. **Description:** A daily newspaper with a weekday circulation of 5,800 and a Sunday circulation of 17,600. **Corporate headquarters location:** Bellevue WA. **Parent company:** Northwest Media. **Operations at this facility include:** Divisional Headquarters. **Number of employees at this location:** 70. **Number of employees nationwide:** 350.

SEATTLE DAILY JOURNAL OF COMMERCE

P.O. Box 11050, Seattle WA 98111. 206/622-8272. **Fax:** 206/622-8416. **Contact:** Hiring Manager. **World Wide Web address:** http://www.djc.com. **Description:** Publishes a daily newspaper with a circulation of approximately 5,000.

SEATTLE FILMWORKS

1260 16th Avenue West, Seattle WA 98119. 206/281-1390. **Fax:** 206/273-8373. **Contact:** Personnel. **E-mail address:** jobs@photoworks.com. **World Wide Web address:** http://www.filmworks.com. **Description:** Processes and sells 35mm film via mail order. Seattle Filmworks has the capabilities to deliver customers' pictures over the Internet. **Positions advertised include:** Vice President of Sales and Marketing. **Corporate headquarters location:** This location. **Operations at this facility include:** Administration; Manufacturing; Research and Development; Sales. **Number of employees at this location:** 400.

SEATTLE POST-INTELLIGENCER

P.O. Box 1909, Seattle WA 98111. 206/448-8000. **Physical address:** 101 Elliott Avenue West, Seattle WA 98119. **Fax:** 206/448-8299. **Contact:** Personnel Manager. **World Wide Web address:** http://www.seattlep-i.com. **Description:** A daily morning newspaper with a weekday circulation in excess of 200,000. *Seattle Post-Intelligencer* is part of the Hearst Newspaper Group. Under terms of a joint operating agreement, circulation, advertising, and production operations for the newspaper are handled by the Seattle Times Company.

THE SEATTLE TIMES COMPANY

P.O. Box 70, Seattle WA 98111. 206/464-2121. **Recorded jobline:** 206/464-2118. **Contact:** Personnel. **World Wide Web address:** http://www.seattletimes.com. **Description:** Publishers of the *Seattle* newspaper. The company also conducts circulation, advertising, and production operations for *Seattle Post-Intelligencer*.

KAYE-SMITH BUSINESS GRAPHICS INC.
P.O. Box 956, Renton WA 98057. 425/228-8600. **Contact:** Human Resources Department. **World Wide Web address:** http://www.kayesmith.com. **Description:** A commercial lithographic printer.

THE SPOKESMAN REVIEW
COWLES PUBLISHING COMPANY
P.O. Box 2160, Spokane WA 99210. 509/459-5000. **Contact:** Human Resources. **World Wide Web address:** http://www.spokesman.net. **Description:** Publishes the *Spokesman Review*, a daily newspaper with a circulation of approximately 98,000.

SUN NEWSPAPER
P.O. Box 259, 545 Fifth Street, Bremerton WA 98337. 206/842-5696. **Contact:** Personnel. **World Wide Web address:** http://www.thesunlink.com. **Description:** Publishes an evening newspaper with a circulation of approximately 40,000. **Number of employees at this location:** 240.

SUNSET MAGAZINE
500 Union Street, Suite 600, Seattle WA 98101. 206/682-3993. **Fax:** 650/324-5727. **Recorded jobline:** 650/324-5706. **Contact:** Personnel Department. **E-mail address:** jobs@sunset.com. **World Wide Web address:** http://www.sunsetmagazine.com. **Description:** Publishes the Pacific Northwest edition of *Sunset Magazine*, focusing on Western cooking, gardening, and travel. **NOTE:** Mail resumes to: 80 Willow Road, Menlo Park CA 94025. For current openings, call the job-line listed above. **Positions advertised include:** Style Editor; Photo Editor; Home Program Manager; Consumer Marketing Manager.

TACOMA NEWS, INC.
P.O. Box 11000, Tacoma WA 98411. 253/597-8575. **Contact:** Human Resources. **World Wide Web address:** http://www.tribnet.com. **Description:** Publishes a morning newspaper with a daily circulation of approximately 122,000 and a circulation of approximately 140,000 on Sunday.

TELDON CALENDARS
250 H Street, P.O. Box 8000, Blaine WA 98230-4033. 360/945-1211. **Toll-free phone:** 800/755-1211. **Contact:** Human Resources Department. **World Wide Web address:** http://www.teldon.com. **Description:** Publishes promotional calendars. **Parent company:** Teldon International Inc. manufactures promotional products, and prints logos on a variety of items including mugs, pens, and towels.

TIME-LIFE LIBRARIES
1100 Olive Way, Suite 320, Seattle WA 98010. 206/748-0626. **Contact:** Human Resources. **Description:** Time-Life Libraries is a book publisher. **Operations at this facility include:** This location is a telemarketing office.

TRI-CITY HERALD
P.O. Box 2608, Tri-Cities WA 99302. 509/582-1500. **Contact:** Kelly Janicek, Human Resources Manager. **World Wide Web address:** http://www.tri-cityherald.com. **Description:** Publishes a daily newspaper with a circulation of over 40,000. **Special programs:** Internships. **Corporate headquarters location:** Sacramento CA. **Parent company:** McClatchey Newspapers Group.

YAKIMA HERALD-REPUBLIC
P.O. Box 9668, Yakima WA 98909. 509/248-1251. **Contact:** Human Resources. **World Wide Web address:** http://www.yakima-herald.com. **Description:** Publishes a daily newspaper with a circulation of approximately 44,000.

REAL ESTATE

You can expect to find the following types of companies in this chapter:

Land Subdividers and Developers
Real Estate Agents, Managers, and Operators
Real Estate Investment Trusts

CAPITAL DEVELOPMENT COMPANY

P.O. Box 3487, Lacey WA 98509-0487. 360/491-6850. **Contact:** Human Resources. **Description:** Engaged in a variety of construction activities including contracting, leasing, and property development and management.

CUSHMAN & WAKEFIELD OF WASHINGTON INC.

700 Fifth Avenue, Suite 2700, Seattle WA 98104-5027. 206/682-0666. **Contact:** Michele Guidinger, Human Resources Department. **World Wide Web address:** http://www.cushwake.com/us. **Description:** A real estate services firm offering sales, property management, and appraisal services. **Corporate headquarters location:** New York NY.

DIAMOND PARKING SERVICES, INC.

3161 Elliott Avenue, Seattle WA 98121. 206/284-3100. **Contact:** Personnel. **World Wide Web address:** http://www.diamondparking. com. **Description:** Owns parking facilities and is involved in real estate. **Corporate headquarters location:** This location. **Number of employees at this location:** 200.

EXPORTS INC.

435 Martin Street, Suite 4000, Blaine WA 98230. 360/332-5239. **Contact:** Human Resources. **Description:** A property management firm involved in the financial management of corporate properties.

OLYMPIC RESOURCE MANAGEMENT

P.O. Box 1780, Poulsbo WA 98370. 206/292-0517. **Physical address:** 19245 10th Avenue NE, Poulsbo WA 98370. **Contact:** Human Resources. **World Wide Web address:** http://www.orm.com. **Description:** Plants and harvests trees sold as timber to the domestic market. This company is also engaged in real estate development.

PRUDENTIAL MACPHERSON

18551 Aurora Avenue North, Suite 100, Shoreline WA 98133. 206/546-4124. **Contact:** Personnel Department. **World Wide Web address:** http://www.macphersons.com. **Description:** A real estate company that also operates apartment buildings and provides related services.

RETAIL

You can expect to find the following types of companies in this chapter:

Catalog Retailers
Department Stores; Specialty Store
Retail Bakeries
Supermarkets

ALBERTSON'S, INC.
14500 15th Avenue NE, Shoreline WA 98155. 206/365-2422. **Contact:** Human Resources. **E-mail address:** employment@ albertsons.com. **World Wide Web address:** http:// www.albertsons. com. **Description:** A full-service supermarket. **Corporate headquarters location:** Portland OR. **Listed on:** New York Stock Exchange. **Stock exchange symbol:** ABS.

ALL-STAR TOYOTA INC.
13355 Lake City Way NE, Seattle WA 98125. 206/367-0080. **Contact:** Personnel Department. **Description:** A retailer and wholesaler of automobile parts and services.

AMAZON.COM, INC.
P.O. Box 81226, Seattle WA 98108-1300. 206/622-2335. **Physical address:** 1200 12th Avenue South, Seattle WA 98144. **Contact:** Strategic Growth. **E-mail address:** jobs@amazon.com. **World Wide Web address:** http://www.amazon.com. **Description:** An online store engaged in the sale of books, videos, music, toys, and electronics. Amazon.com also offers online auctions. Founded in 1995. **NOTE:** If sending a resume via e-mail, please be sure the information is in an ASCII-text format. **Corporate headquarters location:** This location. **Other U.S. locations:** New Castle DE; McDonough GA; Coffeyville KS; Cambellsville KY; Lexington KY; Fernley NV. **International locations:** Europe. **Listed on:** NASDAQ. **Stock exchange symbol:** AMZN. **President/CEO:** Jeffrey Bezos.

BJ'S PAINT'N PLACE INC.
6528 Capitol Boulevard South, Tumwater WA 98501. 360/943-3232. **Contact:** Human Resources. **World Wide Web address:** http:// www.bjspaint.com. **Description:** A retail store offering paints, stains, wallpaper, fabric, finishes, brushes, and similar products.

BARNES & NOBLE BOOKSTORES
626 106th Avenue NE, Bellevue WA 98004. 425/451-8463. **Contact:** Human Resources. **World Wide Web address:** http:// www.bn.com. **Description:** A bookstore chain operating nationwide. This location has a cafe and music department in addition to its book departments. **Corporate headquarters location:** New York NY. **Listed on:** New York Stock Exchange. **Stock exchange symbol:** BKS.

BARTELL DRUGS

4727 Denver Avenue South, Seattle WA 98134. 206/763-2626.
Contact: Personnel Department. **E-mail address:** hr@bartelldrugs.
com. **World Wide Web address:** http://www.bartelldrugs.com.
Description: Operates a chain of drug stores in the Seattle area.
Positions advertised include: Pharmacy Assistant; Pharmacist;
Management Trainee. **Corporate headquarters location:** This
location. **Number of employees nationwide:** 600.

THE BON MARCHE

Third Avenue & Pine, Seattle WA 98181. 206/344-2121. **Contact:**
Personnel. **World Wide Web address:** http://www.federated-fds.com.
Description: Operates a retail department store. **Parent company:**
Federated Department Stores. **Number of employees nationwide:**
3,750.

BEN BRIDGE CORPORATION

P.O. Box 1908, Seattle WA 98111-1908. 206/448-8800. **Contact:**
Human Resources. **World Wide Web address:** http://
www.benbridge.com. **Description:** A retailer of fine jewelry and
related accessories. **Positions advertised include:** Quality Assurance
Specialist; Watchmaker; Clerical and Administrative Associate.
Corporate headquarters location: This location. **Other U.S.
locations:** AL; CA; HI; NV; OR. **Operations at this facility include:**
Administration; Sales. **Number of employees at this location:** 80.
Number of employees nationwide: 475.

COSTCO WHOLESALE

999 Lake Drive, Issaquah WA 98027. 425/313-8100. **Contact:**
Human Resources. **World Wide Web address:** http://www.costco.
com. **Description:** A nationwide retailer of food, clothing, and
numerous other products at wholesale prices. **Corporate
headquarters location:** This location. **Listed on:** NASDAQ. **Stock
exchange symbol:** COST. **Annual sales/revenues:** More than $100
million.

EDDIE BAUER, INC.

P.O. Box 97000, Redmond WA 98073-9700. 425/755-6100.
Physical address: 15010 NE 36th Street, Redmond WA 98052.
Contact: Human Resources. **World Wide Web address:** http://
www.eddiebauer.com. **Description:** A multi-unit, private-label
retailer and catalog company for apparel and home accessories.
Corporate headquarters location: This location. **Other U.S.**

locations: Nationwide. **Parent company:** Spiegel, Inc. **Listed on:** NASDAQ. **Stock exchange symbol:** SPGLE. **Number of employees at this location:** 1,000. **Number of employees nationwide:** 10,000.

FRED MEYER, INC.
14300 First Avenue South, Seattle WA 98168. 206/433-6411. **Contact:** Personnel Department. **E-mail address:** fredmeyer@webhire.com. **World Wide Web address:** http://www.fredmeyer.com. **Description:** A major retailer of food and general merchandise on the West Coast operating through more than 400 stores in 26 states. Products include food, apparel, appliances, jewelry, health and beauty aids, and pharmaceuticals. **Corporate headquarters location:** Portland OR. **Other U.S. locations:** AK; CA; ID; MT; OR; UT. **Parent company:** The Kroger Company. **Listed on:** New York Stock Exchange. **Stock exchange symbol:** KR. **Number of employees nationwide:** 2,440.

HAGGEN, INC.
TOP FOOD & DRUG
P.O. Box 9704, Bellingham WA 98227. 360/733-8720. **Recorded jobline:** 888/HAG-GENS. **Contact:** Human Resources Manager. **E-mail address:** careers@haggen.com. **World Wide Web address:** http://www.haggen.com. **Description:** Operates over 25 grocery stores throughout the Pacific Northwest. **Special programs:** Internships. **Corporate headquarters location:** This location.

LAMONTS APPAREL, INC.
300 Northgate Way, Seattle WA 98125. 206/367-7690. **Contact:** Human Resources Department. **Description:** Owns and operates more than 35 retail clothing stores in the Northwest. This location also hires seasonally. Founded in 1967. **NOTE:** Part-time jobs are offered. **Special programs:** Internships; Training; Summer Jobs. **Office hours:** Monday - Friday, 8:30 a.m. - 5:00 p.m. **Corporate headquarters location:** Fresno CA. **Other U.S. locations:** AK; ID; OR; UT. **Operations at this facility include:** Administration; Service. **Listed on:** NASDAQ. **Annual sales/revenues:** More than $100 million. **Number of employees nationwide:** 1,500.

NORDSTROM RACK
1601 Second Avenue, Seattle WA 98101. 206/448-8522. **Contact:** Human Resources. **World Wide Web address:** http://www.nordstrom.com. **Description:** Nordstom is one of the largest independently-owned fashion retailers in the United States. The

company operates more than 60 full-line stores across the nation along with over 20 clearance, boutique, and leased shoe departments in 12 department stores in Hawaii and Guam. Founded in 1901. **Operations at this facility include:** This location is a discounted outlet store. **Listed on:** New York Stock Exchange. **Stock exchange symbol:** JWN. **Annual sales/revenues:** More than $100 million. **Number of employees at this location:** 500.

NORDSTROM, INC.
100 Bellevue Square, Bellevue WA 98004. 425/455-5800. **Contact:** Human Resources. **World Wide Web address:** http://www.nordstrom.com. **Description:** One of the largest independently-owned fashion retailers in the United States. Founded in 1901. **Corporate headquarters location:** Seattle WA. **Listed on:** New York Stock Exchange. **Stock exchange symbol:** JWN. **Annual sales/revenues:** More than $100 million.

QUALITY FOOD CENTERS
10116 NE Eighth Street, Bellevue WA 98004. 425/455-3761. **Contact:** Human Resources. **World Wide Web address:** http://www.qfconline.com. **Description:** Operates a chain of retail supermarkets. **Corporate headquarters location:** Cincinnati OH. **Parent company:** The Kroger Company. **Number of employees nationwide:** 2,600.

RECREATIONAL EQUIPMENT INC. (REI)
P.O. Box 1938, Sumner WA 98390. 253/395-5965. **Physical address:** 6750 South 228th Street, Kent WA 98032. **Recorded jobline:** 253/395-4694. **Contact:** Human Resources Department. **World Wide Web address:** http://www.rei.com/jobs. **Description:** A retailer of outdoor clothing and a wide variety of recreational equipment. **Corporate headquarters location:** Kent WA. **Operations at this facility include:** Administration. **Number of employees nationwide:** 3,000.

RITE AID CORPORATION
110 SW 148th Street, Burien WA 98166. 206/835-0166. **Fax:** 206/835-0991. **Contact:** Employee Relations Manager. **World Wide Web address:** http://www.riteaid.com. **Description:** Rite Aid Corporation operates 3800 retail drug stores in 30 states and the District of Columbia. Founded in 1939. **Special programs:** Internships. **Corporate headquarters location:** Harrisburg PA. **Other U.S. locations:** Nationwide. **Operations at this facility include:** This

location houses administrative offices. **Listed on:** New York Stock Exchange. **Stock exchange symbol:** RAD. **Number of employees nationwide:** 40,000.

SAFEWAY, INC.
3820 Rainier Avenue South, Seattle WA 98118. 206/725-9575. **Contact:** Human Resources. **World Wide Web address:** http://www.safeway.com. **Description:** Safeway Inc. is one of the world's largest food retailers. The company operates approximately 1,660 stores in the western, Rocky Mountain, southwestern, and mid-Atlantic regions of the United States and in western Canada. In support of its stores, the company has an extensive network of distribution, manufacturing, and food processing facilities. Safeway, Inc. also holds a 49 percent interest in Casa Ley, S.A. de C.V., which operates food/variety, clothing, and wholesale outlet stores in western Mexico. **Subsidiaries include:** Dominick's Supermarkets is a Chicago-area chain with 112 stores. **Listed on:** New York Stock Exchange. **Stock exchange symbol:** SWY.

SEARS, ROEBUCK & CO.
15711 Aurora Avenue North, Seattle WA 98133. 206/364-9000. **Contact:** Human Resources. **World Wide Web address:** http://www.sears.com. **Description:** The company's structure is divided into three groups: Sears Merchandise Group, Allstate Insurance Group, and Corporate Business. With its network of mall-based stores, Sears is a leading retailer of apparel, home, and automotive products and related services for families throughout North America. **Positions advertised include:** District Technical Manager. **Corporate headquarters location:** Chicago IL. **Subsidiaries include:** Allstate Insurance Group is one of the nation's largest publicly held property and casualty insurance companies, with more than 20 million customers and approximately 14,600 full-time agents in the United States and Canada. Founded in 1931 by Sears, Roebuck & Co., which owns 80 percent, Allstate is also a major life insurer. Allstate offers automobile insurance, homeowners insurance, life insurance, annuity and pension products, business insurance for small and mid-size businesses, as well as reinsurance for other insurers, and mortgage guaranty insurance through Allstate's wholly-owned subsidiary, PMI Mortgage Insurance Company. Sears, Roebuck & Co. also operates or holds interests in related businesses in real estate, computer, and information services that extend or support its core businesses. Homart is one of the country's leading developers, owners, and managers of regional shopping malls and community

centers. Prodigy, a Sears/IBM partnership, is one of the nation's largest home computer networks, providing a wide variety of interactive personal services including news, shopping, bulletin boards, travel ticketing, brokerage, banking, and electronic mail services. Advantis, another Sears/IBM partnership, is a networking technology company that provides businesses with data, voice, and multimedia services. **Listed on:** New York Stock Exchange. **Stock exchange symbol:** S.

7-ELEVEN, INC.
2089 72nd Avenue South, Kent WA 98032. 253/796-7111. **Fax:** 253/796-7120. **Contact:** Human Resources. **World Wide Web address:** http://www.7-eleven.com. **Description:** Owns and operates 7-Eleven convenience stores. **Corporate headquarters location:** Dallas TX.

SOUND FORD INC.
750 Rainier Avenue South, Renton WA 98055. 425/235-1000. **Contact:** Human Resources. **World Wide Web address:** http://www.soundford.com. **Description:** An automotive dealership.

STARBUCKS COFFEE CORPORATION
P.O. Box 34067, Seattle WA 98124. 206/447-1575. **Physical address:** 2401 Utah Avenue South, Seattle WA 98134. **Recorded jobline:** 206/447-4123. **Contact:** Human Resources. **World Wide Web address:** http://www.starbucks.com. **Description:** Sells whole-bean coffees, along with hot coffees and Italian-style espresso beverages through more than 2,500 retail stores worldwide. The company purchases green coffee beans for its coffee varieties from coffee-producing regions throughout the world and custom roasts them. In addition to coffee beans and beverages, the company's stores offer a selection of coffee-making equipment, accessories, pastries, and confections. Also, the company sells whole-bean coffees through specialty sales groups, a national mail-order operation, and supermarkets. **Corporate headquarters location:** This location. **Other U.S. locations:** Nationwide. **International locations:** Worldwide. **Number of employees worldwide:** 37,000.

SUPERVALU INC.
1525 East D Street, Tacoma WA 98421. 253/593-3200. **Fax:** 253/404-4288. **Contact:** Human Resources Manager. **World Wide Web address:** http://www.supervalu.com. **Description:** SUPERVALU Inc. is one of the nation's largest food retailers and distribution

companies, supplying grocery, health and beauty, and general merchandise products to over 6,100 customers. In the corporate retail sector, SUPERVALU operates over 1,100 stores under the Bigg's, Cub Foods, Shop'n Save, Save-A-Lot, Scott's Foods, Laneco, and Hornbachers names. **Special programs:** Internships. **Corporate headquarters location:** Eden Prairie MN. **Subsidiaries include:** Hazelwood Farms Bakeries manufactures frozen bakery products. **Operations at this facility include:** This location houses administrative offices. **Listed on:** New York Stock Exchange. **Stock exchange symbol:** SVU. **Number of employees at this location:** 935.

THRIFTWAY STORES INC.
P.O. Box 3763, Seattle WA 98124. 206/783-7922. **Fax:** 206/767-8955. **Contact:** Personnel. **World Wide Web address:** http://www.thriftway.com. **Description:** Operates a retail grocery chain with over 100 outlets.

TIME OIL COMPANY
P.O. 24447, Seattle WA 98124. 206/285-2400. **Physical address:** 2737 West Commodore Way, Seattle WA 98199. **Contact:** Personnel Department. **World Wide Web address:** http://www.timeoil.com. **Description:** Operates retail gasoline service stations, wholesales petroleum products, and retails fuel oil heaters.

TRI NORTH DEPARTMENT STORES
5700 Sixth Avenue South, Suite 214, Seattle WA 98108-2511. 206/767-7600. **Contact:** Human Resources. **Description:** Owns and operates a chain of retail clothing department stores located primarily throughout the Pacific Northwest. **Corporate headquarters location:** This location.

URM STORES, INC.
P.O. Box 3365, Spokane WA 99220. 509/467-2620. **Contact:** Personnel Department. **World Wide Web address:** http://www.urmstores.com. **Description:** A grocery and general merchandise business. **Number of employees nationwide:** 2,000.

STONE, CLAY, GLASS, AND CONCRETE PRODUCTS

You can expect to find the following types of companies in this chapter:

Cement, Tile, Sand, and Gravel
Crushed and Broken Stone
Glass and Glass Products
Mineral Products

ASH GROVE CEMENT COMPANY
3801 East Marginal Way South, Seattle WA 98134. 206/623-5596. **Contact:** Human Resources. **World Wide Web address:** http://www.ashgrove.com. **Description:** Operates cement and lime plants in nine states across the country. With an annual production capacity of more than 4.6 million tons of cement, Ash Grove is one of the largest cement manufacturers in the United States. The Portland and masonry cements produced at the company's plants are used in the construction of highways, bridges, commercial and industrial complexes, residential homes, and a myriad of other structures. In addition to cement operations, the company operates two lime plants with total production capacity of 270,000 tons per year. Ash Grove lime products are used in steel and paper manufacturing, municipal water treatment, agriculture, and construction. **Positions advertised include:** Plant Manager; Product Manager; Maintenance Manager; Process Engineer; Chief Chemist; Human Resources Manager. **Office hours:** Monday - Friday, 7:00 a.m. - 4:00 p.m. **Corporate headquarters location:** Overland Park KS.

CONCRETE TECHNOLOGY CORPORATION
P.O. Box 2259, Tacoma WA 98401-2259. 253/383-3545. **Physical address:** 1123 Port of Tacoma Road, Tacoma WA 98421. **Contact:** Personnel Director. **World Wide Web address:** http://www.concretetech.com. **Description:** Manufactures concrete for a variety of end-use applications. **Corporate headquarters location:** This location.

HEMPHILL BROTHERS INC.
P.O. Box 80786, Seattle WA 98108. 206/762-7622. **Contact:** Personnel Department. **Description:** A manufacturer of crushed limestone and silica sand. **Corporate headquarters location:** This location.

LAFARGE CORPORATION
5400 West Marginal Way SW, Seattle WA 98106. 206/937-8025. **Contact:** Human Resources. **World Wide Web address:** http://www.lafarge-na.com. **Description:** Produces cement, concrete, aggregates, and related products. The company operates 15 full-production cement plants and 420 construction materials facilities. **Corporate headquarters location:** Reston VA. **Subsidiaries include:** Systech Environmental Corporation is a processor and recycler of industrial waste products into fuel for cement kilns. **Listed on:** New York Stock Exchange. **Stock exchange symbol:** LAF.

NORTHWESTERN INDUSTRIES INC.

2500 West Jameson Street, Seattle WA 98199. 206/285-3140. **Fax:** 206/285-4798. **Toll-free phone:** 800/426-2771. **Contact:** Scott Gaynor, Human Resources. **World Wide Web address:** http://www.nwindust.com. **Description:** One of the largest glass fabricators in the United States. The company offers tempered, laminated, and insulated glass products. Founded in 1975. **Corporate headquarters location:** This location.

SAINT-GOBAIN GLASS CONTAINER CORPORATION

5801 East Marginal Way South, Seattle WA 98134-2413. 206/762-0660. **Fax:** 206/768-6266. **Contact:** Jason Noble, Human Resources Manager. **Description:** Manufactures glass bottles and jars. **Parent company:** The Ball Corporation manufactures metal and glass packaging products, primarily for food and beverages, and provides aerospace and communications products and services to government and commercial customers. The Metal Beverage Container Division produces aluminum beverage cans and easy-open can ends for brewers and soft drink companies such as Anheuser-Busch, Coca-Cola, and Pepsi. The Metal Food Containers and Specialty Products Division services food processing, household products, and personal care products markets; and produces three-piece and two-piece steel food and aerosol cans. The company also produces glass bottles and jars for food, juice, wine, and liquor in the Glass Containers Division for bottlers such as Campbell Soup, Ocean Spray, Welch's, and Clorox. The Aerospace and Communications Division provides solutions to complex space, defense, and communication challenges including spacecraft and space systems, scientific and defense instrumentation, military video, government and commercial antennas, electro-optic devices, cryogenic systems, systems engineering, and remote sensing for geographic information systems.

TRANSPORTATION/TRAVEL

You can expect to find the following types of companies in this chapter:

Air, Railroad, and Water Transportation Services
Courier Services
Local and Interurban Passenger Transit
Ship Building and Repair
Transportation Equipment Travel Agencies
Trucking
Warehousing and Storage

AAA SEATTLE

330 Sixth Avenue North, Seattle WA 98109. 206/448-5353. **Contact:** Human Resources. **E-mail address:** hr@aaawa.com. **World Wide Web address:** http://www.aaawa.com. **Description:** Provides insurance, travel, and a wide variety of services to motorists through a network of over 50 branch offices. **Corporate headquarters location:** Heathrow FL.

AIR VAN LINES

P.O. Box 3447, Bellevue WA 98009. 425/453-5560. **Contact:** Personnel Director. **World Wide Web address:** http://www.navlagent.com/airvan. **Description:** A freight forwarding company with operations in domestic moving services. **Corporate headquarters location:** This location.

AIRBORNE EXPRESS

P.O. Box 662, Seattle WA 98111-0662. 206/830-4600. **Physical address:** 3101 Western Avenue, Seattle WA 98121. **Contact:** Recruiting. **E-mail address:** goa.recruiter@airborne.com. **World Wide Web address:** http://www.airborne.com. **Description:** A domestic and international air express, air, and ocean freight services company. Operations include both domestic and international door-to-door, next-day delivery, and door-to-airport freight services. Airborne Express operates a fleet of more than 14,000 delivery vehicles. **Positions advertised include:** Claims Examiner; Corporate Accountant; Customer Service Representative; International Accounting Specialist; Payroll Coordinator. **Corporate headquarters location:** This location. **Listed on:** New York Stock Exchange. **Stock exchange symbol:** ABF. **Number of employees worldwide:** 24,000.

AMERICAN AIRLINES, INC.

Seattle-Tacoma International Airport, Seattle WA 98158-1277. 206/433-3951. **Contact:** Human Resources. **World Wide Web address:** http://www.americanair.com. **Description:** Provides scheduled jet service to more than 170 destinations throughout North America, the Caribbean, Latin America, Europe, and the Pacific. **NOTE:** All resumes should be sent to: American Airlines, Inc., Human Resources, P.O. Box 619616, Mail Drop 5105, DFW Airport TX 75261-9040. **Corporate headquarters location:** Fort Worth TX. **Parent company:** AMR Corporation's operations fall within three major lines of business: the Air Transportation Group, the SABRE Group, and the AMR Management Services Group.

BEKINS NORTHWEST
6501 216th Street SW, Mount Lake Terrace WA 98043. 425/775-8950. **Fax:** 206/527-1429. **Contact:** Personnel Director. **E-mail address:** hr@nekins.net. **World Wide Web address:** http://www.bekinsnorthwest.com. **Description:** Engaged in the transporting and warehousing of household goods, office and industrial equipment, electronics, and business records. Founded in 1903. **Corporate headquarters location:** Seattle WA.

CONSOLIDATED FREIGHTWAYS
P.O. Box 3585, Seattle WA 98124. 206/763-1517. **Contact:** Personnel. **E-mail address:** jobs@cf.com. **World Wide Web address:** http://www.cfwy.com. **Description:** A motor freight carrier and air freight forwarder operating in all 50 states. Operations include export/import brokerage, overseas forwarding, and warehousing and distribution services. **Corporate headquarters location:** Vancouver WA. **Listed on:** NASDAQ. **Stock exchange symbol:** CFWY.

CONTINENTAL VAN LINES INC.
P.O. Box 3963, Seattle WA 98124-3963. 206/937-2261. **Contact:** Personnel. **World Wide Web address:** http://www.continentalvan.com. **Description:** Engaged in interstate moving and storage. **Corporate headquarters location:** Fort Wayne IN.

DANZAS AEI
600 Oakesdale Avenue SW, Suite 101, Renton WA 98055. 425/917-2600. **Contact:** Personnel. **World Wide Web address:** http://www.danzas.com. **Description:** A leading provider of logistics solutions. Services include air, road, rail, and sea transportation, as well as distribution and warehousing. **Corporate headquarters location:** Darien CT. **International locations:** Worldwide.

EZ LOADER BOAT TRAILERS INC.
P.O. Box 3263, Spokane WA 99220-3263. 509/489-0181. **Physical address:** 717 North Hamilton Street, Spokane WA 99202. **Contact:** Carol Mueller, Director of Human Resources Department. **World Wide Web address:** http://www.ezloader.com. **Description:** Manufactures boat trailers. **Corporate headquarters location:** This location. **Operations at this facility include:** Administration; Manufacturing; Research and Development.

EXPEDITORS INTERNATIONAL OF WASHINGTON, INC.

1015 Third Avenue, 12th Floor, Seattle WA 98104. 206/246-3711. **Contact:** Personnel. **World Wide Web address:** http://www.expd. com. **Description:** Engaged in the business of international air and ocean freight forwarding. The company also acts as a customs broker in its domestic overseas offices. **Positions advertised include:** Staff Accountant; Administrative Assistant; EDI Coordinator; Database Administrator; Senior JAVA Developer; IS Project Manager; UI Designer. **Corporate headquarters location:** This location. **Listed on:** NASDAQ. **Stock exchange symbol:** EXPD.

FOSS MARITIME

660 West Ewing Street, Seattle WA 98119. 206/281-3800. **Contact:** Personnel Department. **E-mail address:** fossjobs@foss.com. **World Wide Web address:** http://www.fossmaritime.com. **Description:** Provides maritime carrier services; deep-sea forum services; domestic, coastwide, and intercoastal transportation; and ship repair and services. **Corporate headquarters location:** This location.

HOLLAND AMERICA LINE WESTOURS

300 Elliott Avenue West, Seattle WA 98119. 206/281-3535. **Contact:** Personnel. **World Wide Web address:** http:// www.hollandamerica.com. **Description:** Owns hotels, cruise ships, and sail ships, and operates a motor coach transportation division.

HORIZON AIR

P.O. Box 48309, Seattle WA 98148. 206/241-6757. **Contact:** Human Resources. **World Wide Web address:** http:// www.horizonair.com. **Description:** A passenger and freight air transportation company.

LAIDLAW TRANSIT INC.

13525 Lake City Way NE, Seattle WA 98125-1586. 206/365-7300. **Contact:** Human Resources. **World Wide Web address:** http:// www.laidlawtransit.com. **Description:** Provides bus service for Seattle and charter bus service to private customers. The company is also a school bus contractor. **Parent company:** Laidlaw, Inc. provides solid waste collection, compaction, transportation, treatment, transfer, and disposal services; provides hazardous waste services; operates hazardous waste facilities and wastewater treatment plants; and operates passenger and school buses, transit system buses, and tour and charter buses. **Corporate headquarters**

location: Mt. Lake Terrace WA. **Listed on:** American Stock Exchange. **Stock exchange symbol:** GLL.

LYNDEN INC.

P.O. Box 3757, Seattle WA 98124-3757. 206/241-8778. **Physical address:** 1800 International Boulevard, Suite 800, Seattle WA 98188. **Contact:** Personnel Department. **World Wide Web address:** http://www.lynden.com. **Description:** Provides transportation and construction services for barge, air freight, and trucking companies. **Corporate headquarters location:** This location.

ORIENT OVERSEAS CONTAINER LINE INC. (OOCL)

18912 North Creek Parkway, Suite 208, Bothell WA 98011. 425/488-5080. **Contact:** Human Resources. **World Wide Web address:** http://www.oocl.com. **Description:** An international containerized transportation company. OOCL owns and operates several container vessels, terminals, and chassis throughout the world. The company also maintains a support group consisting of several depots, warehouses, and trucking companies to support its ocean-based transport operations. **Corporate headquarters location:** Hong Kong. **International locations:** Worldwide.

PRINCESS TOURS

2815 Second Avenue, Suite 400, Seattle WA 98121. 206/336-6000. **Fax:** 206/336-6100. **Contact:** Personnel. **World Wide Web address:** http://www.princess.com. **Description:** Operates rail and motorcoach tours in Alaska and the Canadian Rockies for land-only touring, or in conjunction with cruise ships. The company also owns and operates seasonal and year-round hotels in Alaska. **Corporate headquarters location:** This location. **Other U.S. locations:** AK. **Operations at this facility include:** Administration; Sales. **Number of employees at this location:** 150. **Number of employees nationwide:** 300.

PUGET SOUND FREIGHT LINES INC.

P.O. Box 24526, Seattle WA 98124. 206/623-1600. **Contact:** Personnel Department. **E-mail address:** hr@psfl.com. **World Wide Web address:** http://www.psfl.com. **Description:** A regional common carrier using both company drivers and owner/operators in truckload operations. **Corporate headquarters location:** This location. **Other U.S. locations:** OR.

SAS CARGO

2427 South 161st Street, Seattle WA 98158. 206/433-5151. **Fax:** 201/896-3724. **Contact:** Human Resources. **World Wide Web address:** http://www.sascargo.com. **Description:** A cargo shipping company.

SCANDINAVIAN AIRLINES

1301 Fifth Avenue, Suite 3101, Seattle WA 98101. 206/682-5250. **Fax:** 206/625-9057. **Contact:** Human Resources. **World Wide Web address:** http://www.scandinavian.net. **Description:** Scandinavian Airlines is an air transport company. **Operations at this facility include:** This location is the western regional sales office.

SEATTLE MARINE FISHING SUPPLY COMPANY

P.O. Box 99098, Seattle WA 98199-0098. 206/285-5010. **Physical address:** 2121 West Commodore Way, Seattle WA 98199. **Fax:** 206/285-7925. **Contact:** Personnel Department. **World Wide Web address:** http://www.seamar.com. **Description:** A wholesaler of marine supplies and hardware.

SHURGARD STORAGE CENTERS INC.

1155 Valley Street, Suite 400, Seattle WA 98109. 206/624-8100. **Fax:** 206/652-3800. **Contact:** Human Resources. **World Wide Web address:** http://www.shurgard.com. **Description:** Specializes in the self-storage industry. Shurgard Storage Centers Inc. is a self-administered, real estate investment trust. As one of the largest self-storage center operators in the United States, the company operates over 280 storage centers nationally and abroad. Shurgard owns approximately 60 percent of these centers. **Corporate headquarters location:** This location. **Listed on:** New York Stock Exchange. **Stock exchange symbol:** SHU.

SOCIETY EXPEDITIONS, INC.

2001 Western Avenue, Suite 300, Seattle WA 98121. 206/728-9400. **Contact:** Human Resources Manager. **World Wide Web address:** http://www.societyexpeditions.com. **Description:** An expedition cruise line offering service to Alaska, Antarctica, and the South Pacific. **Positions advertised include:** Expedition Leader; Staff Assistant; Lecturer.

TODD PACIFIC SHIPYARDS CORPORATION

1806 16th Avenue SW, Seattle WA 98134. 206/623-1635. **Fax:** 206/442-8503. **Contact:** Personnel. **E-mail address:**

jobs@toddpacific.com. **World Wide Web address:** http://www.toddpacific.com. **Description:** Engaged in the construction, maintenance, and repair of commercial ships, both domestic and foreign, and of ships for the U.S. Navy and other government agencies. **Positions advertised include:** Project Manager; Senior Financial Analyst; CVN Zone Manager.

US AIRWAYS, INC.
Seattle-Tacoma International Airport, Seattle WA 98158. 206/433-7858. **Contact:** Manager. **World Wide Web address:** http://www.usairways.com. **Description:** US Airways offers service to 155 cities in the United States, Canada, the Bahamas, Bermuda, Puerto Rico, the Virgin Islands, France, and Germany. The company's primary hubs are located in Charlotte, Pittsburgh, Baltimore/Washington, and Philadelphia. **Corporate headquarters location:** Arlington VA. **Parent company:** United Airlines, Inc.

UTILITIES: ELECTRIC/GAS/WATER

You can expect to find the following types of companies in this chapter:

Gas, Electric, and Fuel Companies; Other Energy-Producing Companies
Public Utility Holding Companies
Water Utilities

Avista Corporation
1411 East Mission Avenue, Spokane WA 99220-3727. 509/489-0500. **Contact:** Employment. **World Wide Web address:** http://www.avistacorp.com. **Description:** Provides natural gas and electricity to customers in eastern Washington, northern Idaho, Oregon, and Northern California. **NOTE:** This firm does not accept unsolicited resumes. Please only respond to advertised openings. **Positions advertised include:** Large Format Copy Technician. **Special programs:** Internships. **Corporate headquarters location:** This location. **Other U.S. locations:** South Lake Tahoe CA; Medford CT; Klammath OR. **Operations at this facility include:** Administration. **Listed on:** New York Stock Exchange. **Stock exchange symbol:** AVA. **Number of employees at this location:** 900. **Number of employees nationwide:** 1,400.

CASCADE NATURAL GAS CORPORATION
P.O. Box 24464, Seattle WA 98124-0464. 206/624-3900. **Physical address:** 222 Fairview Avenue North, Seattle WA 98109. **Contact:** Personnel Director. **World Wide Web address:** http://www.cngc.com. **Description:** Engaged in the distribution and transportation of natural gas to customers. **Corporate headquarters location:** This location. **Operations at this facility include:** Administration. **Listed on:** New York Stock Exchange. **Stock exchange symbol:** CGC.

NORTHSHORE UTILITY DISTRICT
6830 NE 185th Street, Kenmore WA 98028-2701. 425/398-4400. **Contact:** Human Resources. **World Wide Web address:** http://www.nud.net. **Description:** A special purpose water and sewer utility company. **Positions advertised include:** Meter Technician.

TACOMA PUBLIC UTILITIES
747 Market Street, Room 1336, Tacoma WA 98402-3764. 253/591-5400. **Recorded jobline:** 253/591-5795. **Contact:** Human Resources. **World Wide Web address:** http://www.cityoftacoma.org. **Description:** Provides water and electricity services.

MISCELLANEOUS WHOLESALING

You can expect to find the following types of companies in this chapter:

Exporters and Importers
General Wholesale Distribution Companies

ABATIX ENVIRONMENTAL CORPORATION

1808 B Street NW, Suite 190, Auburn WA 98001. 253/872-6955. **Fax:** 214/381-9513. **Contact:** Human Resources. **E-mail address:** hr@abatix.com. **World Wide Web address:** http://www.abatix.com. **Description:** A full-line supplier of durable and nondurable supplies to the asbestos and lead abatement, hazardous material remediation, and construction industries. Products include industrial safety supplies, construction tools, general safety products such as protective clothing and eyewear, and clean-up equipment. **Corporate headquarters location:** Dallas TX. **Listed on:** NASDAQ. **Stock exchange symbol:** ABIX.

APPLIED INDUSTRIAL TECHNOLOGIES

2747A R.W. Johnson Boulevard SW, Olympia WA 98512. 360/754-4363. **Contact:** Human Resources. **E-mail address:** career@ apzapplied.com. **World Wide Web address:** http:// www.appliedindustrial.com. **Description:** A distributor of bearings, power transmitters, hydraulic power units, and rubber products for use in various industries. **Corporate headquarters location:** Cleveland OH. **Listed on:** New York Stock Exchange. **Stock exchange symbol:** AIT.

FISHERIES SUPPLY COMPANY

1900 North Northlake Way, Suite 10, Seattle WA 98103. 206/632-4462. **Contact:** Personnel Department. **World Wide Web address:** http://www.fisheries-supply.com. **Description:** A wholesaler of marine hardware and supplies. **Corporate headquarters location:** This location.

GRAINGER

5706 East Broadway Avenue, Spokane WA 99212. 509/535-9882. **Contact:** Human Resources. **World Wide Web address:** http:// www.grainger.com. **Description:** Distributes a variety of equipment and components to the industrial, commercial, contracting, and institutional markets nationwide. Products include equipment and components for motors, air tools, hydraulic products, refrigeration items, power and hand tools, office equipment, computer supplies, storage equipment, replacement parts, industrial products, safety items, cold weather clothing, and sanitary supplies. **Positions advertised include:** Outside Sales Account Manager; Market Development Specialist. **Corporate headquarters location:** Chicago IL. **Listed on:** New York Stock Exchange. **Stock exchange symbol:** GWW.

JENSEN DISTRIBUTION SERVICES
P.O. Box 3708, Spokane WA 99220. 509/624-1321. **Contact:** Personnel. **World Wide Web address:** http://www.jensenonline. com. **Description:** A wholesale distributor of hardware goods. **Corporate headquarters location:** This location.

KEY INDUSTRIES INC.
dba LIBERTY EQUIPMENT & SUPPLY CO.
P.O. Box 24848, Seattle WA 98124. 206/682-8700. **Physical address:** 4100 West Marginal Way SW, Seattle WA 98106. **Contact:** Administrative Manager. **World Wide Web address:** http:// www.libertyeq.com. **Description:** A wholesale distributor of industrial pipe, valves, and fittings for commercial, industrial, marine, and nuclear applications. The company is also engaged in the distribution of valve automation products. **Corporate headquarters location:** This location. **Operations at this facility include:** Administration; Sales.

NC MACHINERY COMPANY
P.O. Box 3562, Seattle WA 98124. 425/251-9800. **Contact:** Human Resources. **World Wide Web address:** http://www.ncmachinery. com. **Description:** Sells heavy equipment including generators, backhoes, and asphalt cutters as part of Caterpillar's worldwide dealer network. **Number of employees nationwide:** 600.

EQUIPMENT
22431 83rd Avenue South, Kent WA 98032. 253/872-3500. **Fax:** 253/872-3519. **Contact:** Human Resources. **World Wide Web address:** http://www.pneco.com. **Description:** Engaged in the sale and service of construction and logging equipment.

WESTERN UTILITIES SUPPLY COMPANY
10013 Martin Luther King Jr. Way South, Seattle WA 98178. 206/722-4800. **Contact:** Personnel. **Description:** A company engaged in the wholesale of industrial waterworks supplies. **Corporate headquarters location:** This location. **Operations at this facility include:** Administration; Sales; Service.

Seattle Choral Company/77
The Seattle Mariners/77
The Summit at Snoqualmie/77
Woodland Park Zoo/78

AUTOMOTIVE

Cummins Northwest/80
Kenworth Truck Company/80
Mar Lac Parts Plus/80
PACCAR Inc./80
Red Dot Corporation/81
Six States Distributors/81
Western Recreational Vehicle Inc./81

BANKING/SAVINGS & LOANS/ OTHER DEPOSITORY INSTITUTIONS (MISC.)

Americanwest Bancorporation/83
Bank of America/83
Columbia Bank/83
First Mutual Bank/83
The Image Bank/83
KeyBank N.A./84
Pacific Northwest Bank/85
PEMCO Financial Services/85
Sterling Savings Association/85
U.S. Bank of Washington/85
United Savings and Loan Bank/86
Washington Federal Savings & Loan
    Association/86
Washington Mutual Savings Bank/86

BIOTECHNOLOGY/ PHARMACEUTICALS/ SCIENTIFIC R&D (MISC.)

Bio-Rad Laboratories/88
Cardinal Distribution/88
Cell Therapeutics, Inc./88
Dynacare Laboratory/88
Epoch Pharmaceuticals, Inc./89
Hollister-Stier Laboratories, LLC/89
ICOS Corporation/89
Immunex Corporation/90
Laboratory Corporation of America
    (LabCorp)/90
MDS Pharma Services/90
Meridian Valley Clinical Lab, Inc./91
NeoRx Corporation/91

Pacific Northwest National
    Laboratory/91
Pathology Associates Medical
    Laboratories/91
Quest Diagnostics Incorporated/92
Targeted Genetics Corporation/92
TriPath Imaging, Inc./92

BUSINESS SERVICES/ NON-SCIENTIFIC RESEARCH

ADT Security Services/95
APS Pinkerton/95
Labor Ready, Inc./95
LYNX Medical Systems/95
Muzak LLC/96
Northwest Protective Services, Inc./
    96
Siemens Business Services/96
Venturi Technology Partners/96
Verisign/97
The Wackenhut Corporation/97

CHARITIES/SOCIAL SERVICES

American Red Cross/99
Childcare International/99
Goodwill Industries/99
IAM Cares/99
Lifelong Aids Alliance/99
Lutheran Community Services/100
Overlake Service League/100
Tacoma Goodwill Industries/100
    Rehabilitation Center Inc./ 100
The West Seattle Helpline/100
YMCA of Greater Seattle/100

CHEMICALS/RUBBER AND PLASTICS

Air Liquide Corporation/103
Alcide Corporation/103
Atofina Chemicals Incorporated/103
BOC Gases/103
Bunzl Extrusion/104
Foamex International, Inc./104
Gaco Western Inc./104
General Chemical Corporation/104
Hexcel Corporation/105
Kelly-Moore Preservative Paints/105

ELECTRONIC/INDUSTRIAL ELECTRICAL EQUIPMENT AND COMPONENTS

ENVIRONMENTAL & WASTE MANAGEMENT SERVICES

FABRICATED METAL PRODUCTS AND PRIMARY METALS

FINANCIAL SERVICES (MISC.)

FOOD AND BEVERAGES/ AGRICULTURE

GOVERNMENT

HEALTH CARE: SERVICES, EQUIPMENT, AND PRODUCTS (MISC.)

HOTELS AND RESTAURANTS

PRINTING AND PUBLISHING

REAL ESTATE

RETAIL

STONE, CLAY, GLASS, AND CONCRETE PRODUCTS

Your Job Hunt
Your Feedback

*Comments, questions, or suggestions? We want to hear from you!
Please complete this questionnaire and mail it to:*

The JobBank Staff
Adams Media Corporation
57 Littlefield Street
Avon, MA 02322

or send us an e-mail at **jobbank@adamsmedia.com**

*Did this book provide helpful advice and valuable information which you used in
your job search? What did you like about it?*

*How could we improve this book to help you in your job search? Is there a
specific company we left out or an industry you'd like to see more of in a future
edition? No suggestion is too small or too large.*

Would you recommend this book to a friend beginning a job hunt?

Name:

Occupation:

Which JobBank did you use?

Mailing address:

E-mail address:

Daytime phone:

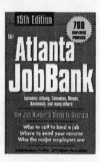  

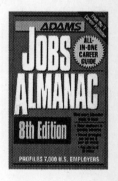